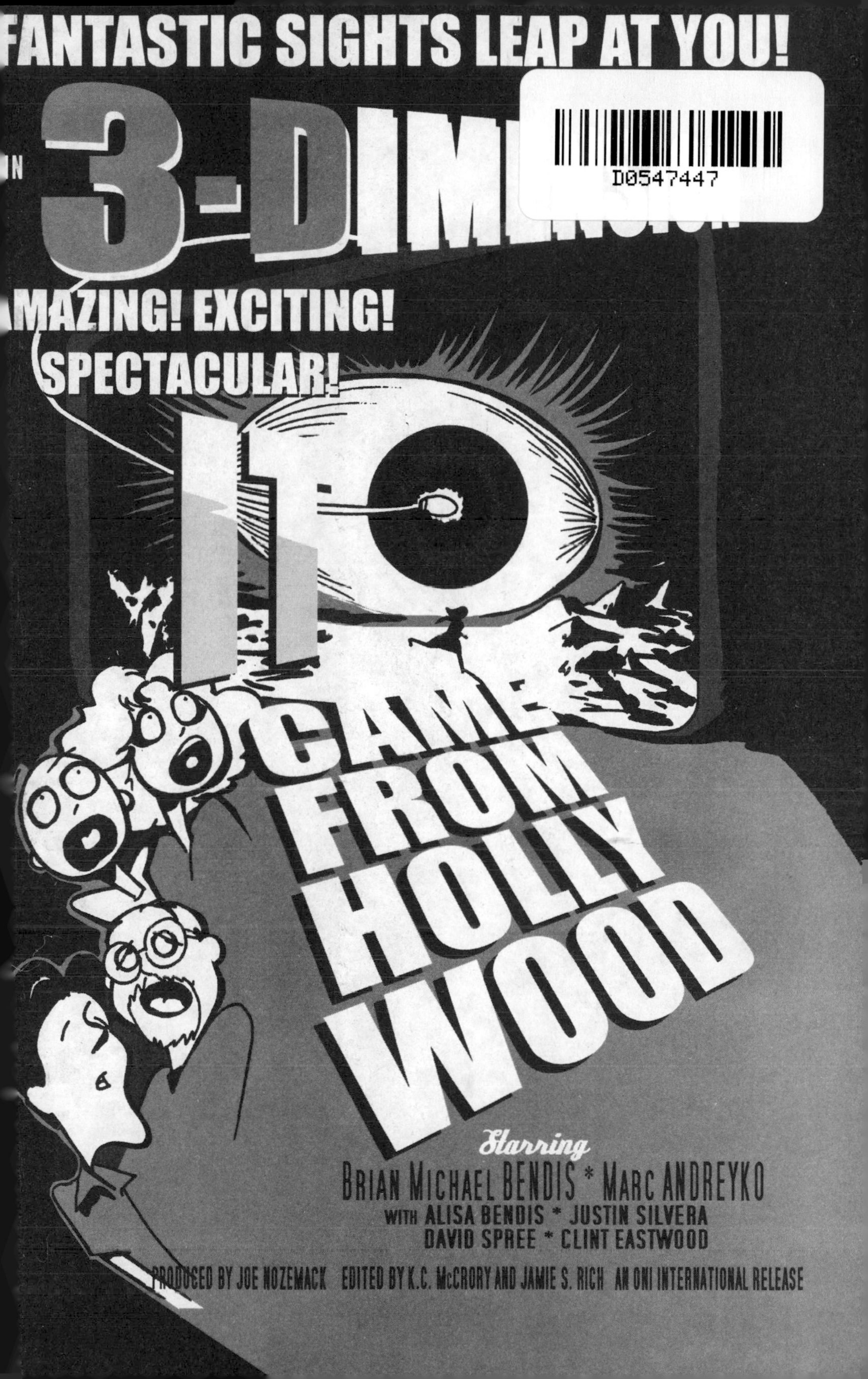
FANTASTIC SIGHTS LEAP AT YOU!
IN 3-DIMENSION
AMAZING! EXCITING! SPECTACULAR!
IT CAME FROM HOLLYWOOD
Starring
BRIAN MICHAEL BENDIS * MARC ANDREYKO
WITH ALISA BENDIS * JUSTIN SILVERA
DAVID SPREE * CLINT EASTWOOD
PRODUCED BY JOE NOZEMACK EDITED BY K.C. McCRORY AND JAMIE S. RICH AN ONI INTERNATIONAL RELEASE

Additional production assistance provided by Steven Birch @ Servo

Published by Oni Press, Inc.
Joe Nozemack, publisher
Jamie S. Rich, editor in chief
James Lucas Jones, webmaster

This book collects issues 1-3 of the Oni Press series Fortune & Glory.

Oni Press, Inc.
6336 SE Milwaukie Avenue, PMB30
Portland, OR 97202
USA

www.onipress.com

First edition, June 2000
ISBN 1-929998-06-6

1 3 5 7 9 10 8 6 4 2
PRINTED IN CANADA

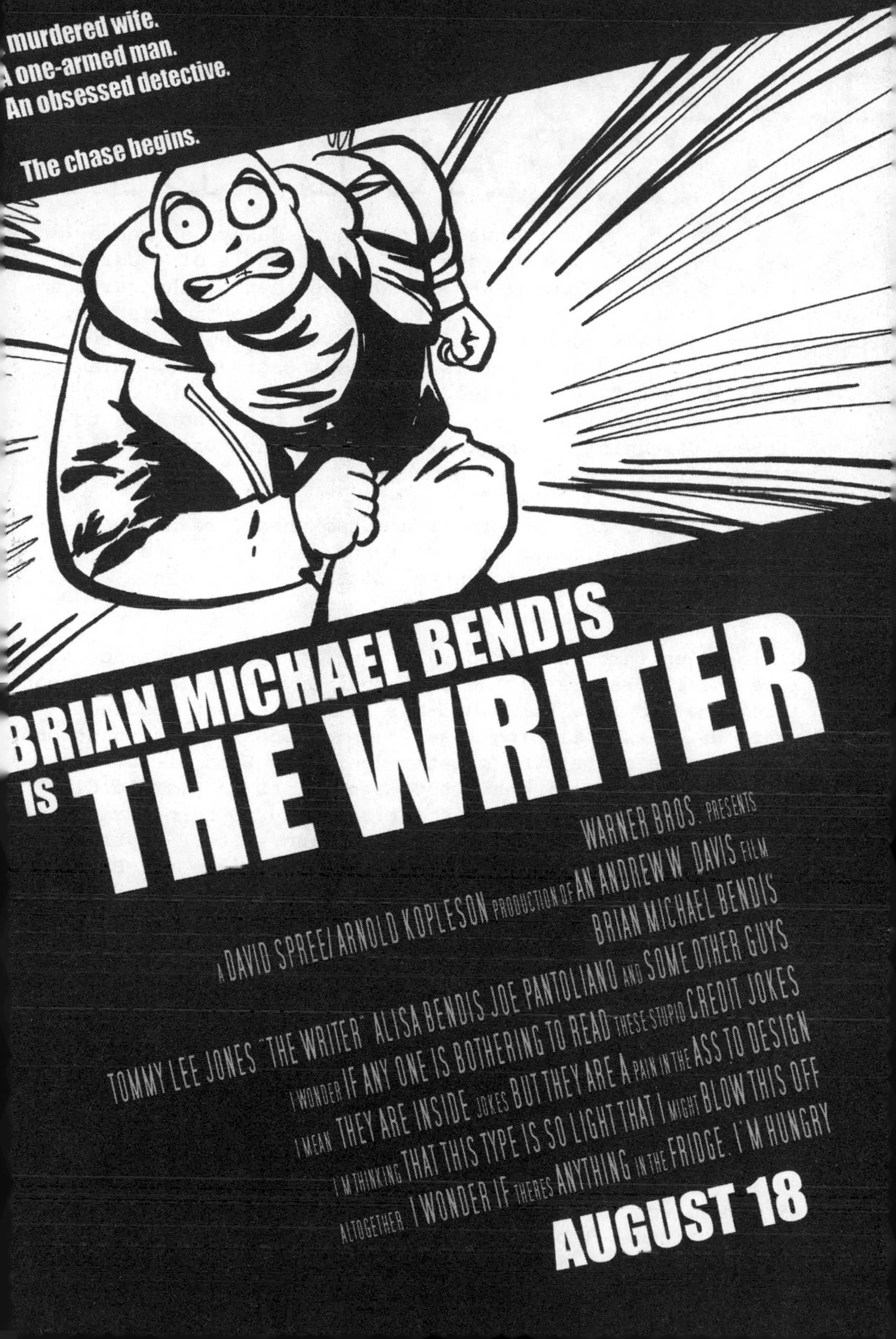
murdered wife.
A one-armed man.
An obsessed detective.
The chase begins.
BRIAN MICHAEL BENDIS
IS THE WRITER
WARNER BROS. PRESENTS
A DAVID SPREE/ARNOLD KOPLESON PRODUCTION OF AN ANDREW W. DAVIS FILM
BRIAN MICHAEL BENDIS
TOMMY LEE JONES "THE WRITER" ALISA BENDIS JOE PANTOLIANO AND SOME OTHER GUYS
I WONDER IF ANY ONE IS BOTHERING TO READ THESE STUPID CREDIT JOKES
I MEAN THEY ARE INSIDE JOKES BUT THEY ARE A PAIN IN THE ASS TO DESIGN
I'M THINKING THAT THIS TYPE IS SO LIGHT THAT I MIGHT BLOW THIS OFF
ALTOGETHER. I WONDER IF THERES ANYTHING IN THE FRIDGE. I'M HUNGRY
AUGUST 18

introduction
by PAUL DIN

There's an old Looney Tune wherein Bugs Bunny, en route to Miami, mistakenly burrows up in the middle of a desert and encounters an enemy who spends the rest of the cartoon trying to destroy him. After finally vanquishing his foe, Bugs heads back to his hole only to see a gleeful Daffy Duck pop out and dash across the desert screaming, "Miami Beach at last!" Bugs tries to stop Daffy, but the duck is too enraptured with finally gaining the promised land to listen. Shrugging to the audience, Bugs says Daffy will have to figure it out for himself.

That's roughly the same feeling I had when I read *Fortune & Glory*, Brian Michael Bendis' funny, sobering, and ultimately brilliant account of his first foray into Hollywood.

Having been through the Hollywood wringer once or twice, I can easily relate to the emotional odyssey Brian's cartoon alter ego endures. Hollywood has spent the last hundred years or so establishing itself (in our collective conscious, if nowhere else) as the creative person's Land of Oz. Beneath its glistening hilltop sign exists an Emerald City whose benevolent wizards labor tirelessly to turn our dreams into realities. No one can tell aspiring writers anything different and what's more, they want to believe it. But this is show business, and the frustrations, setbacks, and heartbreaks of that business walk hand in hand with our dreams like the school bully with the prom queen. Is it all bad? Of course not. But like Daffy Duck looking for the beach that isn't there, newcomers will have to figure out the lay of the land for themselves.

Fortunately, Bendis is a fast learner, and in *Fortune & Glory*, he's created a great primer for any show biz hopeful to follow. The book is an astute, painfully funny, and all too real account of the struggle and insanity that awaits 99.9% of the creative people when they first get involved with Hollywood. And if the other .01% don't get the treatment the first time, I promise you they will on the second.

Brian has perfectly captured the emotional highs and
lows of a writer on the Hollywood see-saw. He also
deftly skewers a number of the irritating nuances I've
come to know and hate about LA. There's the hungry,
desperate way the movers, shakers, and fakers that haunt
trendy restaurants instantly scan your face and discard you
as you enter, unless your last name is DiCaprio, of course.
And let's not forget the strange paradox that while every
agent, producer, and development person in town is a
tremendous fan of the idea of your work as reported
in a magazine or TV spot, none of them have actually sat
down to read the work itself.

Riddle me that, huh?

Bendis' dry wit is perfectly matched by his clean, minimalist
artwork. His round-headed caricature evokes both the innocent
child and the shell-shocked war veteran. Another great visual
touch I loved was the way Brian drew no development person or
producer with their eyes open. I believe it was David Geffen
who pioneered the sleepy-eyed, semi-conscious, semi-
contemptuous air of casual disinterest which most
power wannabes now adopt.

In fact, I am reasonably sure they offer classes on
mastering this attitude through the Hollywood Learning Annex.

In any event, congratulations to Brian on both the book and the
well-deserved praise it has thus far received. I only hope the
producers don't force him to write a happier ending for the
movie version.

Paul Dini

Paul Dini has written a number of books, cartoons, comics,
and screenplays. He is currently in turn-around.

FOR
ALISA

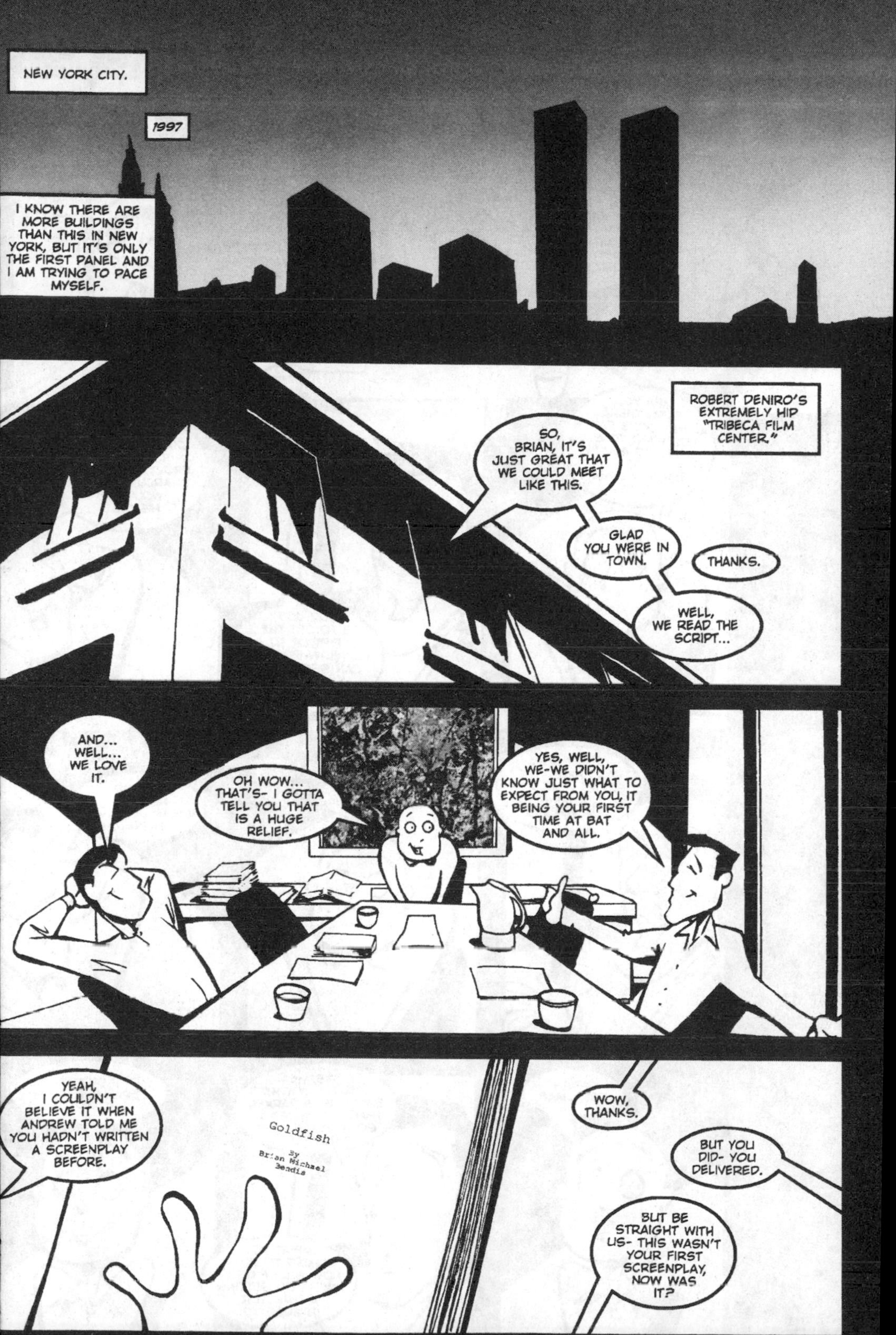

NEW YORK CITY.
1997
I KNOW THERE ARE MORE BUILDINGS THAN THIS IN NEW YORK, BUT IT'S ONLY THE FIRST PANEL AND I AM TRYING TO PACE MYSELF.
ROBERT DENIRO'S EXTREMELY HIP "TRIBECA FILM CENTER."
SO, BRIAN, IT'S JUST GREAT THAT WE COULD MEET LIKE THIS.
GLAD YOU WERE IN TOWN.
THANKS.
WELL, WE READ THE SCRIPT...
AND... WELL... WE LOVE IT.
OH WOW... THAT'S- I GOTTA TELL YOU THAT IS A HUGE RELIEF.
YES, WELL, WE-WE DIDN'T KNOW JUST WHAT TO EXPECT FROM YOU, IT BEING YOUR FIRST TIME AT BAT AND ALL.
YEAH, I COULDN'T BELIEVE IT WHEN ANDREW TOLD ME YOU HADN'T WRITTEN A SCREENPLAY BEFORE.
Goldfish
By Brian Michael Bendis
WOW, THANKS.
BUT YOU DID- YOU DELIVERED.
BUT BE STRAIGHT WITH US- THIS WASN'T YOUR FIRST SCREENPLAY, NOW WAS IT?

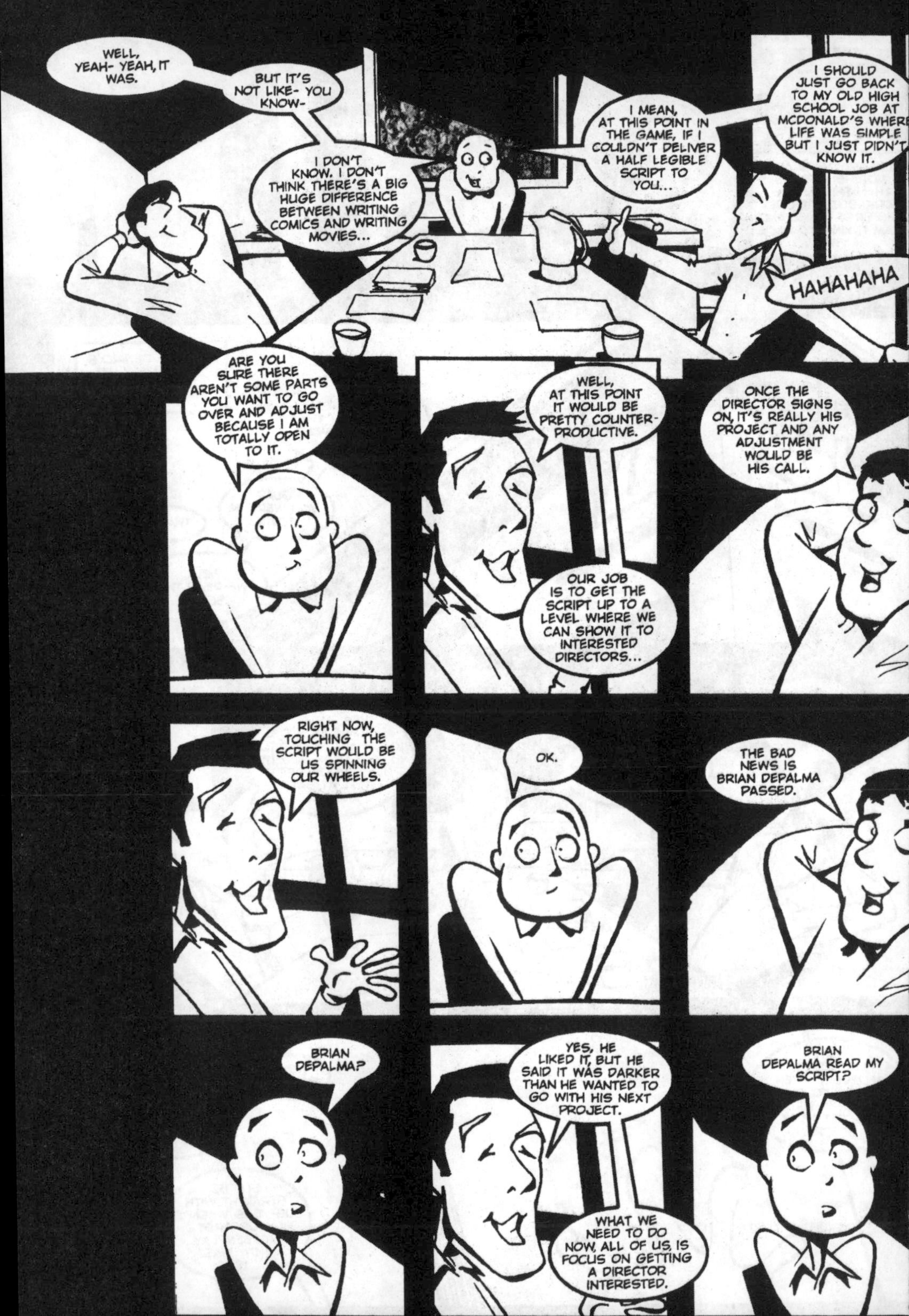
WELL, YEAH- YEAH, IT WAS.
BUT IT'S NOT LIKE- YOU KNOW-
I DON'T KNOW. I DON'T THINK THERE'S A BIG HUGE DIFFERENCE BETWEEN WRITING COMICS AND WRITING MOVIES...
I MEAN, AT THIS POINT IN THE GAME, IF I COULDN'T DELIVER A HALF LEGIBLE SCRIPT TO YOU...
I SHOULD JUST GO BACK TO MY OLD HIGH SCHOOL JOB AT MCDONALD'S WHERE LIFE WAS SIMPLE BUT I JUST DIDN'T KNOW IT.
HAHAHAHA
ARE YOU SURE THERE AREN'T SOME PARTS YOU WANT TO GO OVER AND ADJUST BECAUSE I AM TOTALLY OPEN TO IT.
WELL, AT THIS POINT IT WOULD BE PRETTY COUNTER-PRODUCTIVE.
OUR JOB IS TO GET THE SCRIPT UP TO A LEVEL WHERE WE CAN SHOW IT TO INTERESTED DIRECTORS...
ONCE THE DIRECTOR SIGNS ON, IT'S REALLY HIS PROJECT AND ANY ADJUSTMENT WOULD BE HIS CALL.
RIGHT NOW, TOUCHING THE SCRIPT WOULD BE US SPINNING OUR WHEELS.
OK.
THE BAD NEWS IS BRIAN DEPALMA PASSED.
BRIAN DEPALMA?
YES, HE LIKED IT, BUT HE SAID IT WAS DARKER THAN HE WANTED TO GO WITH HIS NEXT PROJECT.
WHAT WE NEED TO DO NOW, ALL OF US, IS FOCUS ON GETTING A DIRECTOR INTERESTED.
BRIAN DEPALMA READ MY SCRIPT?

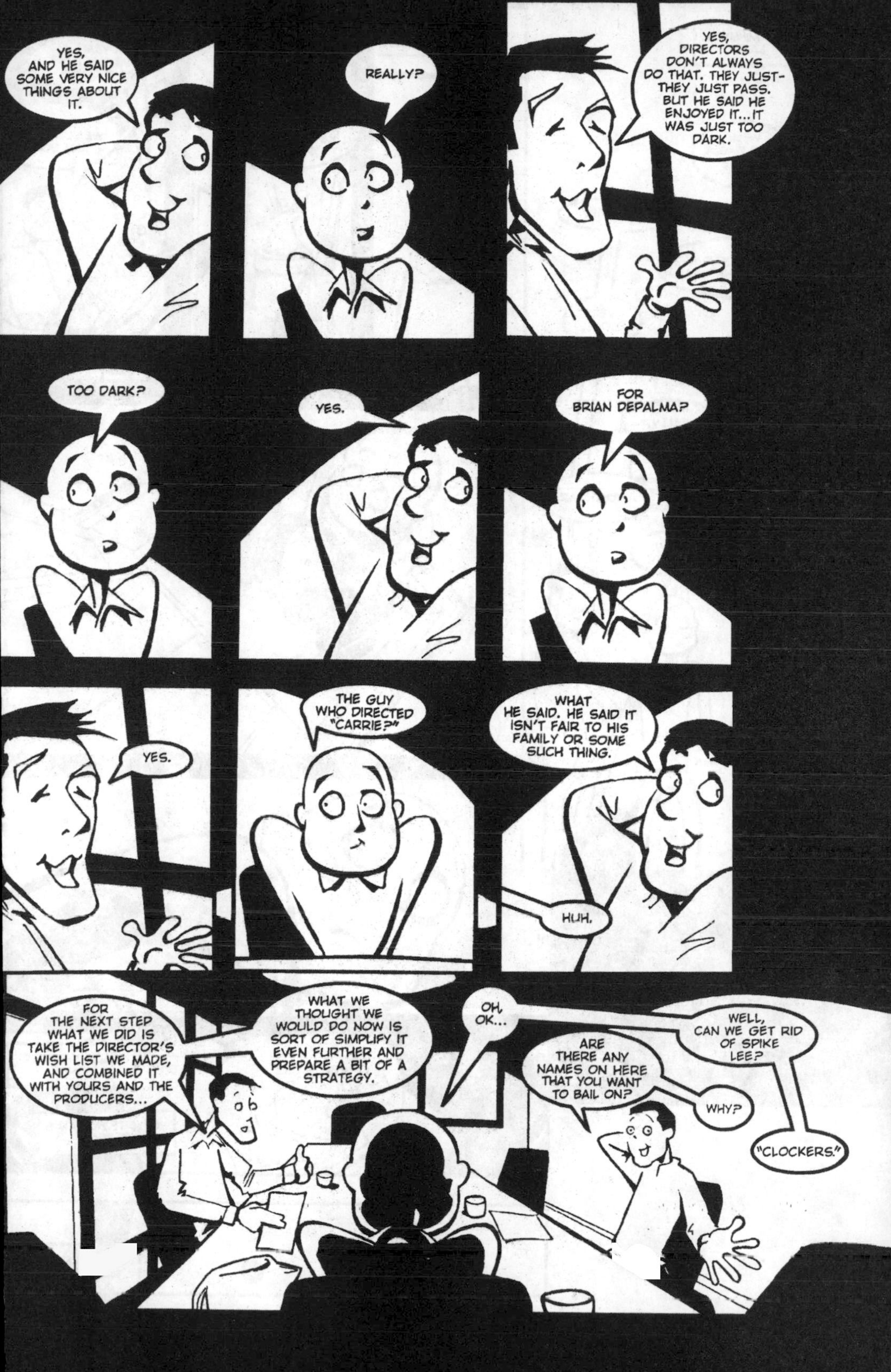
YES, AND HE SAID SOME VERY NICE THINGS ABOUT IT.
REALLY?
YES, DIRECTORS DON'T ALWAYS DO THAT. THEY JUST- THEY JUST PASS. BUT HE SAID HE ENJOYED IT... IT WAS JUST TOO DARK.
TOO DARK?
YES.
FOR BRIAN DEPALMA?
YES.
THE GUY WHO DIRECTED "CARRIE?"
WHAT HE SAID. HE SAID IT ISN'T FAIR TO HIS FAMILY OR SOME SUCH THING.
HUH.
FOR THE NEXT STEP WHAT WE DID IS TAKE THE DIRECTOR'S WISH LIST WE MADE, AND COMBINED IT WITH YOURS AND THE PRODUCERS...
WHAT WE THOUGHT WE WOULD DO NOW IS SORT OF SIMPLIFY IT EVEN FURTHER AND PREPARE A BIT OF A STRATEGY.
OH, OK...
ARE THERE ANY NAMES ON HERE THAT YOU WANT TO BAIL ON?
WELL, CAN WE GET RID OF SPIKE LEE?
WHY?
"CLOCKERS."

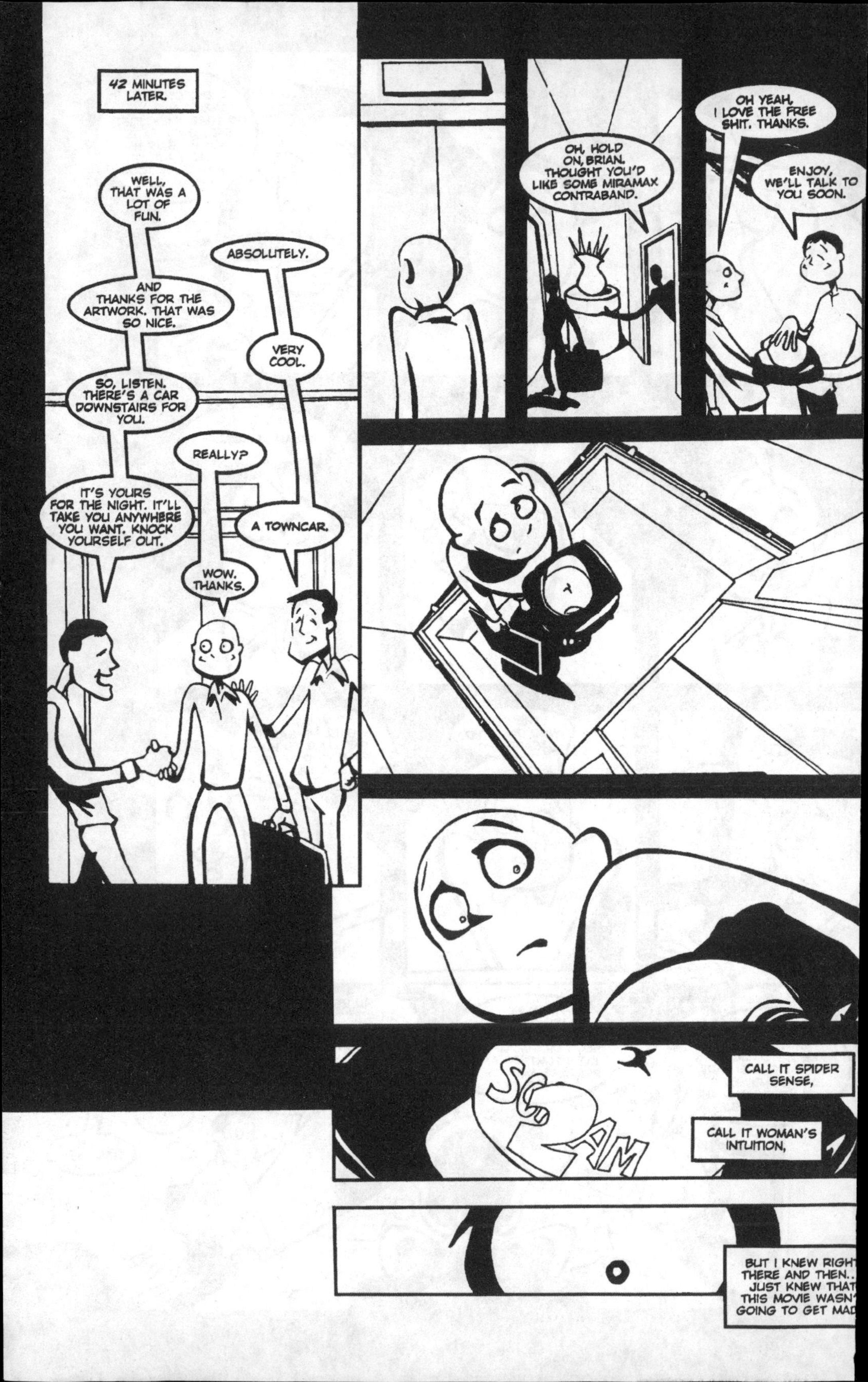

42 MINUTES LATER.
WELL, THAT WAS A LOT OF FUN.
AND THANKS FOR THE ARTWORK. THAT WAS SO NICE.
ABSOLUTELY.
VERY COOL.
SO, LISTEN. THERE'S A CAR DOWNSTAIRS FOR YOU.
REALLY?
IT'S YOURS FOR THE NIGHT. IT'LL TAKE YOU ANYWHERE YOU WANT. KNOCK YOURSELF OUT.
A TOWNCAR.
WOW. THANKS.
OH, HOLD ON, BRIAN. THOUGHT YOU'D LIKE SOME MIRAMAX CONTRABAND.
OH YEAH, I LOVE THE FREE SHIT. THANKS.
ENJOY, WE'LL TALK TO YOU SOON.
SCLAM
CALL IT SPIDER SENSE,
CALL IT WOMAN'S INTUITION,
BUT I KNEW RIGHT THERE AND THEN.. JUST KNEW THAT THIS MOVIE WASN'T GOING TO GET MAD

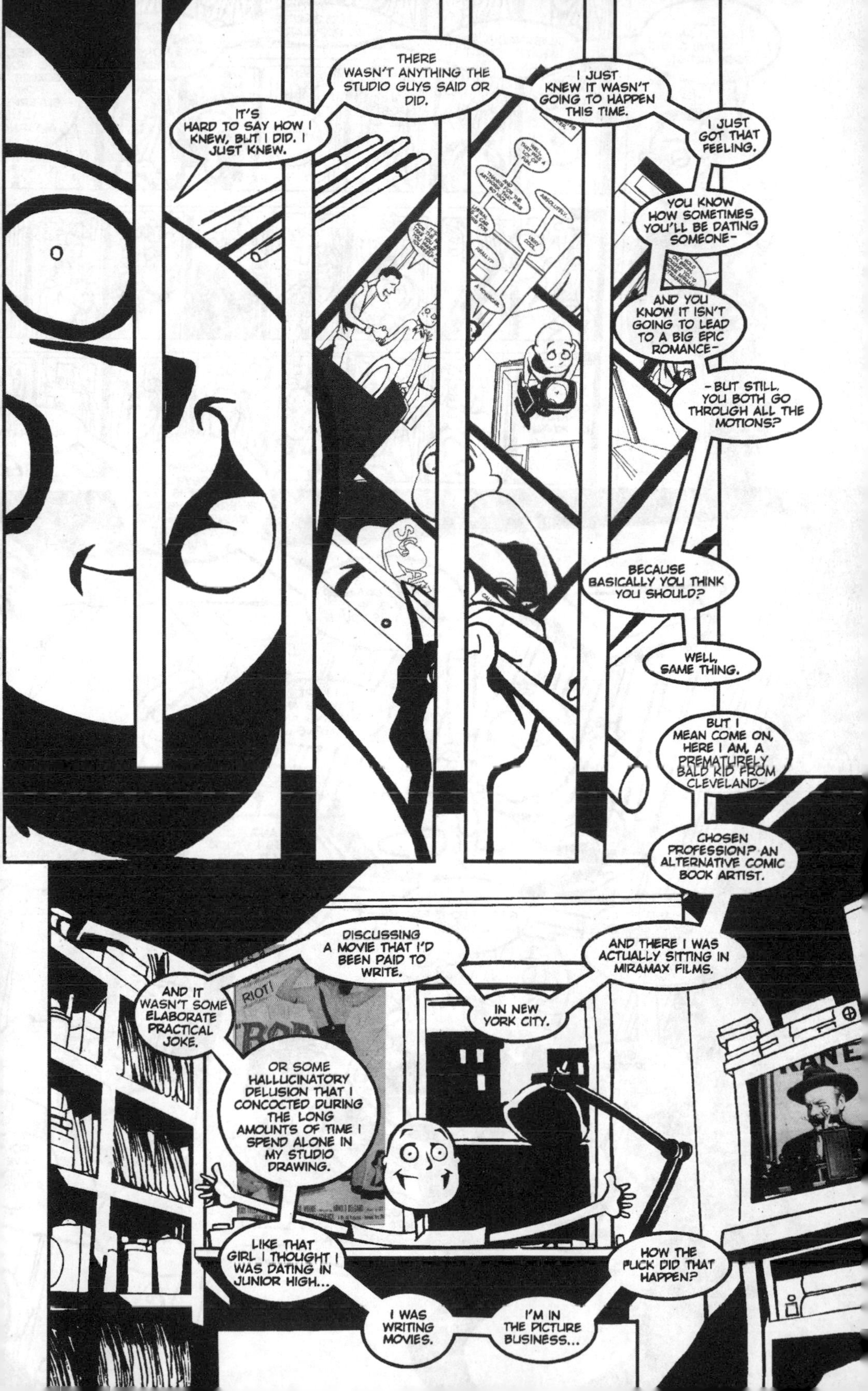
IT'S HARD TO SAY HOW I KNEW, BUT I DID. I JUST KNEW.
THERE WASN'T ANYTHING THE STUDIO GUYS SAID OR DID.
I JUST KNEW IT WASN'T GOING TO HAPPEN THIS TIME.
I JUST GOT THAT FEELING.
YOU KNOW HOW SOMETIMES YOU'LL BE DATING SOMEONE-
AND YOU KNOW IT ISN'T GOING TO LEAD TO A BIG EPIC ROMANCE-
-BUT STILL, YOU BOTH GO THROUGH ALL THE MOTIONS?
BECAUSE BASICALLY YOU THINK YOU SHOULD?
WELL, SAME THING.
BUT I MEAN COME ON, HERE I AM, A PREMATURELY BALD KID FROM CLEVELAND-
CHOSEN PROFESSION? AN ALTERNATIVE COMIC BOOK ARTIST.
AND THERE I WAS ACTUALLY SITTING IN MIRAMAX FILMS.
IN NEW YORK CITY.
DISCUSSING A MOVIE THAT I'D BEEN PAID TO WRITE.
AND IT WASN'T SOME ELABORATE PRACTICAL JOKE.
OR SOME HALLUCINATORY DELUSION THAT I CONCOCTED DURING THE LONG AMOUNTS OF TIME I SPEND ALONE IN MY STUDIO DRAWING.
LIKE THAT GIRL I THOUGHT I WAS DATING IN JUNIOR HIGH...
I WAS WRITING MOVIES.
I'M IN THE PICTURE BUSINESS...
HOW THE FUCK DID THAT HAPPEN?
RIOT!
KANE

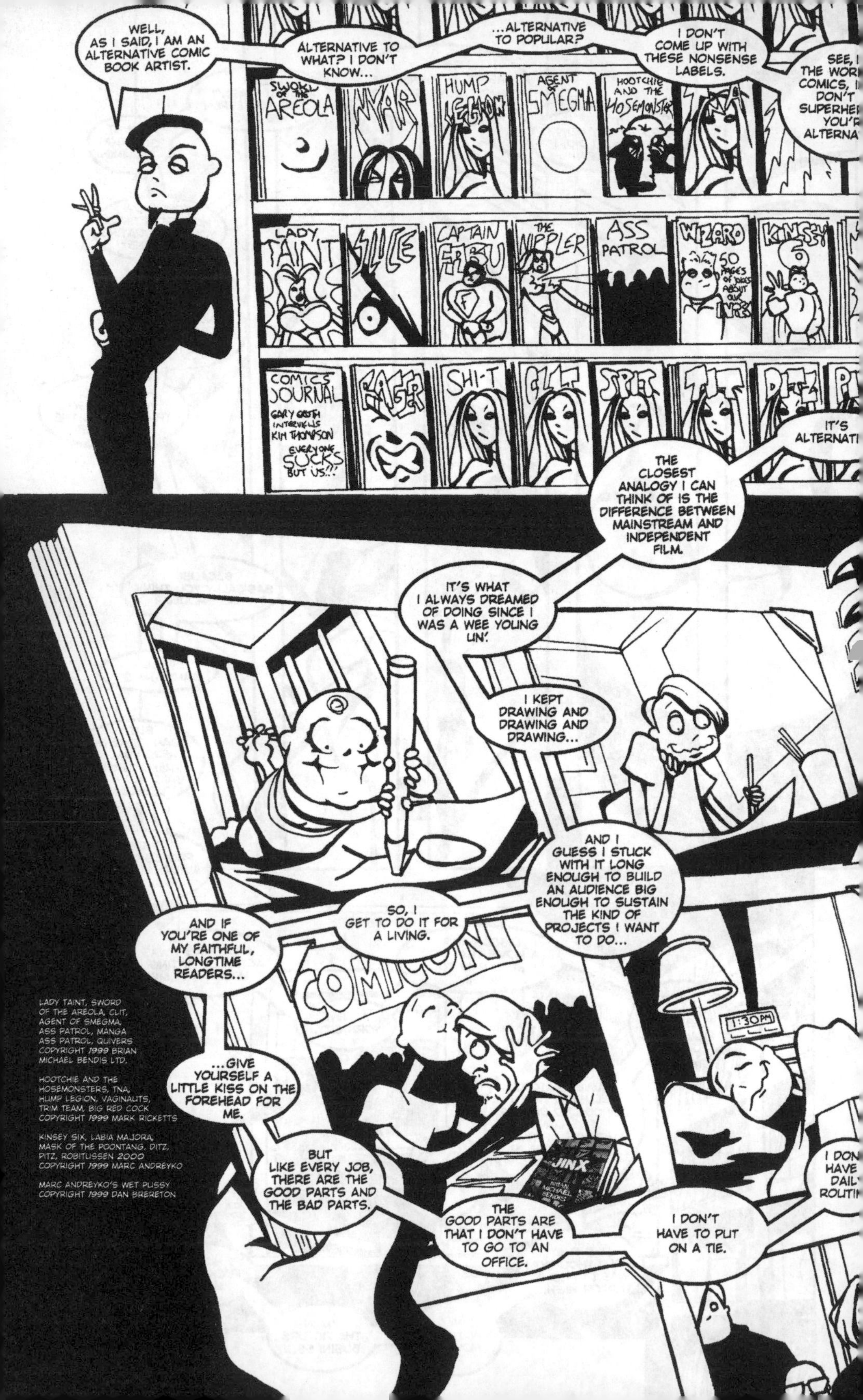
WELL, AS I SAID, I AM AN ALTERNATIVE COMIC BOOK ARTIST.
ALTERNATIVE TO WHAT? I DON'T KNOW...
...ALTERNATIVE TO POPULAR?
I DON'T COME UP WITH THESE NONSENSE LABELS.
AREOLA
HUMP
AGENT OF SMEGMA
HOOTCHIE AND THE
LADY TAINT
SLICE
CAPTAIN
THE NIPPLER
ASS PATROL
WIZARD
50 PAGES OF JOKES ABOUT OUR
COMICS JOURNAL
GARY GROTH INTERVIEWS KIM THOMPSON
EVERYONE SUCKS BUT US!!!
SHI-T
THE CLOSEST ANALOGY I CAN THINK OF IS THE DIFFERENCE BETWEEN MAINSTREAM AND INDEPENDENT FILM.
IT'S WHAT I ALWAYS DREAMED OF DOING SINCE I WAS A WEE YOUNG UN'.
I KEPT DRAWING AND DRAWING AND DRAWING...
AND I GUESS I STUCK WITH IT LONG ENOUGH TO BUILD AN AUDIENCE BIG ENOUGH TO SUSTAIN THE KIND OF PROJECTS I WANT TO DO...
SO, I GET TO DO IT FOR A LIVING.
AND IF YOU'RE ONE OF MY FAITHFUL, LONGTIME READERS...
...GIVE YOURSELF A LITTLE KISS ON THE FOREHEAD FOR ME.
COMICON
1:30 PM
JINX
BRIAN MICHAEL BENDIS
BUT LIKE EVERY JOB, THERE ARE THE GOOD PARTS AND THE BAD PARTS.
THE GOOD PARTS ARE THAT I DON'T HAVE TO GO TO AN OFFICE.
I DON'T HAVE TO PUT ON A TIE.

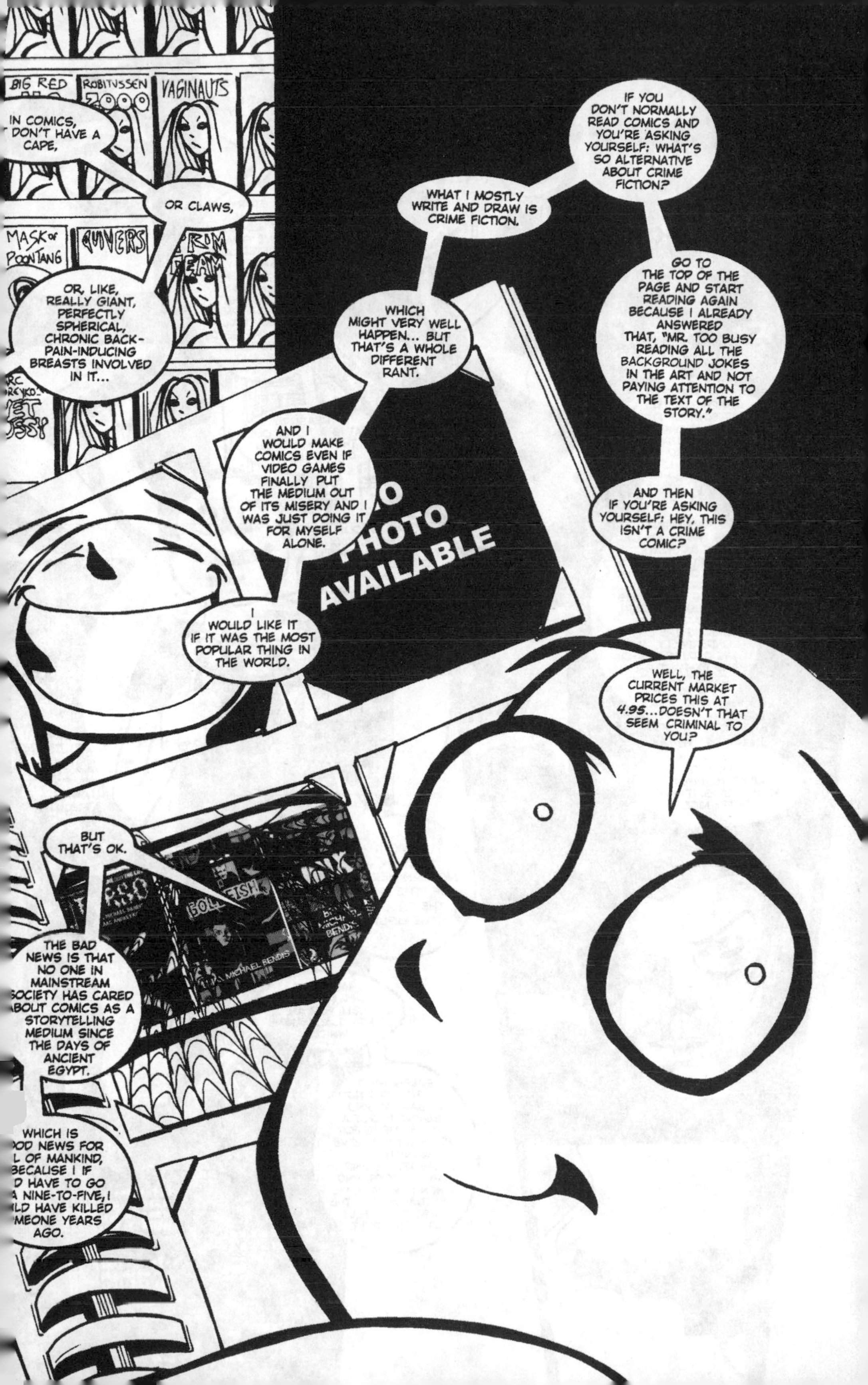

BIG RED
ROBITUSSEN 2000
VAGINAUTS
IN COMICS, T DON'T HAVE A CAPE,
OR CLAWS,
MASK of POONTANG
QUIVERS
OR, LIKE, REALLY GIANT, PERFECTLY SPHERICAL, CHRONIC BACK-PAIN-INDUCING BREASTS INVOLVED IN IT...
BUT THAT'S OK.
THE BAD NEWS IS THAT NO ONE IN MAINSTREAM OCIETY HAS CARED BOUT COMICS AS A STORYTELLING MEDIUM SINCE THE DAYS OF ANCIENT EGYPT.
WHICH IS OOD NEWS FOR L OF MANKIND, BECAUSE I IF D HAVE TO GO A NINE-TO-FIVE, I LD HAVE KILLED MEONE YEARS AGO.
MICHAEL BENDIS
I WOULD LIKE IT IF IT WAS THE MOST POPULAR THING IN THE WORLD.
AND I WOULD MAKE COMICS EVEN IF VIDEO GAMES FINALLY PUT THE MEDIUM OUT OF ITS MISERY AND I WAS JUST DOING IT FOR MYSELF ALONE.
PHOTO AVAILABLE
WHICH MIGHT VERY WELL HAPPEN... BUT THAT'S A WHOLE DIFFERENT RANT.
WHAT I MOSTLY WRITE AND DRAW IS CRIME FICTION.
IF YOU DON'T NORMALLY READ COMICS AND YOU'RE ASKING YOURSELF: WHAT'S SO ALTERNATIVE ABOUT CRIME FICTION?
GO TO THE TOP OF THE PAGE AND START READING AGAIN BECAUSE I ALREADY ANSWERED THAT, "MR. TOO BUSY READING ALL THE BACKGROUND JOKES IN THE ART AND NOT PAYING ATTENTION TO THE TEXT OF THE STORY."
AND THEN IF YOU'RE ASKING YOURSELF: HEY, THIS ISN'T A CRIME COMIC?
WELL, THE CURRENT MARKET PRICES THIS AT 4.95...DOESN'T THAT SEEM CRIMINAL TO YOU?

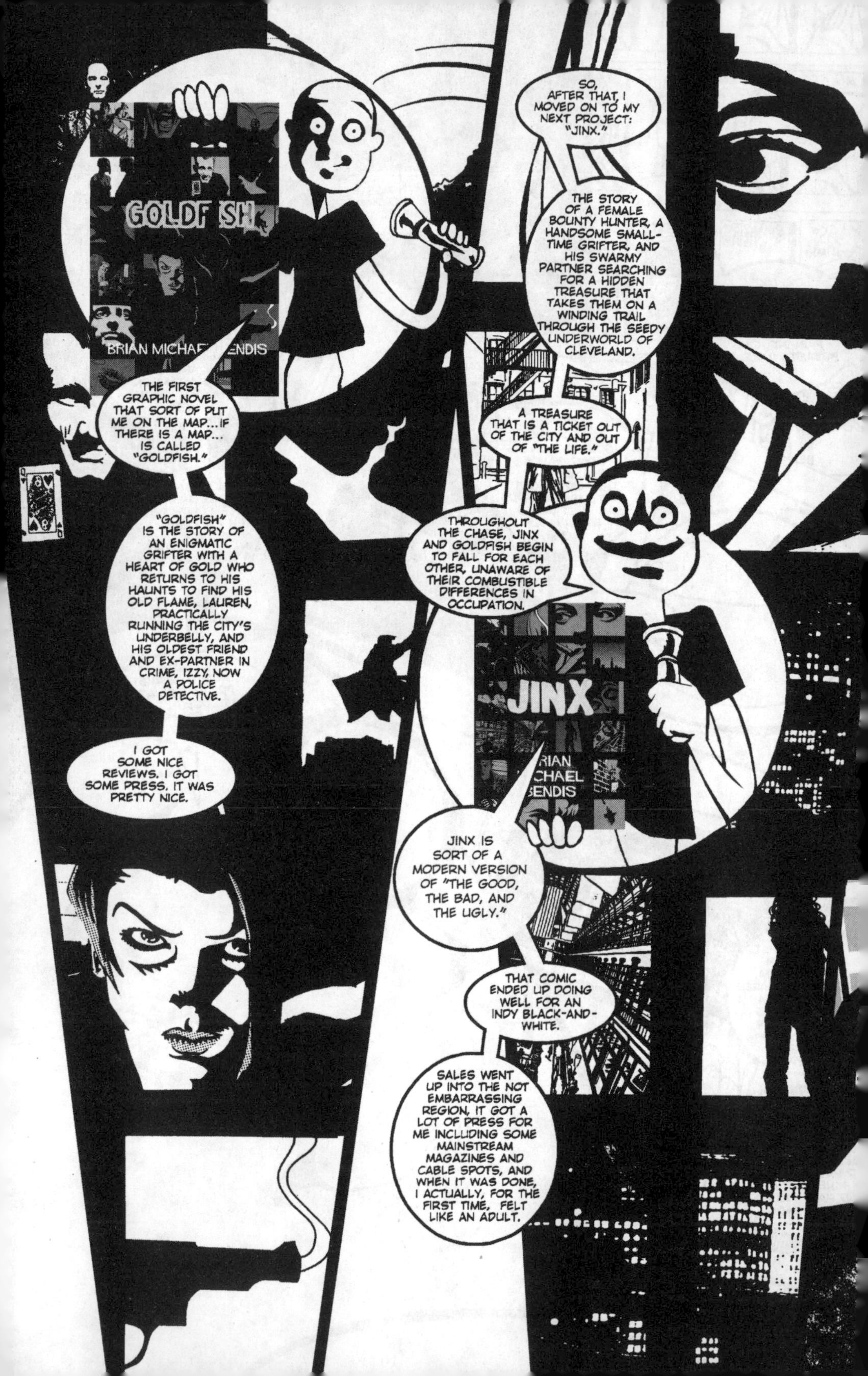
GOLDFISH
BRIAN MICHAEL BENDIS
THE FIRST GRAPHIC NOVEL THAT SORT OF PUT ME ON THE MAP... IF THERE IS A MAP... IS CALLED "GOLDFISH."
"GOLDFISH" IS THE STORY OF AN ENIGMATIC GRIFTER WITH A HEART OF GOLD WHO RETURNS TO HIS HAUNTS TO FIND HIS OLD FLAME, LAUREN, PRACTICALLY RUNNING THE CITY'S UNDERBELLY, AND HIS OLDEST FRIEND AND EX-PARTNER IN CRIME, IZZY, NOW A POLICE DETECTIVE.
I GOT SOME NICE REVIEWS. I GOT SOME PRESS. IT WAS PRETTY NICE.
SO, AFTER THAT, I MOVED ON TO MY NEXT PROJECT: "JINX."
THE STORY OF A FEMALE BOUNTY HUNTER, A HANDSOME SMALL-TIME GRIFTER, AND HIS SWARMY PARTNER SEARCHING FOR A HIDDEN TREASURE THAT TAKES THEM ON A WINDING TRAIL THROUGH THE SEEDY UNDERWORLD OF CLEVELAND.
A TREASURE THAT IS A TICKET OUT OF THE CITY AND OUT OF "THE LIFE."
THROUGHOUT THE CHASE, JINX AND GOLDFISH BEGIN TO FALL FOR EACH OTHER, UNAWARE OF THEIR COMBUSTIBLE DIFFERENCES IN OCCUPATION.
JINX
JINX IS SORT OF A MODERN VERSION OF "THE GOOD, THE BAD, AND THE UGLY."
THAT COMIC ENDED UP DOING WELL FOR AN INDY BLACK-AND-WHITE.
SALES WENT UP INTO THE NOT EMBARRASSING REGION, IT GOT A LOT OF PRESS FOR ME INCLUDING SOME MAINSTREAM MAGAZINES AND CABLE SPOTS, AND WHEN IT WAS DONE, I ACTUALLY, FOR THE FIRST TIME, FELT LIKE AN ADULT.

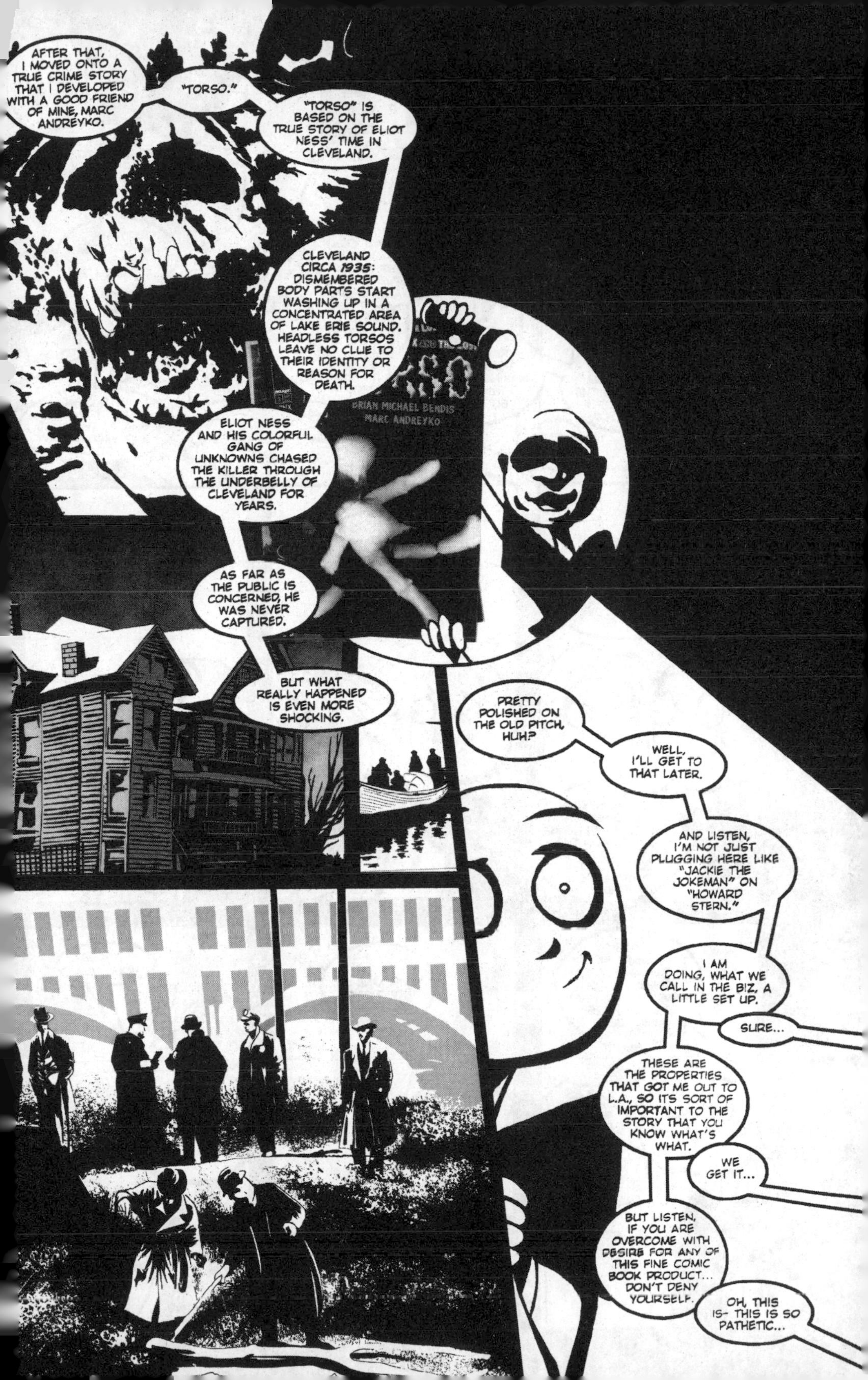
AFTER THAT, I MOVED ONTO A TRUE CRIME STORY THAT I DEVELOPED WITH A GOOD FRIEND OF MINE, MARC ANDREYKO.
"TORSO."
"TORSO" IS BASED ON THE TRUE STORY OF ELIOT NESS' TIME IN CLEVELAND.
CLEVELAND CIRCA 1935: DISMEMBERED BODY PARTS START WASHING UP IN A CONCENTRATED AREA OF LAKE ERIE SOUND. HEADLESS TORSOS LEAVE NO CLUE TO THEIR IDENTITY OR REASON FOR DEATH.
BRIAN MICHAEL BENDIS
MARC ANDREYKO
ELIOT NESS AND HIS COLORFUL GANG OF UNKNOWNS CHASED THE KILLER THROUGH THE UNDERBELLY OF CLEVELAND FOR YEARS.
AS FAR AS THE PUBLIC IS CONCERNED, HE WAS NEVER CAPTURED.
BUT WHAT REALLY HAPPENED IS EVEN MORE SHOCKING.
PRETTY POLISHED ON THE OLD PITCH, HUH?
WELL, I'LL GET TO THAT LATER.
AND LISTEN, I'M NOT JUST PLUGGING HERE LIKE "JACKIE THE JOKEMAN" ON "HOWARD STERN."
I AM DOING, WHAT WE CALL IN THE BIZ, A LITTLE SET UP.
SURE...
THESE ARE THE PROPERTIES THAT GOT ME OUT TO L.A., SO ITS SORT OF IMPORTANT TO THE STORY THAT YOU KNOW WHAT'S WHAT.
WE GET IT...
BUT LISTEN, IF YOU ARE OVERCOME WITH DESIRE FOR ANY OF THIS FINE COMIC BOOK PRODUCT... DON'T DENY YOURSELF.
OH, THIS IS- THIS IS SO PATHETIC...

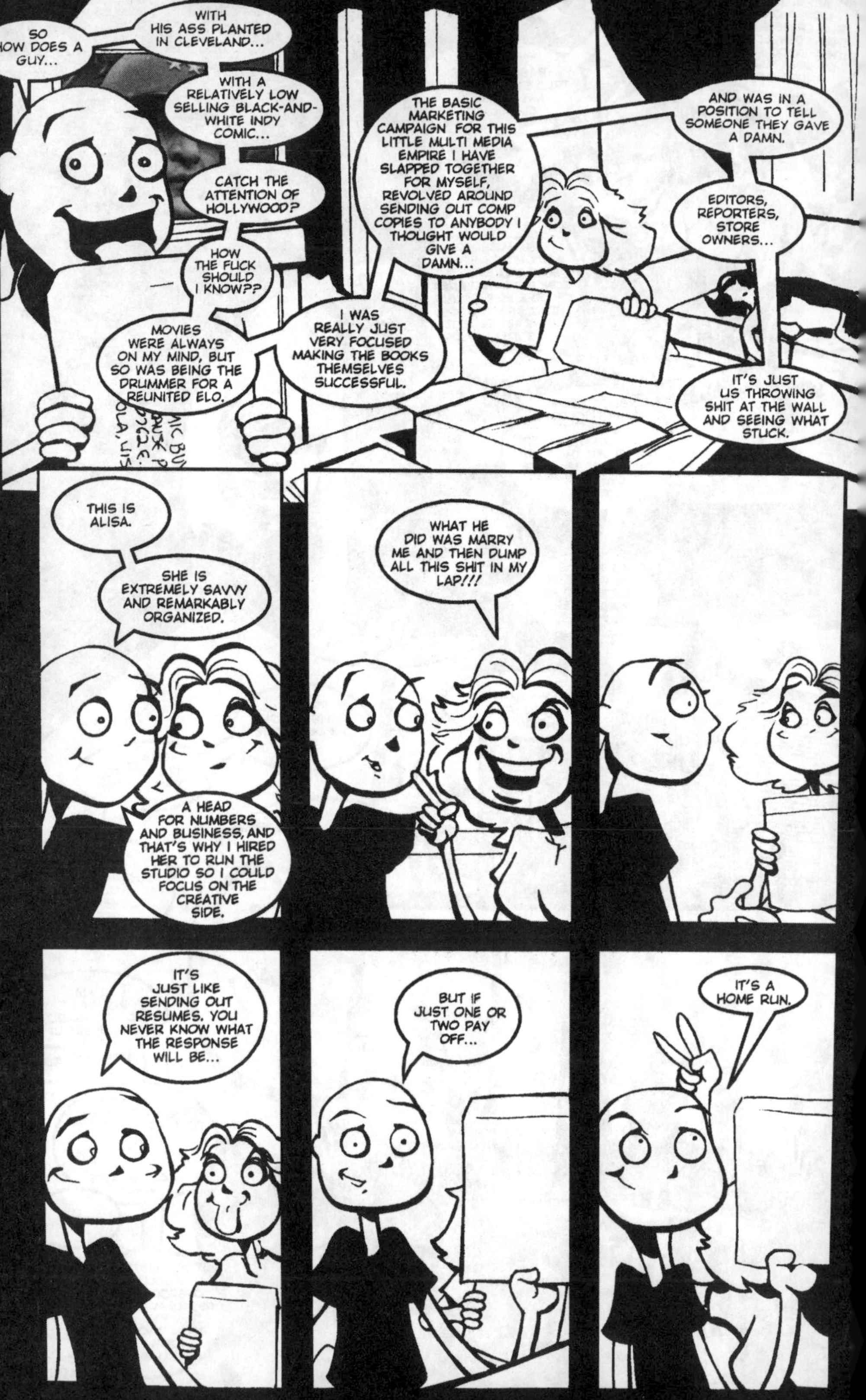
SO HOW DOES A GUY...
WITH HIS ASS PLANTED IN CLEVELAND...
WITH A RELATIVELY LOW SELLING BLACK-AND-WHITE INDY COMIC...
CATCH THE ATTENTION OF HOLLYWOOD?
HOW THE FUCK SHOULD I KNOW??
MOVIES WERE ALWAYS ON MY MIND, BUT SO WAS BEING THE DRUMMER FOR A REUNITED ELO.
I WAS REALLY JUST VERY FOCUSED MAKING THE BOOKS THEMSELVES SUCCESSFUL.
THE BASIC MARKETING CAMPAIGN FOR THIS LITTLE MULTI MEDIA EMPIRE I HAVE SLAPPED TOGETHER FOR MYSELF, REVOLVED AROUND SENDING OUT COMP COPIES TO ANYBODY I THOUGHT WOULD GIVE A DAMN...
AND WAS IN A POSITION TO TELL SOMEONE THEY GAVE A DAMN.
EDITORS, REPORTERS, STORE OWNERS...
IT'S JUST US THROWING SHIT AT THE WALL AND SEEING WHAT STUCK.
THIS IS ALISA.
SHE IS EXTREMELY SAVVY AND REMARKABLY ORGANIZED.
A HEAD FOR NUMBERS AND BUSINESS, AND THAT'S WHY I HIRED HER TO RUN THE STUDIO SO I COULD FOCUS ON THE CREATIVE SIDE.
WHAT HE DID WAS MARRY ME AND THEN DUMP ALL THIS SHIT IN MY LAP!!!
IT'S JUST LIKE SENDING OUT RESUMES. YOU NEVER KNOW WHAT THE RESPONSE WILL BE...
BUT IF JUST ONE OR TWO PAY OFF...
IT'S A HOME RUN.

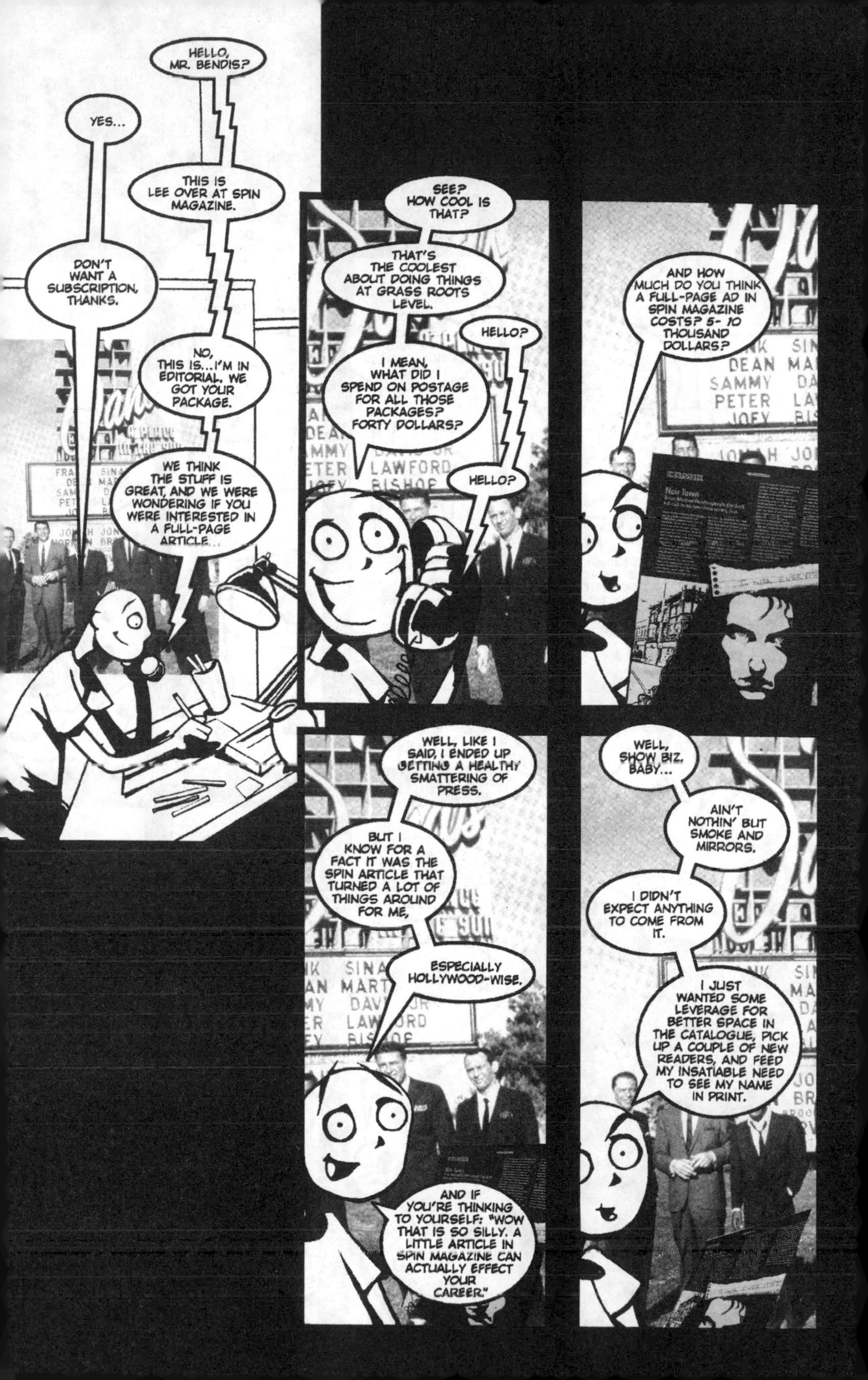
HELLO, MR. BENDIS?
YES...
THIS IS LEE OVER AT SPIN MAGAZINE.
DON'T WANT A SUBSCRIPTION, THANKS.
NO, THIS IS...I'M IN EDITORIAL. WE GOT YOUR PACKAGE.
WE THINK THE STUFF IS GREAT, AND WE WERE WONDERING IF YOU WERE INTERESTED IN A FULL-PAGE ARTICLE...
SEE? HOW COOL IS THAT?
THAT'S THE COOLEST ABOUT DOING THINGS AT GRASS ROOTS LEVEL.
I MEAN, WHAT DID I SPEND ON POSTAGE FOR ALL THOSE PACKAGES? FORTY DOLLARS?
HELLO?
HELLO?
AND HOW MUCH DO YOU THINK A FULL-PAGE AD IN SPIN MAGAZINE COSTS? 5- 10 THOUSAND DOLLARS?
WELL, LIKE I SAID, I ENDED UP GETTING A HEALTHY SMATTERING OF PRESS.
BUT I KNOW FOR A FACT IT WAS THE SPIN ARTICLE THAT TURNED A LOT OF THINGS AROUND FOR ME,
ESPECIALLY HOLLYWOOD-WISE.
AND IF YOU'RE THINKING TO YOURSELF: "WOW THAT IS SO SILLY. A LITTLE ARTICLE IN SPIN MAGAZINE CAN ACTUALLY EFFECT YOUR CAREER."
WELL, SHOW BIZ, BABY...
AIN'T NOTHIN' BUT SMOKE AND MIRRORS.
I DIDN'T EXPECT ANYTHING TO COME FROM IT.
I JUST WANTED SOME LEVERAGE FOR BETTER SPACE IN THE CATALOGUE, PICK UP A COUPLE OF NEW READERS, AND FEED MY INSATIABLE NEED TO SEE MY NAME IN PRINT.

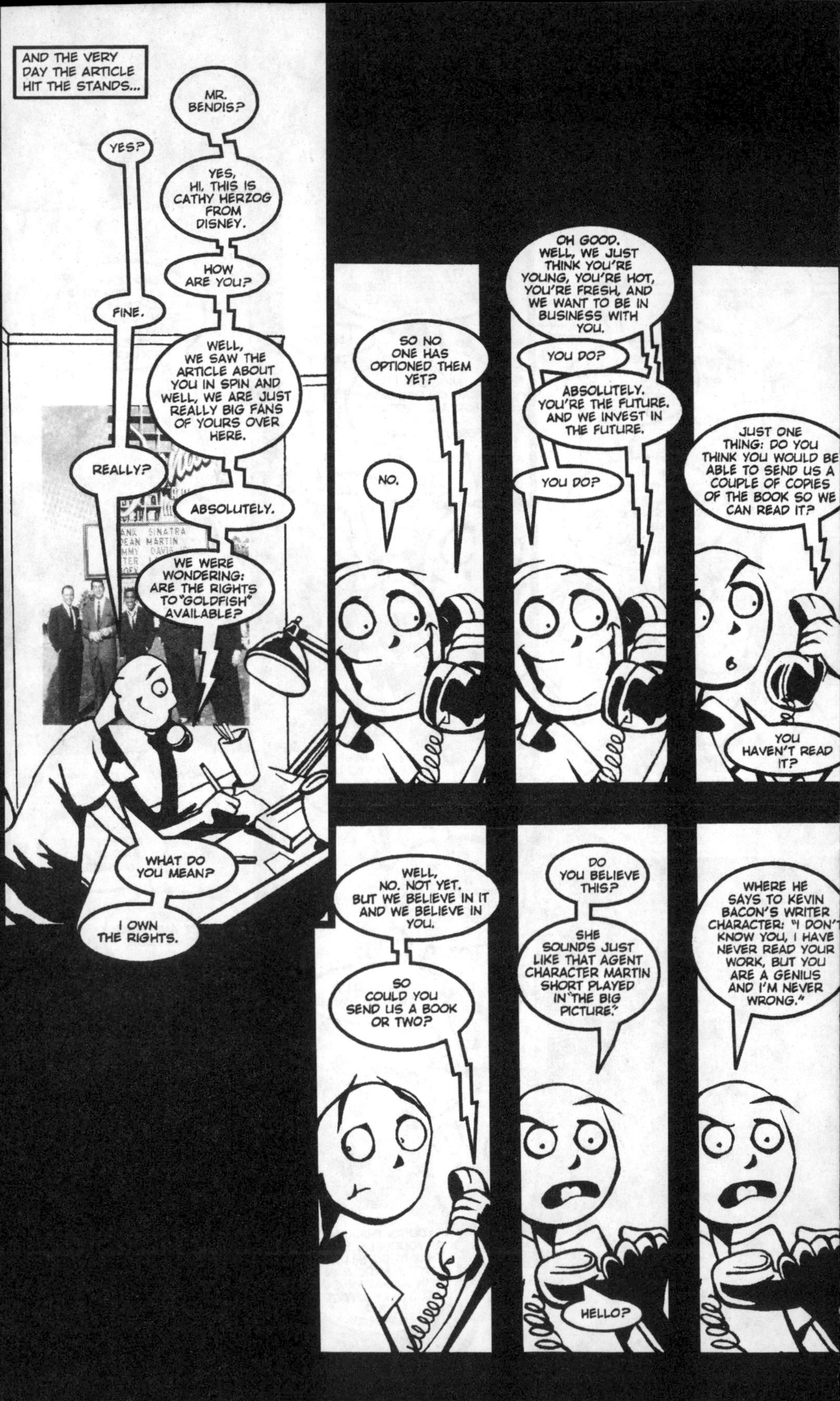
AND THE VERY DAY THE ARTICLE HIT THE STANDS...
MR. BENDIS?
YES?
YES, HI. THIS IS CATHY HERZOG FROM DISNEY.
HOW ARE YOU?
FINE.
WELL, WE SAW THE ARTICLE ABOUT YOU IN SPIN AND WELL, WE ARE JUST REALLY BIG FANS OF YOURS OVER HERE.
REALLY?
ABSOLUTELY.
WE WERE WONDERING: ARE THE RIGHTS TO "GOLDFISH" AVAILABLE?
WHAT DO YOU MEAN?
I OWN THE RIGHTS.
SO NO ONE HAS OPTIONED THEM YET?
NO.
OH GOOD. WELL, WE JUST THINK YOU'RE YOUNG, YOU'RE HOT, YOU'RE FRESH, AND WE WANT TO BE IN BUSINESS WITH YOU.
YOU DO?
ABSOLUTELY. YOU'RE THE FUTURE. AND WE INVEST IN THE FUTURE.
YOU DO?
JUST ONE THING: DO YOU THINK YOU WOULD BE ABLE TO SEND US A COUPLE OF COPIES OF THE BOOK SO WE CAN READ IT?
YOU HAVEN'T READ IT?
WELL, NO. NOT YET. BUT WE BELIEVE IN IT AND WE BELIEVE IN YOU.
SO COULD YOU SEND US A BOOK OR TWO?
DO YOU BELIEVE THIS?
SHE SOUNDS JUST LIKE THAT AGENT CHARACTER MARTIN SHORT PLAYED IN "THE BIG PICTURE."
HELLO?
WHERE HE SAYS TO KEVIN BACON'S WRITER CHARACTER: "I DON'T KNOW YOU, I HAVE NEVER READ YOUR WORK, BUT YOU ARE A GENIUS AND I'M NEVER WRONG."

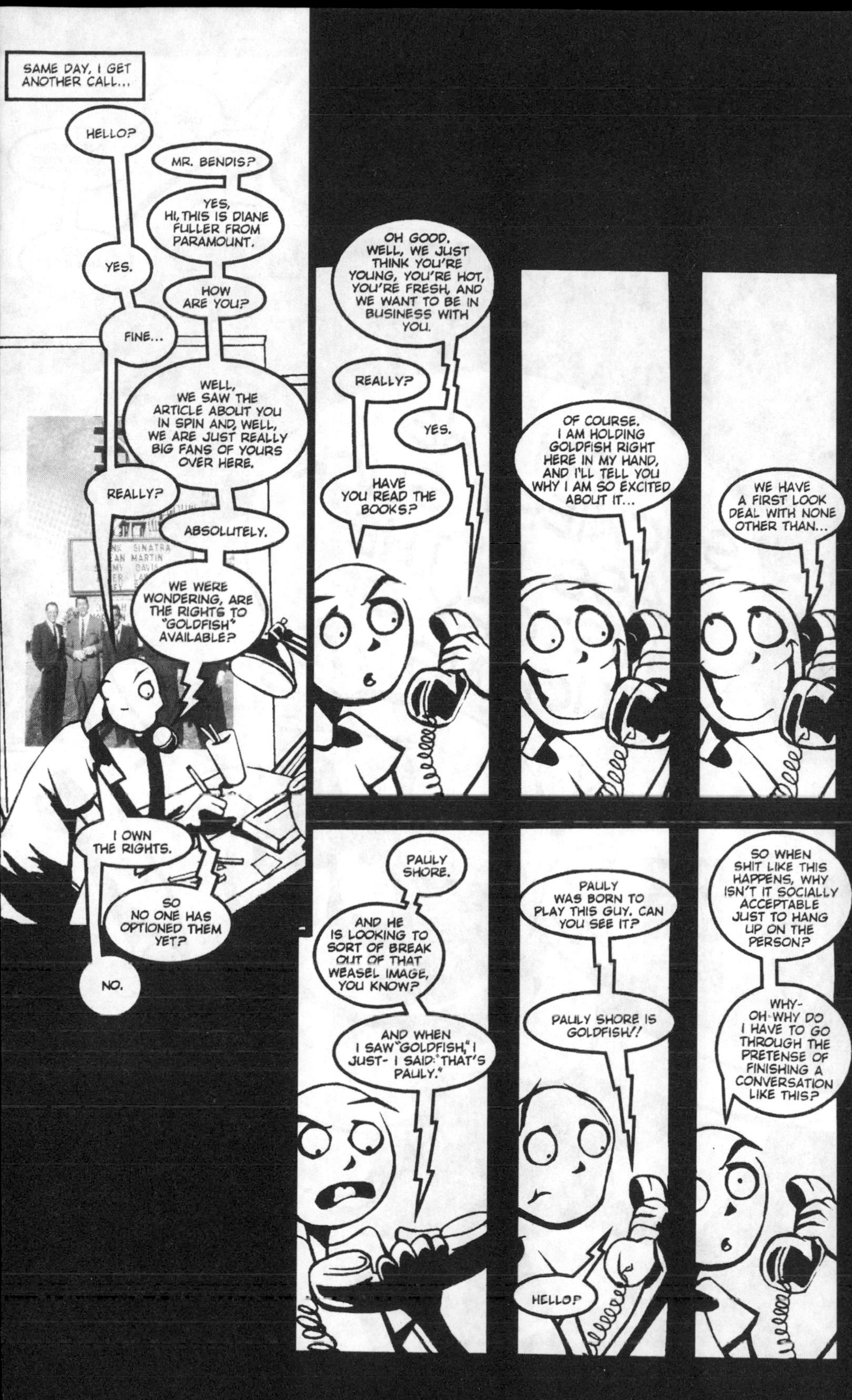
SAME DAY, I GET ANOTHER CALL...
HELLO?
MR. BENDIS?
YES.
YES, HI, THIS IS DIANE FULLER FROM PARAMOUNT.
HOW ARE YOU?
FINE...
WELL, WE SAW THE ARTICLE ABOUT YOU IN SPIN AND, WELL, WE ARE JUST REALLY BIG FANS OF YOURS OVER HERE.
REALLY?
ABSOLUTELY.
WE WERE WONDERING, ARE THE RIGHTS TO "GOLDFISH" AVAILABLE?
I OWN THE RIGHTS.
SO NO ONE HAS OPTIONED THEM YET?
NO.
OH GOOD. WELL, WE JUST THINK YOU'RE YOUNG, YOU'RE HOT, YOU'RE FRESH, AND WE WANT TO BE IN BUSINESS WITH YOU.
REALLY?
YES.
HAVE YOU READ THE BOOKS?
OF COURSE. I AM HOLDING GOLDFISH RIGHT HERE IN MY HAND, AND I'LL TELL YOU WHY I AM SO EXCITED ABOUT IT...
WE HAVE A FIRST LOOK DEAL WITH NONE OTHER THAN...
PAULY SHORE.
AND HE IS LOOKING TO SORT OF BREAK OUT OF THAT WEASEL IMAGE, YOU KNOW?
AND WHEN I SAW "GOLDFISH," I JUST- I SAID: "THAT'S PAULY."
PAULY WAS BORN TO PLAY THIS GUY. CAN YOU SEE IT?
PAULY SHORE IS GOLDFISH!!
HELLO?
SO WHEN SHIT LIKE THIS HAPPENS, WHY ISN'T IT SOCIALLY ACCEPTABLE JUST TO HANG UP ON THE PERSON?
WHY- OH-WHY DO I HAVE TO GO THROUGH THE PRETENSE OF FINISHING A CONVERSATION LIKE THIS?

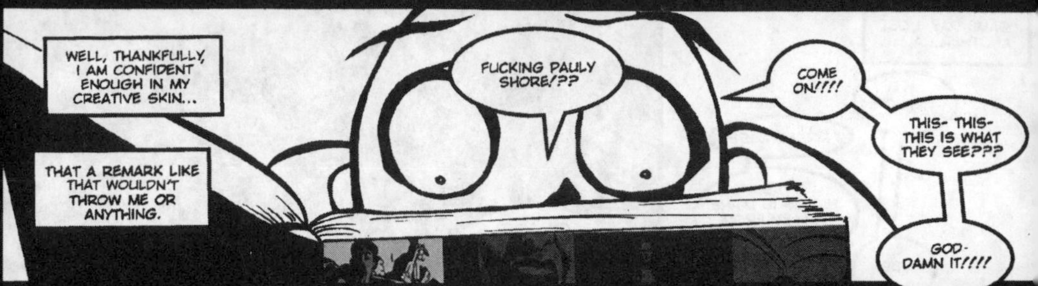
WELL, THANKFULLY, I AM CONFIDENT ENOUGH IN MY CREATIVE SKIN...
THAT A REMARK LIKE THAT WOULDN'T THROW ME OR ANYTHING.
FUCKING PAULY SHORE!??
COME ON!!!!
THIS- THIS- THIS IS WHAT THEY SEE???
GOD-DAMN IT!!!!

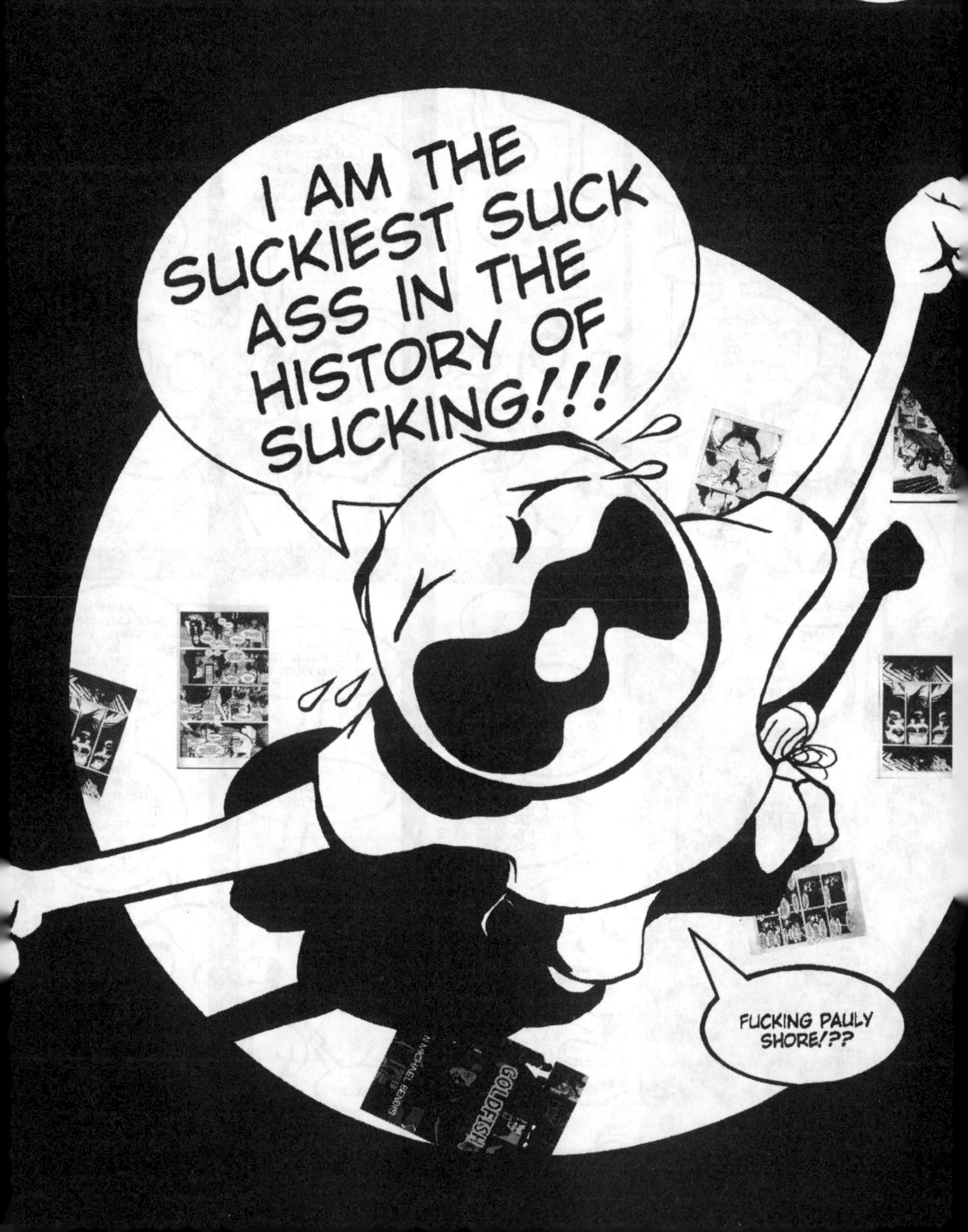
I AM THE SUCKIEST SUCK ASS IN THE HISTORY OF SUCKING!!!
FUCKING PAULY SHORE!??
GOLDFISH

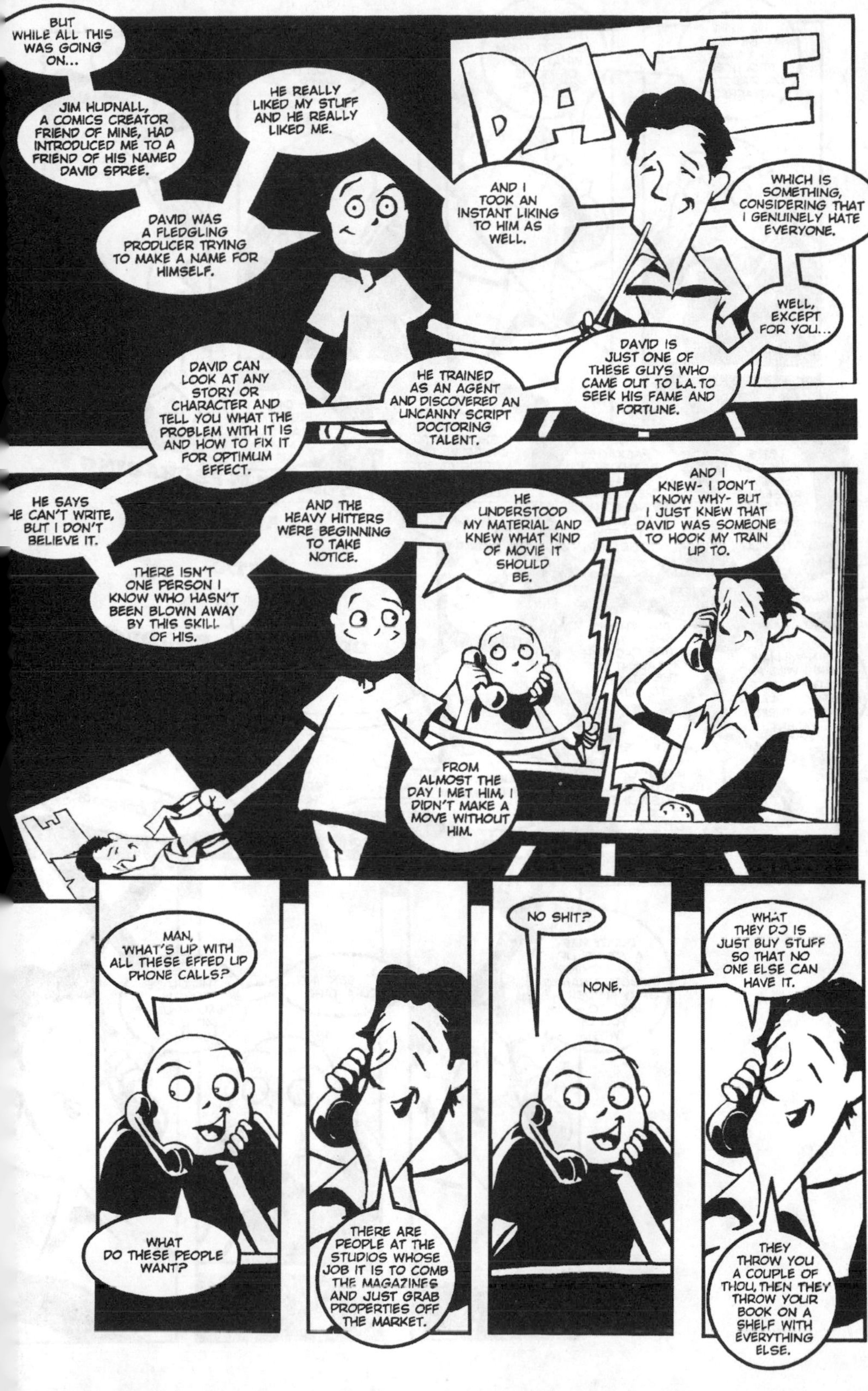
BUT WHILE ALL THIS WAS GOING ON...
JIM HUDNALL, A COMICS CREATOR FRIEND OF MINE, HAD INTRODUCED ME TO A FRIEND OF HIS NAMED DAVID SPREE.
HE REALLY LIKED MY STUFF AND HE REALLY LIKED ME.
DAVID WAS A FLEDGLING PRODUCER TRYING TO MAKE A NAME FOR HIMSELF.
DAVE
AND I TOOK AN INSTANT LIKING TO HIM AS WELL.
WHICH IS SOMETHING, CONSIDERING THAT I GENUINELY HATE EVERYONE.
WELL, EXCEPT FOR YOU...
DAVID IS JUST ONE OF THESE GUYS WHO CAME OUT TO L.A. TO SEEK HIS FAME AND FORTUNE.
HE TRAINED AS AN AGENT AND DISCOVERED AN UNCANNY SCRIPT DOCTORING TALENT.
DAVID CAN LOOK AT ANY STORY OR CHARACTER AND TELL YOU WHAT THE PROBLEM WITH IT IS AND HOW TO FIX IT FOR OPTIMUM EFFECT.
HE SAYS HE CAN'T WRITE, BUT I DON'T BELIEVE IT.
THERE ISN'T ONE PERSON I KNOW WHO HASN'T BEEN BLOWN AWAY BY THIS SKILL OF HIS.
AND THE HEAVY HITTERS WERE BEGINNING TO TAKE NOTICE.
HE UNDERSTOOD MY MATERIAL AND KNEW WHAT KIND OF MOVIE IT SHOULD BE.
AND I KNEW- I DON'T KNOW WHY- BUT I JUST KNEW THAT DAVID WAS SOMEONE TO HOOK MY TRAIN UP TO.
FROM ALMOST THE DAY I MET HIM, I DIDN'T MAKE A MOVE WITHOUT HIM.
MAN, WHAT'S UP WITH ALL THESE EFFED UP PHONE CALLS?
WHAT DO THESE PEOPLE WANT?
THERE ARE PEOPLE AT THE STUDIOS WHOSE JOB IT IS TO COMB THE MAGAZINES AND JUST GRAB PROPERTIES OFF THE MARKET.
NO SHIT?
NONE.
WHAT THEY DO IS JUST BUY STUFF SO THAT NO ONE ELSE CAN HAVE IT.
THEY THROW YOU A COUPLE OF THOU, THEN THEY THROW YOUR BOOK ON A SHELF WITH EVERYTHING ELSE.

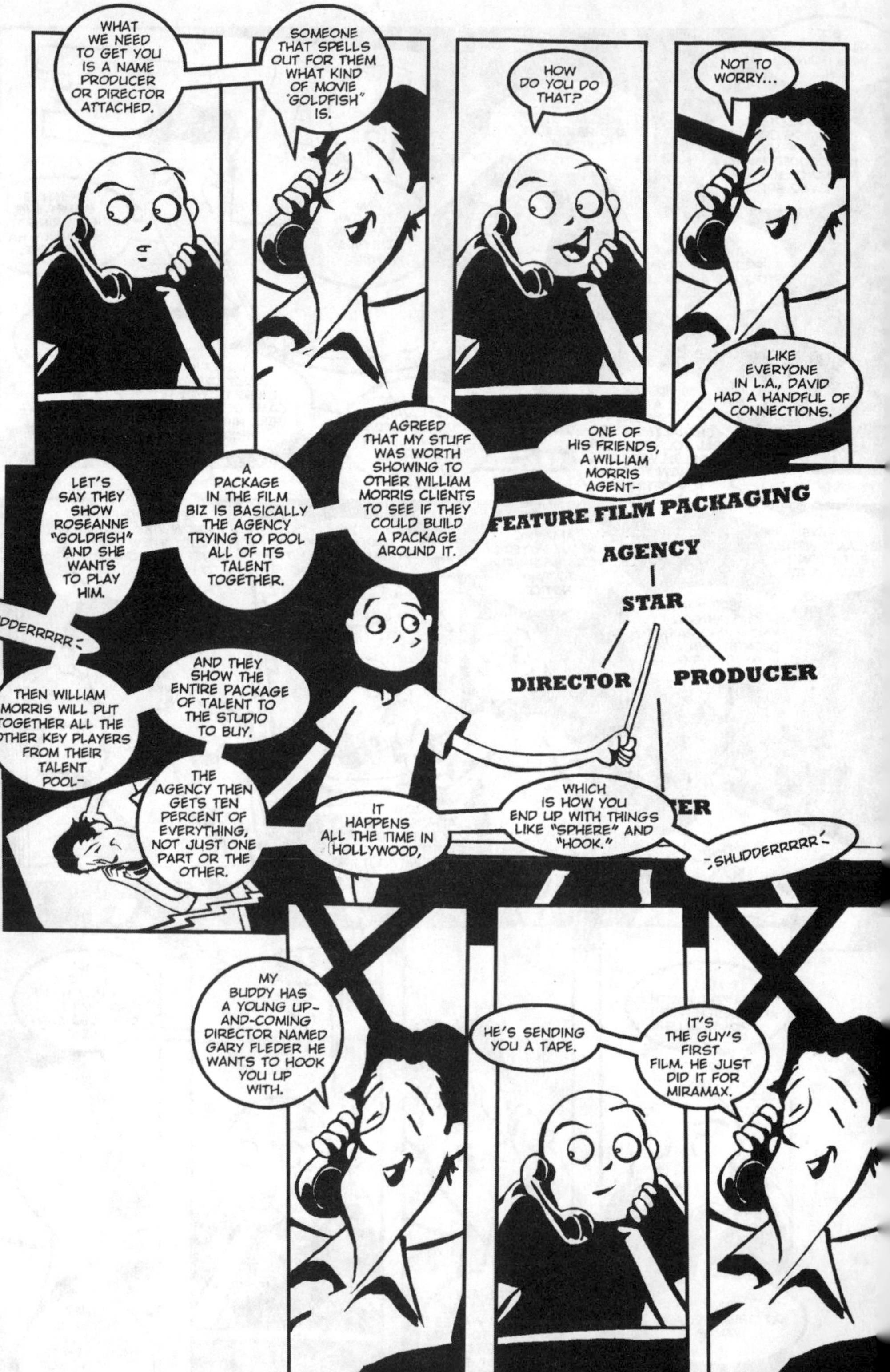

WHAT WE NEED TO GET YOU IS A NAME PRODUCER OR DIRECTOR ATTACHED.
SOMEONE THAT SPELLS OUT FOR THEM WHAT KIND OF MOVIE "GOLDFISH" IS.
HOW DO YOU DO THAT?
NOT TO WORRY...
LIKE EVERYONE IN L.A., DAVID HAD A HANDFUL OF CONNECTIONS.
ONE OF HIS FRIENDS, A WILLIAM MORRIS AGENT-
AGREED THAT MY STUFF WAS WORTH SHOWING TO OTHER WILLIAM MORRIS CLIENTS TO SEE IF THEY COULD BUILD A PACKAGE AROUND IT.
A PACKAGE IN THE FILM BIZ IS BASICALLY THE AGENCY TRYING TO POOL ALL OF ITS TALENT TOGETHER.
LET'S SAY THEY SHOW ROSEANNE "GOLDFISH" AND SHE WANTS TO PLAY HIM.
-SHUDDERRRRR-
THEN WILLIAM MORRIS WILL PUT TOGETHER ALL THE OTHER KEY PLAYERS FROM THEIR TALENT POOL-
AND THEY SHOW THE ENTIRE PACKAGE OF TALENT TO THE STUDIO TO BUY.
THE AGENCY THEN GETS TEN PERCENT OF EVERYTHING, NOT JUST ONE PART OR THE OTHER.
IT HAPPENS ALL THE TIME IN HOLLYWOOD,
WHICH IS HOW YOU END UP WITH THINGS LIKE "SPHERE" AND "HOOK."
-SHUDDERRRRR-
FEATURE FILM PACKAGING
AGENCY
STAR
DIRECTOR
PRODUCER
MY BUDDY HAS A YOUNG UP-AND-COMING DIRECTOR NAMED GARY FLEDER HE WANTS TO HOOK YOU UP WITH.
HE'S SENDING YOU A TAPE.
IT'S THE GUY'S FIRST FILM. HE JUST DID IT FOR MIRAMAX.

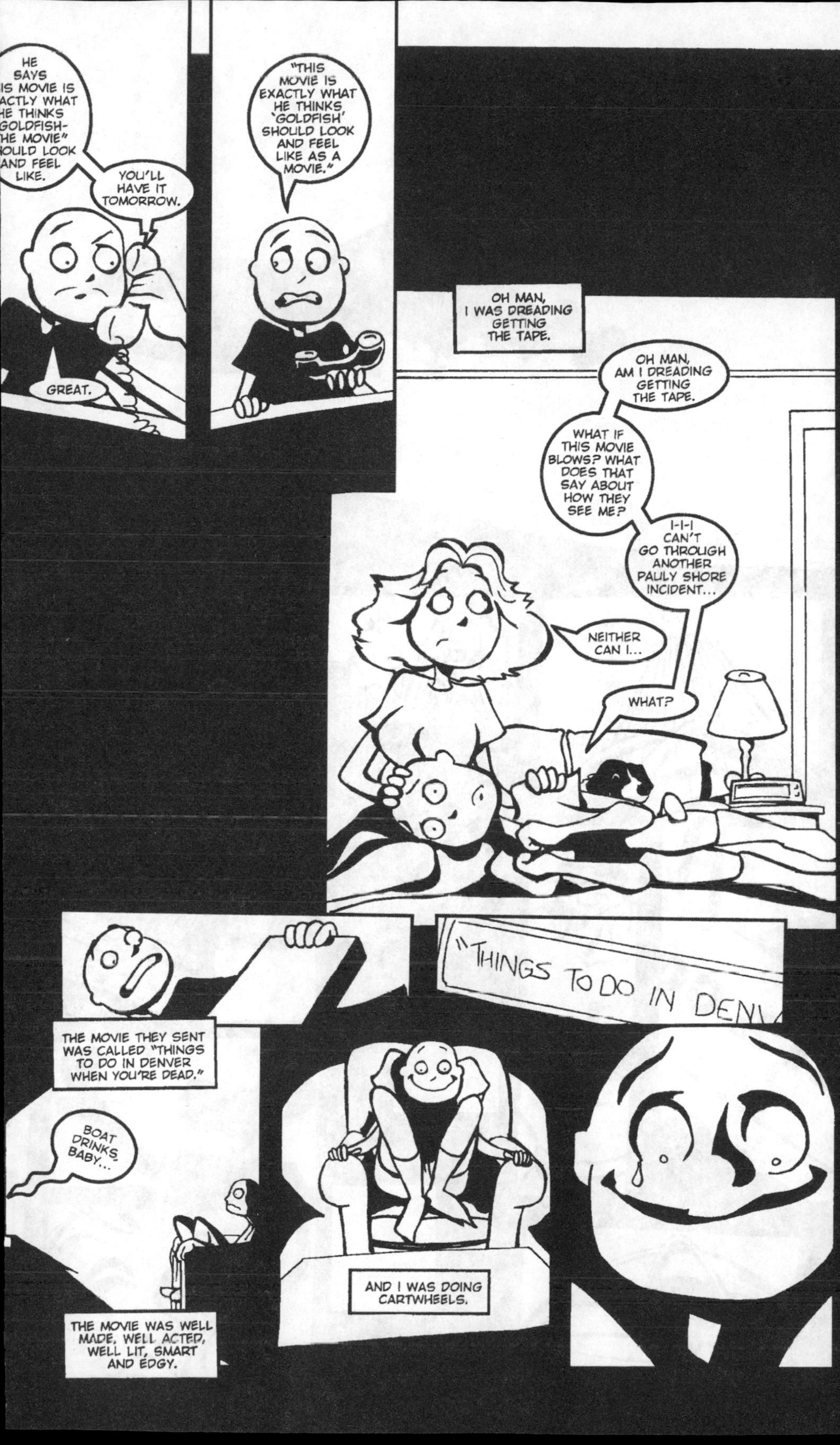
HE SAYS IS MOVIE IS ACTLY WHAT HE THINKS GOLDFISH- HE MOVIE" HOULD LOOK AND FEEL LIKE.
YOU'LL HAVE IT TOMORROW.
GREAT.
"THIS MOVIE IS EXACTLY WHAT HE THINKS 'GOLDFISH' SHOULD LOOK AND FEEL LIKE AS A MOVIE."
OH MAN, I WAS DREADING GETTING THE TAPE.
OH MAN, AM I DREADING GETTING THE TAPE.
WHAT IF THIS MOVIE BLOWS? WHAT DOES THAT SAY ABOUT HOW THEY SEE ME?
I-I-I CAN'T GO THROUGH ANOTHER PAULY SHORE INCIDENT...
NEITHER CAN I...
WHAT?
"THINGS TO DO IN DENV
THE MOVIE THEY SENT WAS CALLED "THINGS TO DO IN DENVER WHEN YOU'RE DEAD."
BOAT DRINKS, BABY...
THE MOVIE WAS WELL MADE, WELL ACTED, WELL LIT, SMART AND EDGY.
AND I WAS DOING CARTWHEELS.

EVERYTHING YOU'VE
EVER HEARD ABOUT
L.A. IS TRUE.

EVERYTHING YOU'VE
EVER SEEN ABOUT
L.A. IS TRUE.

EVERYTHING YOU'VE
EVER READ ABOUT
L.A. IS TRUE.

EVERY CLICHE,
EVERY ANECDOTE,
EVERY OUTRAGEOUS
STEREOTYPE...

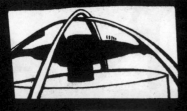

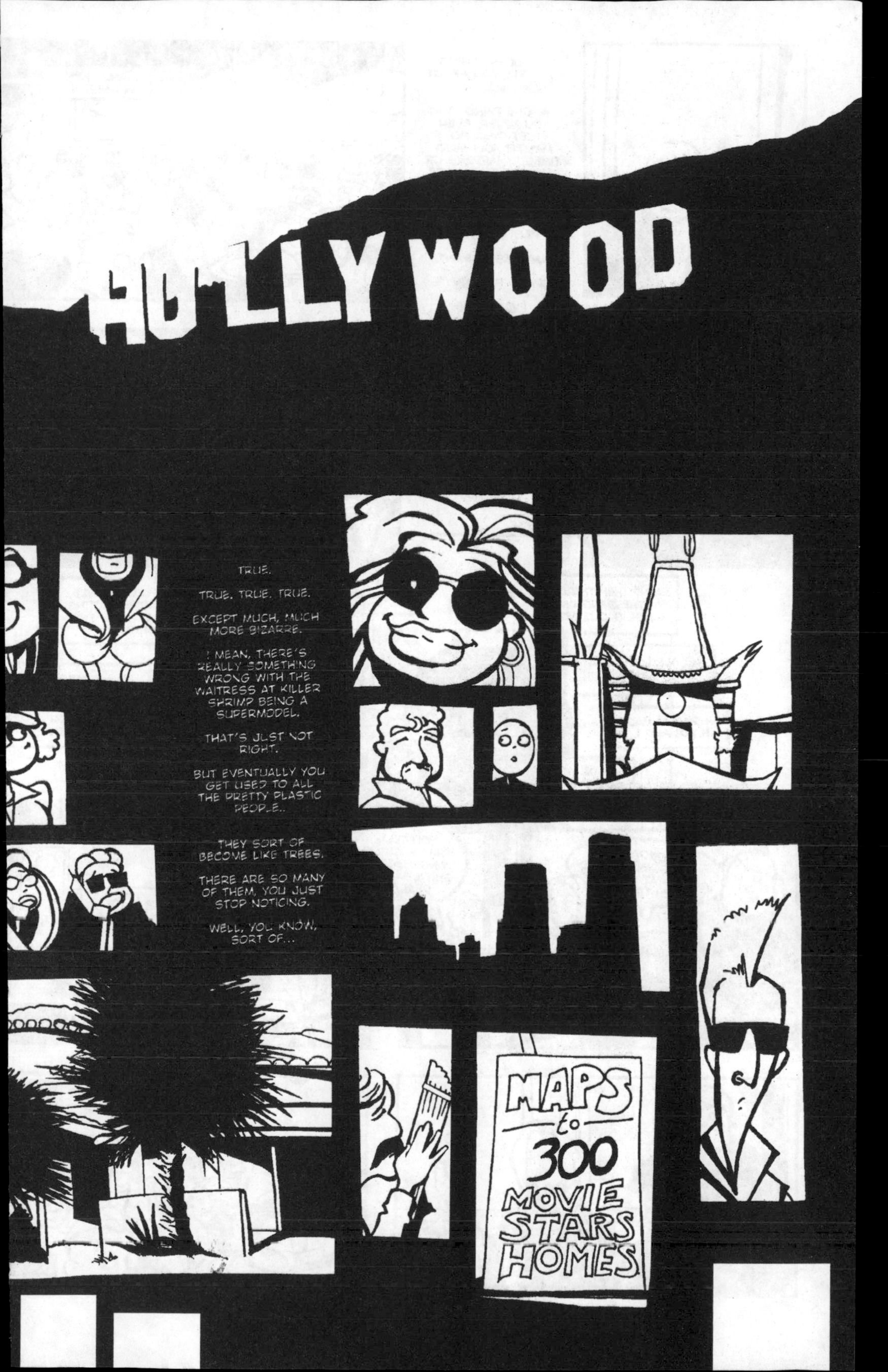
HOLLYWOOD
TRUE.
TRUE. TRUE. TRUE.
EXCEPT MUCH, MUCH MORE BIZARRE.
I MEAN, THERE'S REALLY SOMETHING WRONG WITH THE WAITRESS AT KILLER SHRIMP BEING A SUPERMODEL.
THAT'S JUST NOT RIGHT.
BUT EVENTUALLY YOU GET USED TO ALL THE PRETTY PLASTIC PEOPLE..
THEY SORT OF BECOME LIKE TREES.
THERE ARE SO MANY OF THEM, YOU JUST STOP NOTICING.
WELL, YOU KNOW, SORT OF...
MAPS to 300 MOVIE STARS HOMES

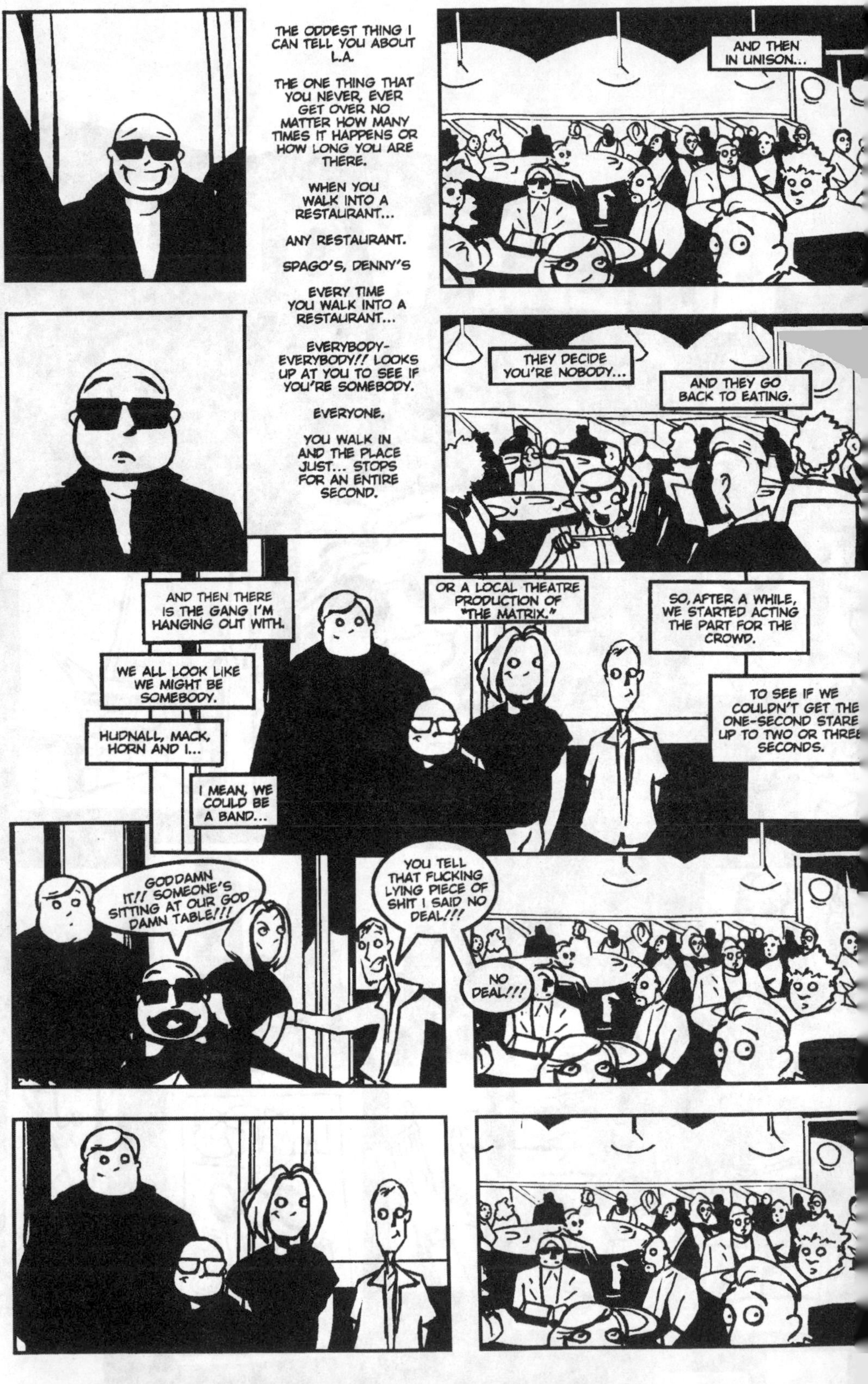
THE ODDEST THING I CAN TELL YOU ABOUT L.A.
THE ONE THING THAT YOU NEVER, EVER GET OVER NO MATTER HOW MANY TIMES IT HAPPENS OR HOW LONG YOU ARE THERE.
WHEN YOU WALK INTO A RESTAURANT...
ANY RESTAURANT.
SPAGO'S, DENNY'S
EVERY TIME YOU WALK INTO A RESTAURANT...
AND THEN IN UNISON...
EVERYBODY- EVERYBODY!! LOOKS UP AT YOU TO SEE IF YOU'RE SOMEBODY.
EVERYONE.
YOU WALK IN AND THE PLACE JUST... STOPS FOR AN ENTIRE SECOND.
THEY DECIDE YOU'RE NOBODY...
AND THEY GO BACK TO EATING.
AND THEN THERE IS THE GANG I'M HANGING OUT WITH.
WE ALL LOOK LIKE WE MIGHT BE SOMEBODY.
HUDNALL, MACK, HORN AND I...
I MEAN, WE COULD BE A BAND...
OR A LOCAL THEATRE PRODUCTION OF "THE MATRIX."
SO, AFTER A WHILE, WE STARTED ACTING THE PART FOR THE CROWD.
TO SEE IF WE COULDN'T GET THE ONE-SECOND STARE UP TO TWO OR THREE SECONDS.
GODDAMN IT!! SOMEONE'S SITTING AT OUR GOD DAMN TABLE!!!
YOU TELL THAT FUCKING LYING PIECE OF SHIT I SAID NO DEAL!!!
NO DEAL!!!

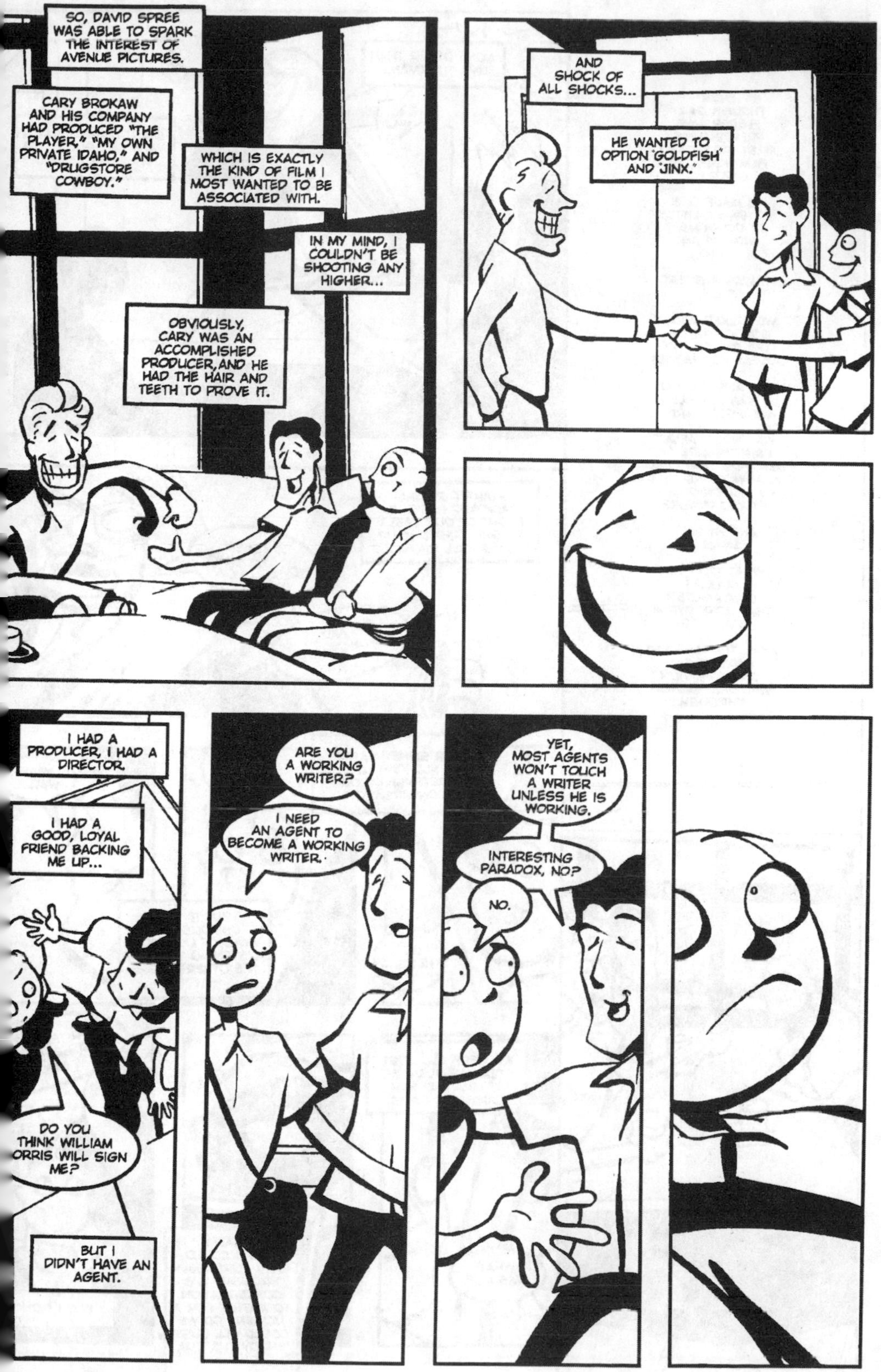
SO, DAVID SPREE WAS ABLE TO SPARK THE INTEREST OF AVENUE PICTURES.
CARY BROKAW AND HIS COMPANY HAD PRODUCED "THE PLAYER," "MY OWN PRIVATE IDAHO," AND "DRUGSTORE COWBOY."
WHICH IS EXACTLY THE KIND OF FILM I MOST WANTED TO BE ASSOCIATED WITH.
IN MY MIND, I COULDN'T BE SHOOTING ANY HIGHER...
OBVIOUSLY, CARY WAS AN ACCOMPLISHED PRODUCER, AND HE HAD THE HAIR AND TEETH TO PROVE IT.
AND SHOCK OF ALL SHOCKS...
HE WANTED TO OPTION "GOLDFISH" AND "JINX."
I HAD A PRODUCER, I HAD A DIRECTOR.
I HAD A GOOD, LOYAL FRIEND BACKING ME UP...
DO YOU THINK WILLIAM ORRIS WILL SIGN ME?
BUT I DIDN'T HAVE AN AGENT.
ARE YOU A WORKING WRITER?
I NEED AN AGENT TO BECOME A WORKING WRITER.
YET, MOST AGENTS WON'T TOUCH A WRITER UNLESS HE IS WORKING.
INTERESTING PARADOX, NO?
NO.

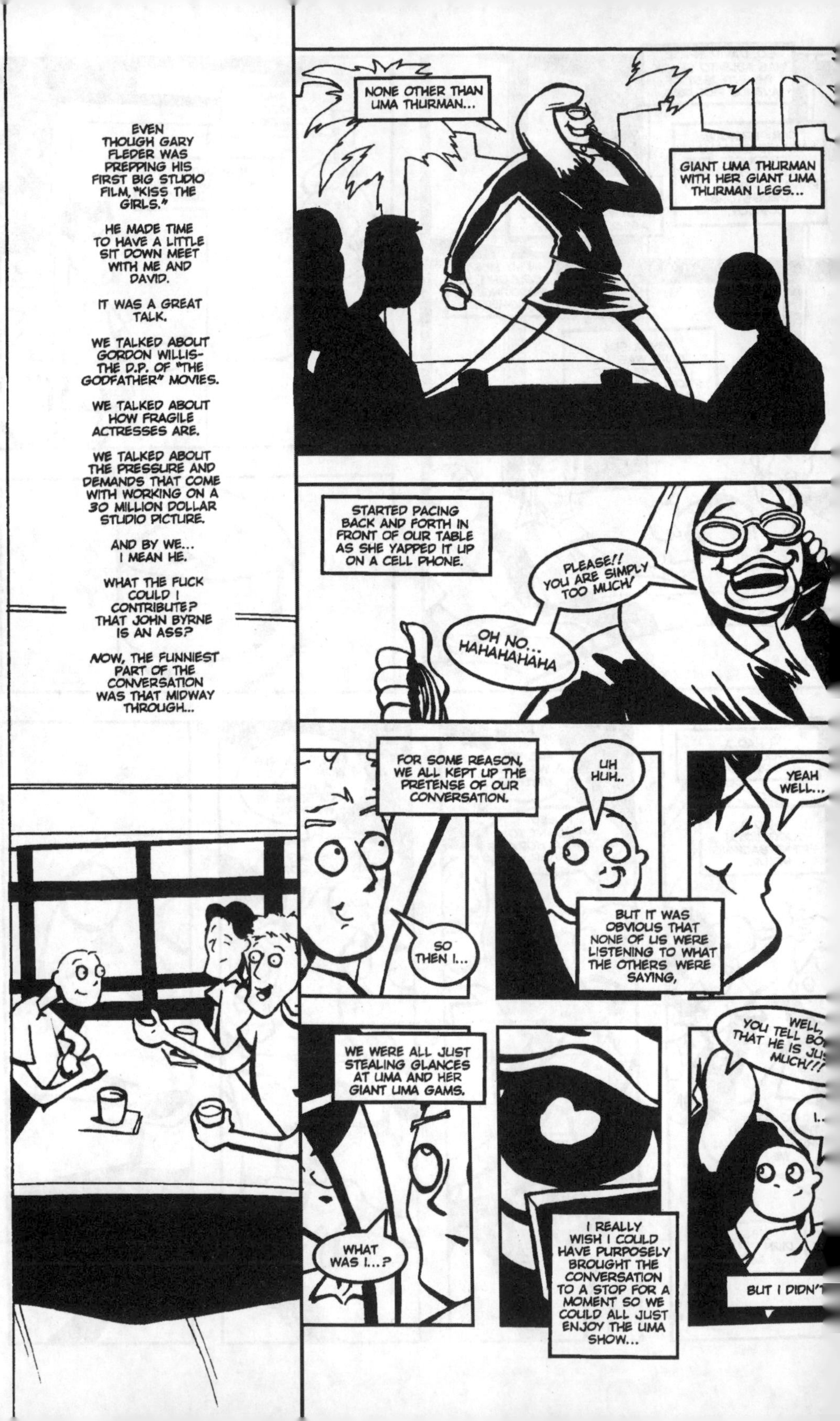

EVEN THOUGH GARY FLEDER WAS PREPPING HIS FIRST BIG STUDIO FILM, "KISS THE GIRLS."
HE MADE TIME TO HAVE A LITTLE SIT DOWN MEET WITH ME AND DAVID.
IT WAS A GREAT TALK.
WE TALKED ABOUT GORDON WILLIS- THE D.P. OF "THE GODFATHER" MOVIES.
WE TALKED ABOUT HOW FRAGILE ACTRESSES ARE.
WE TALKED ABOUT THE PRESSURE AND DEMANDS THAT COME WITH WORKING ON A 30 MILLION DOLLAR STUDIO PICTURE.
AND BY WE... I MEAN HE.
WHAT THE FUCK COULD I CONTRIBUTE? THAT JOHN BYRNE IS AN ASS?
NOW, THE FUNNIEST PART OF THE CONVERSATION WAS THAT MIDWAY THROUGH...
NONE OTHER THAN UMA THURMAN...
GIANT UMA THURMAN WITH HER GIANT UMA THURMAN LEGS...
STARTED PACING BACK AND FORTH IN FRONT OF OUR TABLE AS SHE YAPPED IT UP ON A CELL PHONE.
PLEASE!! YOU ARE SIMPLY TOO MUCH!
OH NO... HAHAHAHAHA
FOR SOME REASON, WE ALL KEPT UP THE PRETENSE OF OUR CONVERSATION.
UH HUH..
YEAH WELL...
SO THEN I...
BUT IT WAS OBVIOUS THAT NONE OF US WERE LISTENING TO WHAT THE OTHERS WERE SAYING,
WE WERE ALL JUST STEALING GLANCES AT UMA AND HER GIANT UMA GAMS.
WHAT WAS I...?
I REALLY WISH I COULD HAVE PURPOSELY BROUGHT THE CONVERSATION TO A STOP FOR A MOMENT SO WE COULD ALL JUST ENJOY THE UMA SHOW...
I...
BUT I DIDN'T

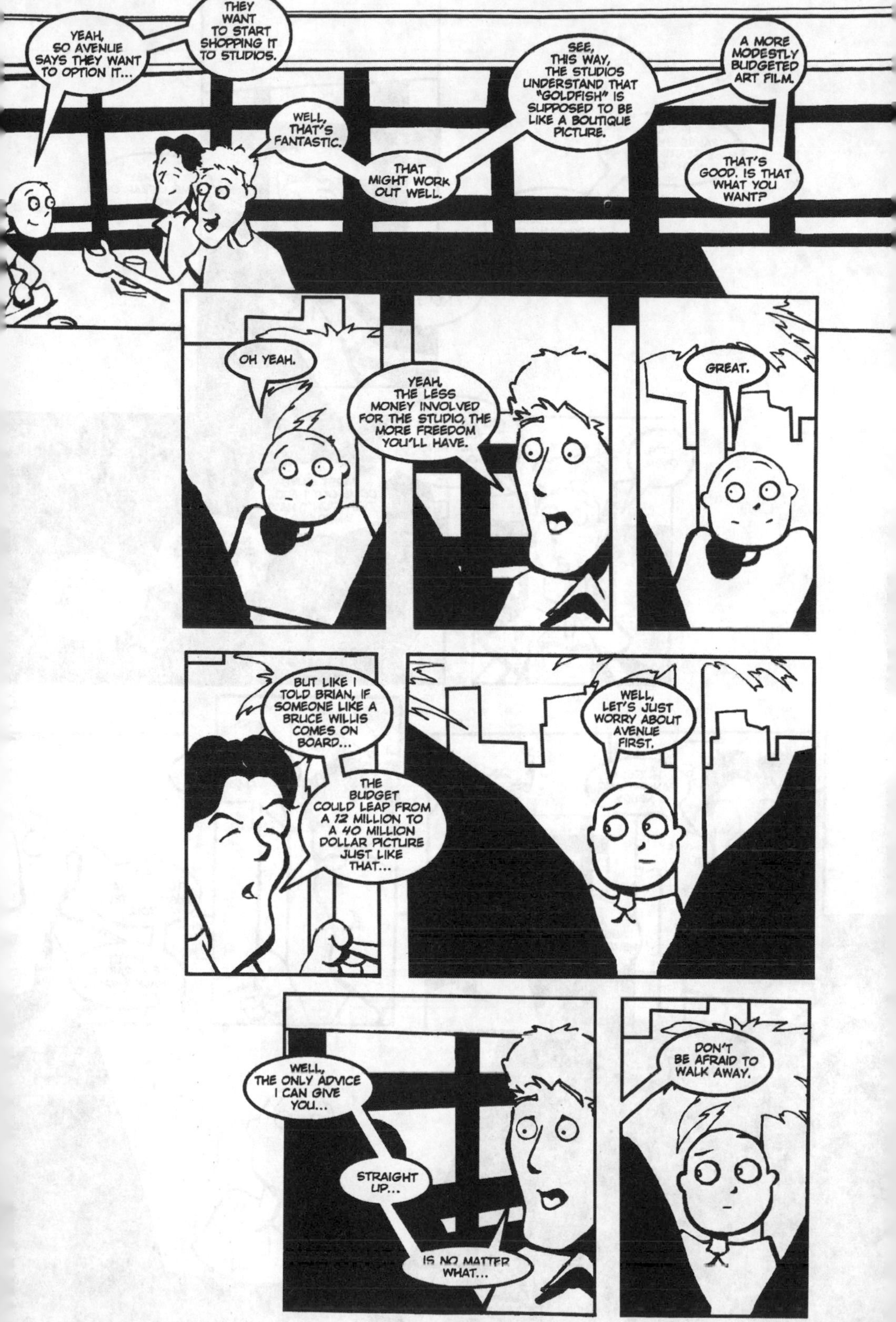
YEAH, SO AVENUE SAYS THEY WANT TO OPTION IT...
THEY WANT TO START SHOPPING IT TO STUDIOS.
WELL, THAT'S FANTASTIC.
THAT MIGHT WORK OUT WELL.
SEE, THIS WAY, THE STUDIOS UNDERSTAND THAT "GOLDFISH" IS SUPPOSED TO BE LIKE A BOUTIQUE PICTURE.
A MORE MODESTLY BUDGETED ART FILM.
THAT'S GOOD. IS THAT WHAT YOU WANT?
OH YEAH.
YEAH, THE LESS MONEY INVOLVED FOR THE STUDIO, THE MORE FREEDOM YOU'LL HAVE.
GREAT.
BUT LIKE I TOLD BRIAN, IF SOMEONE LIKE A BRUCE WILLIS COMES ON BOARD...
THE BUDGET COULD LEAP FROM A 12 MILLION TO A 40 MILLION DOLLAR PICTURE JUST LIKE THAT...
WELL, LET'S JUST WORRY ABOUT AVENUE FIRST.
WELL, THE ONLY ADVICE I CAN GIVE YOU...
STRAIGHT UP...
IS NO MATTER WHAT...
DON'T BE AFRAID TO WALK AWAY.

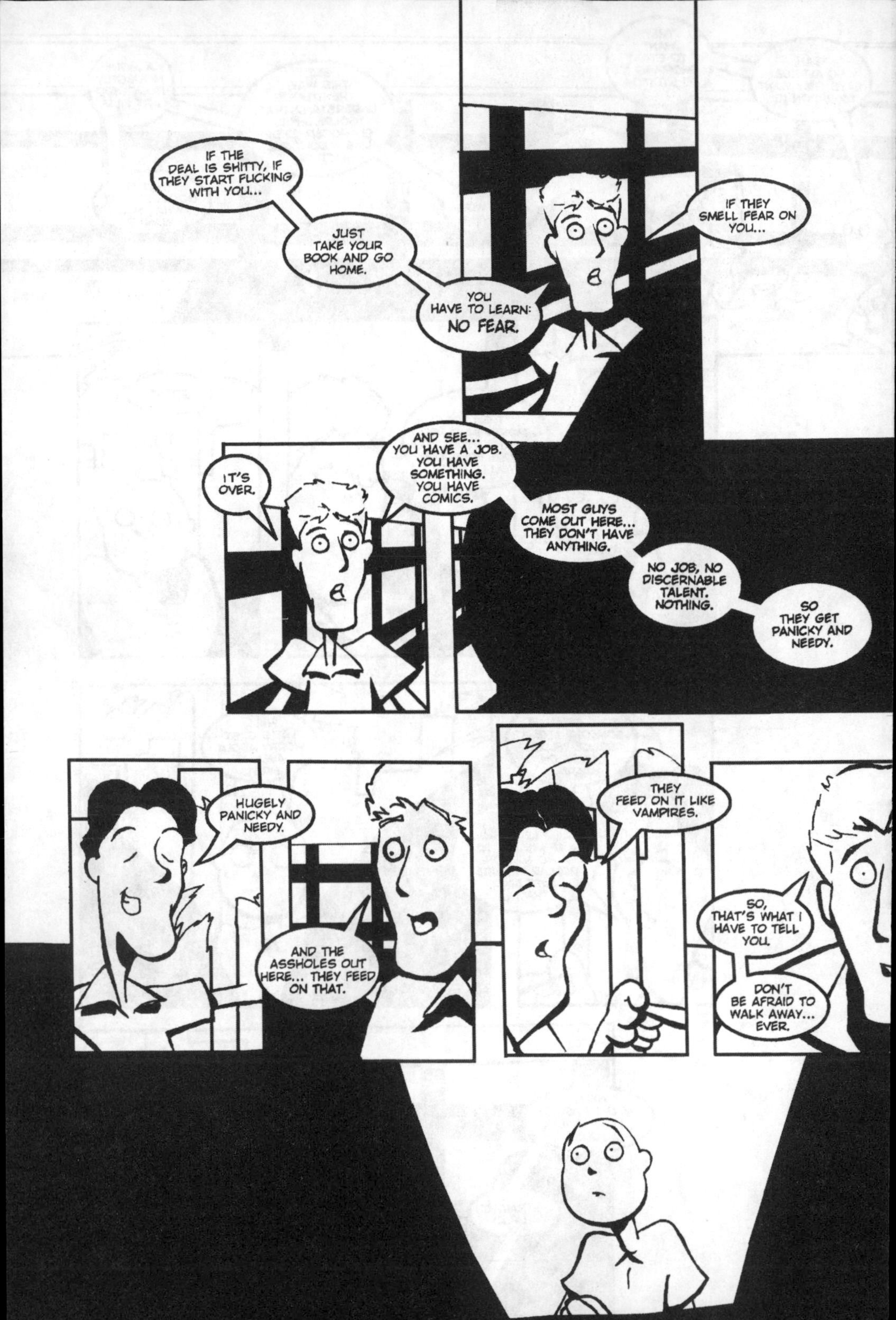
IF THE DEAL IS SHITTY, IF THEY START FUCKING WITH YOU...
JUST TAKE YOUR BOOK AND GO HOME.
YOU HAVE TO LEARN: NO FEAR.
IF THEY SMELL FEAR ON YOU...
IT'S OVER.
AND SEE... YOU HAVE A JOB. YOU HAVE SOMETHING. YOU HAVE COMICS.
MOST GUYS COME OUT HERE... THEY DON'T HAVE ANYTHING.
NO JOB, NO DISCERNABLE TALENT. NOTHING.
SO THEY GET PANICKY AND NEEDY.
HUGELY PANICKY AND NEEDY.
AND THE ASSHOLES OUT HERE... THEY FEED ON THAT.
THEY FEED ON IT LIKE VAMPIRES.
SO, THAT'S WHAT I HAVE TO TELL YOU.
DON'T BE AFRAID TO WALK AWAY... EVER.

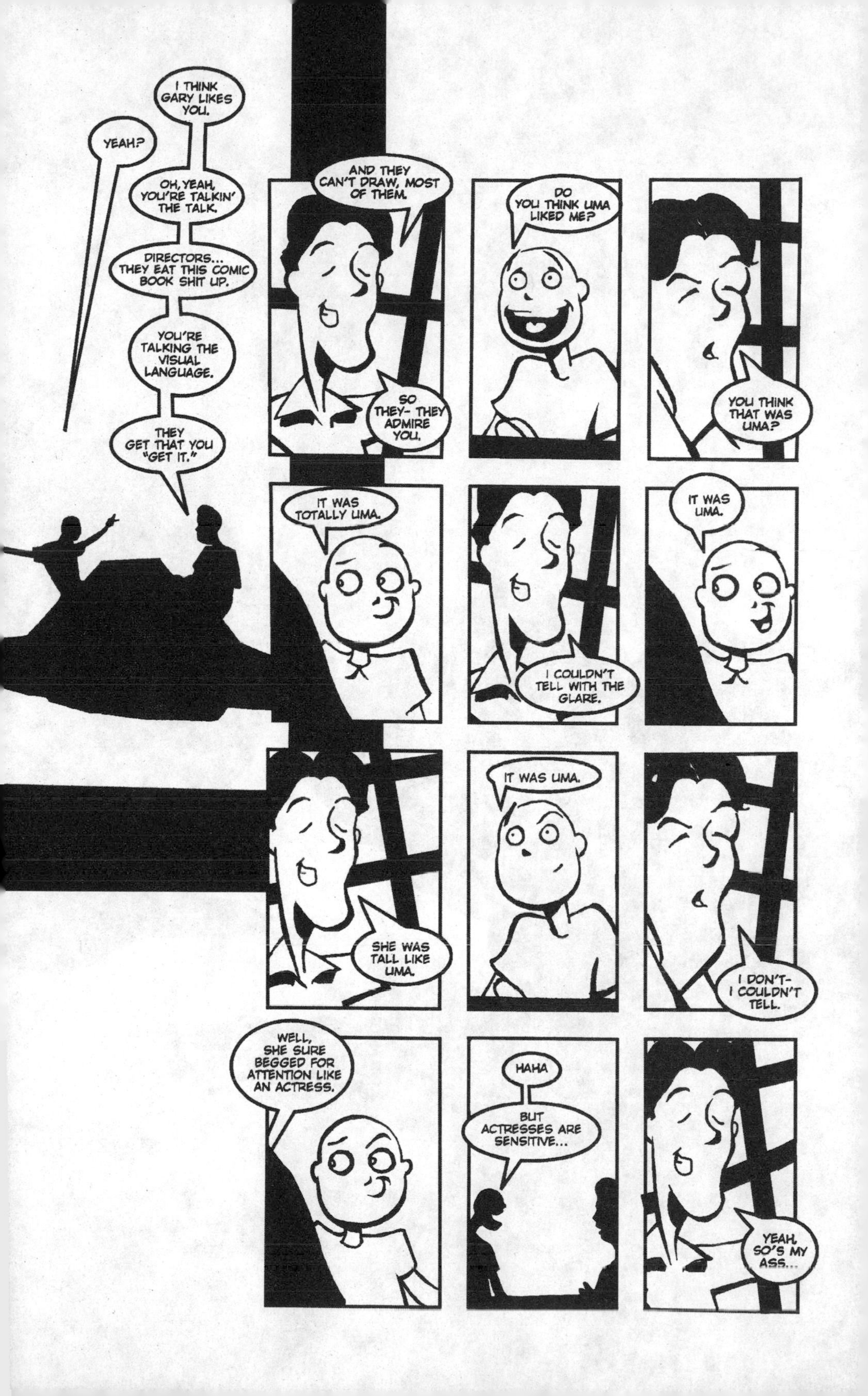
I THINK GARY LIKES YOU.
YEAH?
OH, YEAH, YOU'RE TALKIN' THE TALK.
DIRECTORS... THEY EAT THIS COMIC BOOK SHIT UP.
YOU'RE TALKING THE VISUAL LANGUAGE.
THEY GET THAT YOU "GET IT."
AND THEY CAN'T DRAW, MOST OF THEM.
SO THEY- THEY ADMIRE YOU.
DO YOU THINK UMA LIKED ME?
YOU THINK THAT WAS UMA?
IT WAS TOTALLY UMA.
I COULDN'T TELL WITH THE GLARE.
IT WAS UMA.
SHE WAS TALL LIKE UMA.
IT WAS UMA.
I DON'T- I COULDN'T TELL.
WELL, SHE SURE BEGGED FOR ATTENTION LIKE AN ACTRESS.
HAHA
BUT ACTRESSES ARE SENSITIVE...
YEAH, SO'S MY ASS...

SO I MADE [...]
BACK HOME TO
CLEVELAND WITH MY SOUL
INTACT AND A WHOLE
LOT TO PONDER

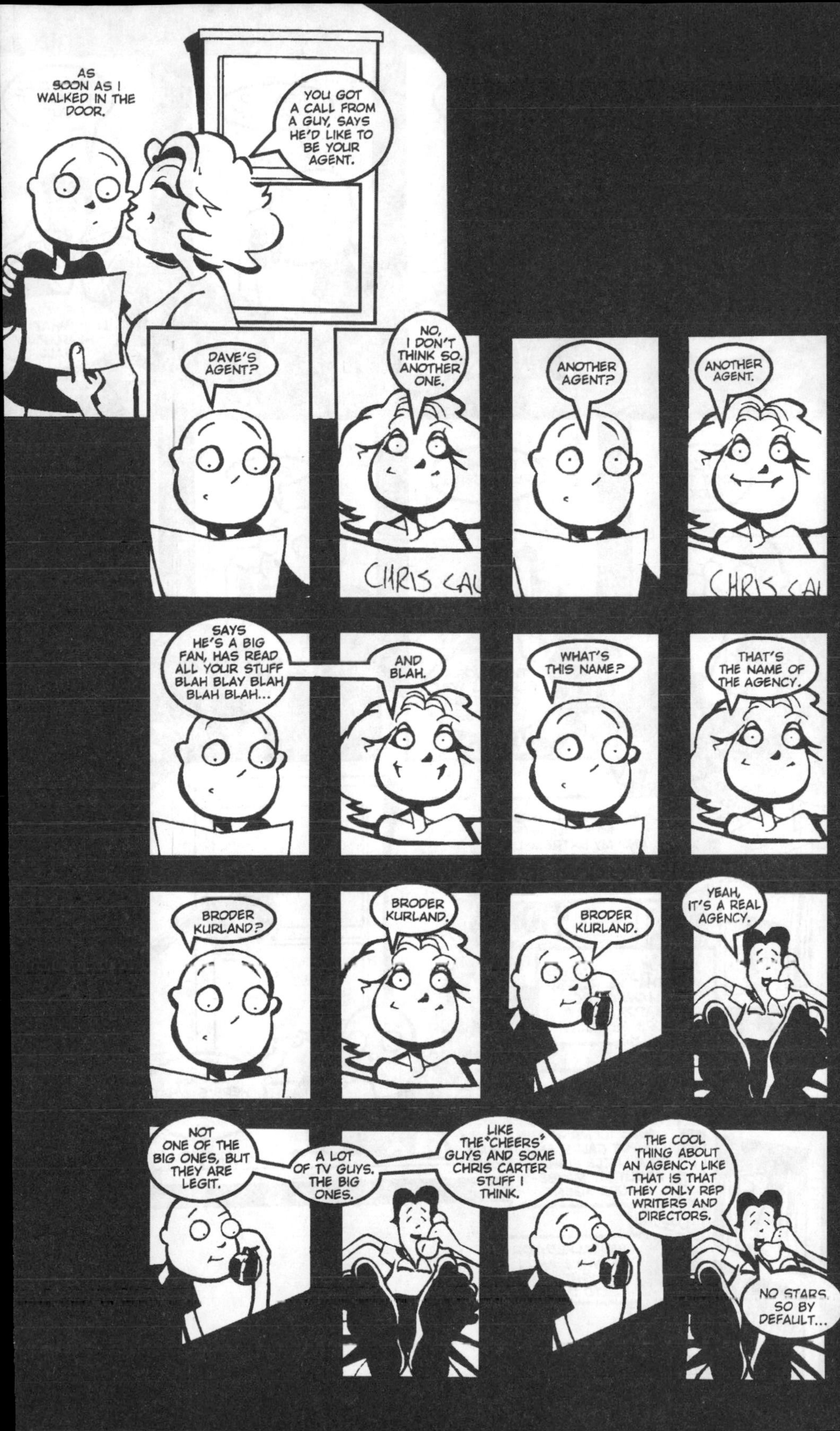

AS SOON AS I WALKED IN THE DOOR.
YOU GOT A CALL FROM A GUY, SAYS HE'D LIKE TO BE YOUR AGENT.
DAVE'S AGENT?
NO, I DON'T THINK SO. ANOTHER ONE.
CHRIS CAL
ANOTHER AGENT?
ANOTHER AGENT.
CHRIS CAL
SAYS HE'S A BIG FAN, HAS READ ALL YOUR STUFF BLAH BLAY BLAH BLAH BLAH...
AND BLAH.
WHAT'S THIS NAME?
THAT'S THE NAME OF THE AGENCY.
BRODER KURLAND?
BRODER KURLAND.
BRODER KURLAND.
YEAH, IT'S A REAL AGENCY.
NOT ONE OF THE BIG ONES, BUT THEY ARE LEGIT.
A LOT OF TV GUYS. THE BIG ONES.
LIKE THE "CHEERS" GUYS AND SOME CHRIS CARTER STUFF I THINK.
THE COOL THING ABOUT AN AGENCY LIKE THAT IS THAT THEY ONLY REP WRITERS AND DIRECTORS.
NO STARS. SO BY DEFAULT...

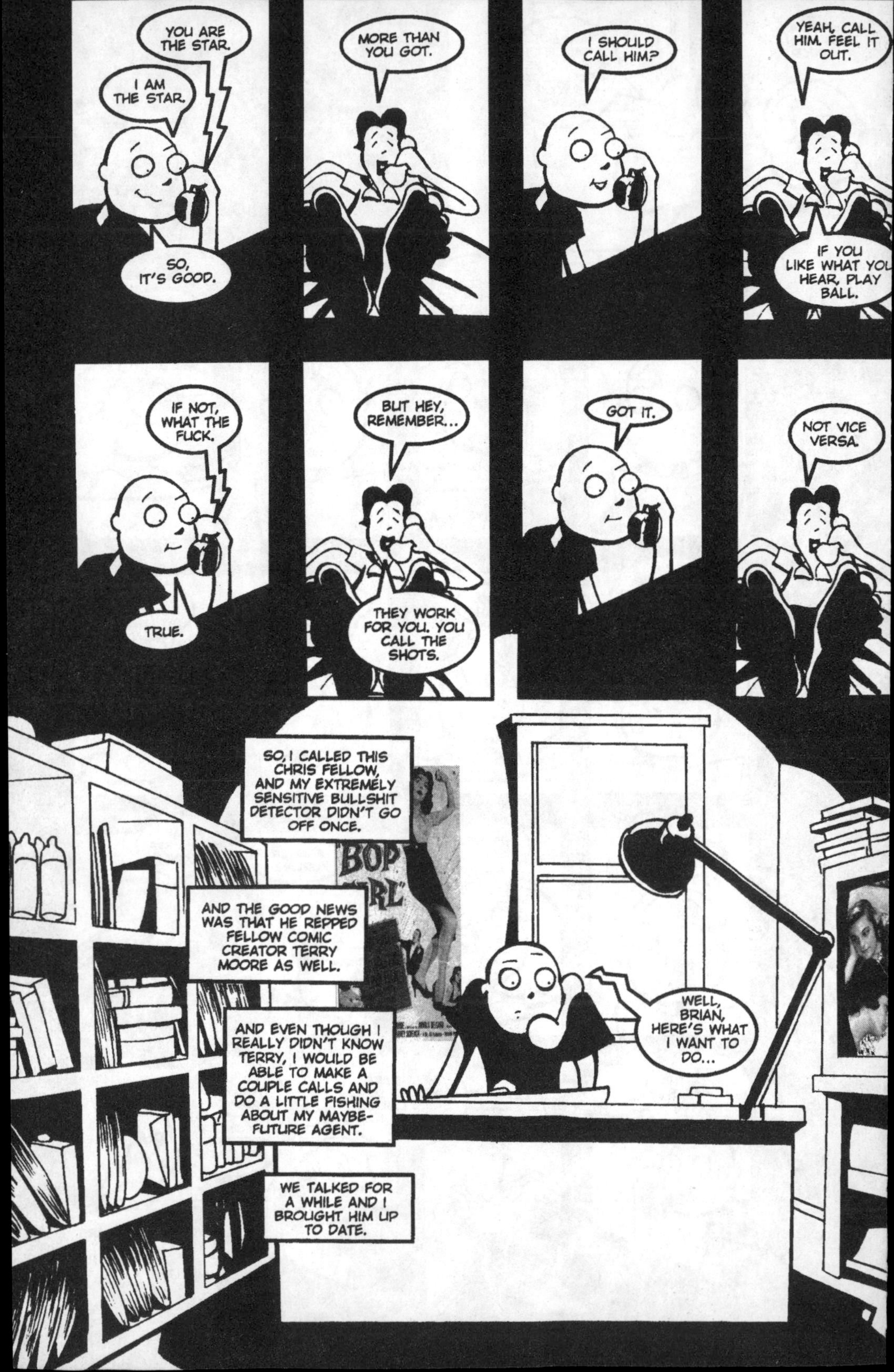
I AM THE STAR.
YOU ARE THE STAR.
SO, IT'S GOOD.
MORE THAN YOU GOT.
I SHOULD CALL HIM?
YEAH, CALL HIM. FEEL IT OUT.
IF YOU LIKE WHAT YOU HEAR, PLAY BALL.
IF NOT, WHAT THE FUCK.
TRUE.
BUT HEY, REMEMBER...
THEY WORK FOR YOU. YOU CALL THE SHOTS.
GOT IT.
NOT VICE VERSA.
SO, I CALLED THIS CHRIS FELLOW, AND MY EXTREMELY SENSITIVE BULLSHIT DETECTOR DIDN'T GO OFF ONCE.
AND THE GOOD NEWS WAS THAT HE REPPED FELLOW COMIC CREATOR TERRY MOORE AS WELL.
AND EVEN THOUGH I REALLY DIDN'T KNOW TERRY, I WOULD BE ABLE TO MAKE A COUPLE CALLS AND DO A LITTLE FISHING ABOUT MY MAYBE-FUTURE AGENT.
WELL, BRIAN, HERE'S WHAT I WANT TO DO...
WE TALKED FOR A WHILE AND I BROUGHT HIM UP TO DATE.

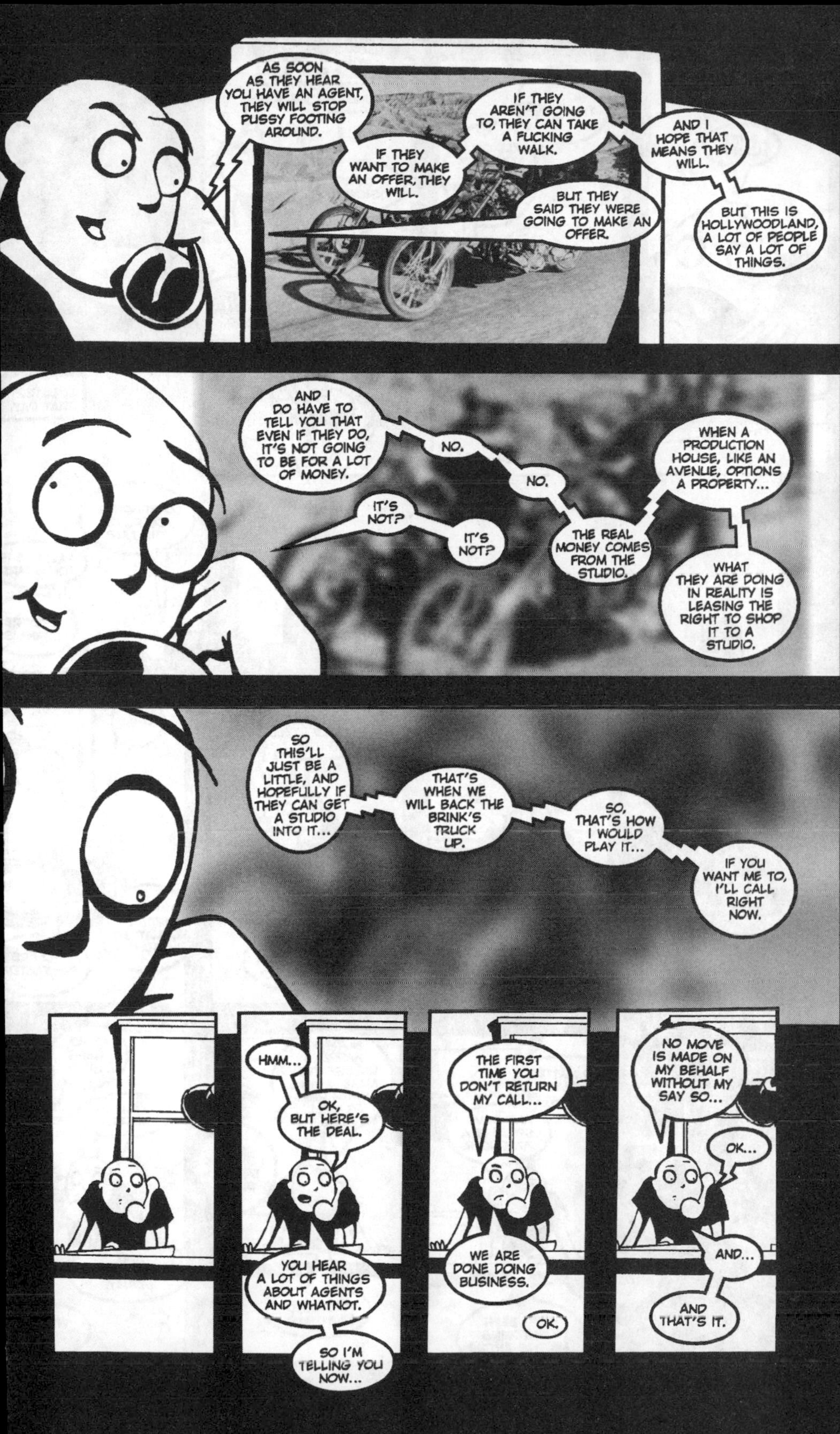

AS SOON AS THEY HEAR YOU HAVE AN AGENT, THEY WILL STOP PUSSY FOOTING AROUND.
IF THEY WANT TO MAKE AN OFFER, THEY WILL.
IF THEY AREN'T GOING TO, THEY CAN TAKE A FUCKING WALK.
BUT THEY SAID THEY WERE GOING TO MAKE AN OFFER.
AND I HOPE THAT MEANS THEY WILL.
BUT THIS IS HOLLYWOODLAND, A LOT OF PEOPLE SAY A LOT OF THINGS.
AND I DO HAVE TO TELL YOU THAT EVEN IF THEY DO, IT'S NOT GOING TO BE FOR A LOT OF MONEY.
IT'S NOT?
NO.
IT'S NOT?
NO.
WHEN A PRODUCTION HOUSE, LIKE AN AVENUE, OPTIONS A PROPERTY...
THE REAL MONEY COMES FROM THE STUDIO.
WHAT THEY ARE DOING IN REALITY IS LEASING THE RIGHT TO SHOP IT TO A STUDIO.
SO THIS'LL JUST BE A LITTLE, AND HOPEFULLY IF THEY CAN GET A STUDIO INTO IT...
THAT'S WHEN WE WILL BACK THE BRINK'S TRUCK UP.
SO, THAT'S HOW I WOULD PLAY IT...
IF YOU WANT ME TO, I'LL CALL RIGHT NOW.
HMM...
OK, BUT HERE'S THE DEAL.
YOU HEAR A LOT OF THINGS ABOUT AGENTS AND WHATNOT.
SO I'M TELLING YOU NOW...
THE FIRST TIME YOU DON'T RETURN MY CALL...
WE ARE DONE DOING BUSINESS.
OK.
NO MOVE IS MADE ON MY BEHALF WITHOUT MY SAY SO...
OK...
AND...
AND THAT'S IT.

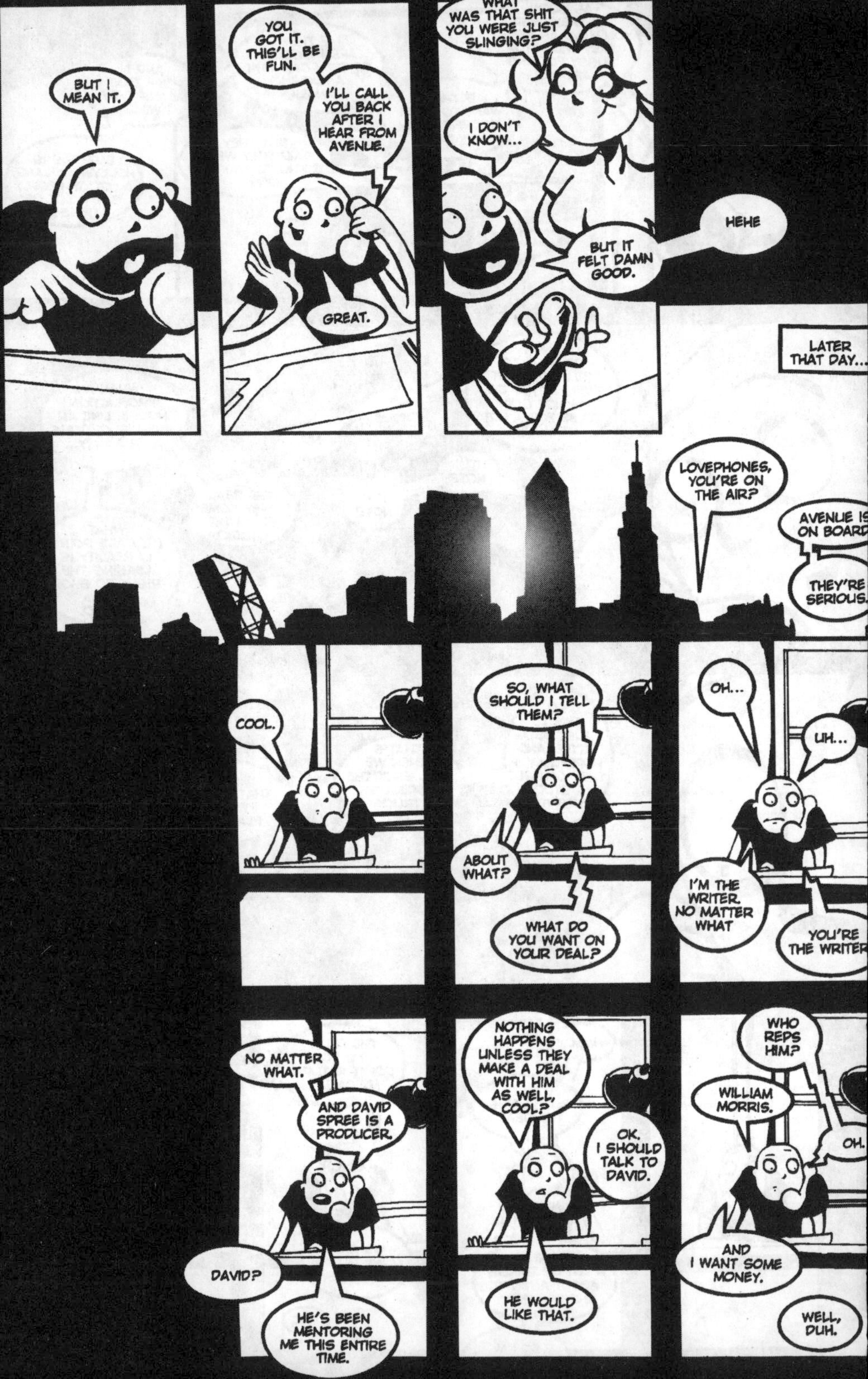
BUT I MEAN IT.
YOU GOT IT. THIS'LL BE FUN.
I'LL CALL YOU BACK AFTER I HEAR FROM AVENUE.
GREAT.
WHAT WAS THAT SHIT YOU WERE JUST SLINGING?
I DON'T KNOW...
BUT IT FELT DAMN GOOD.
HEHE
LATER THAT DAY...
LOVEPHONES, YOU'RE ON THE AIR?
AVENUE IS ON BOARD
THEY'RE SERIOUS.
COOL.
SO, WHAT SHOULD I TELL THEM?
ABOUT WHAT?
WHAT DO YOU WANT ON YOUR DEAL?
OH...
UH...
I'M THE WRITER NO MATTER WHAT
YOU'RE THE WRITER
NO MATTER WHAT.
AND DAVID SPREE IS A PRODUCER.
DAVID?
HE'S BEEN MENTORING ME THIS ENTIRE TIME.
NOTHING HAPPENS UNLESS THEY MAKE A DEAL WITH HIM AS WELL, COOL?
OK. I SHOULD TALK TO DAVID.
HE WOULD LIKE THAT.
WHO REPS HIM?
WILLIAM MORRIS.
OH.
AND I WANT SOME MONEY.
WELL, DUH.

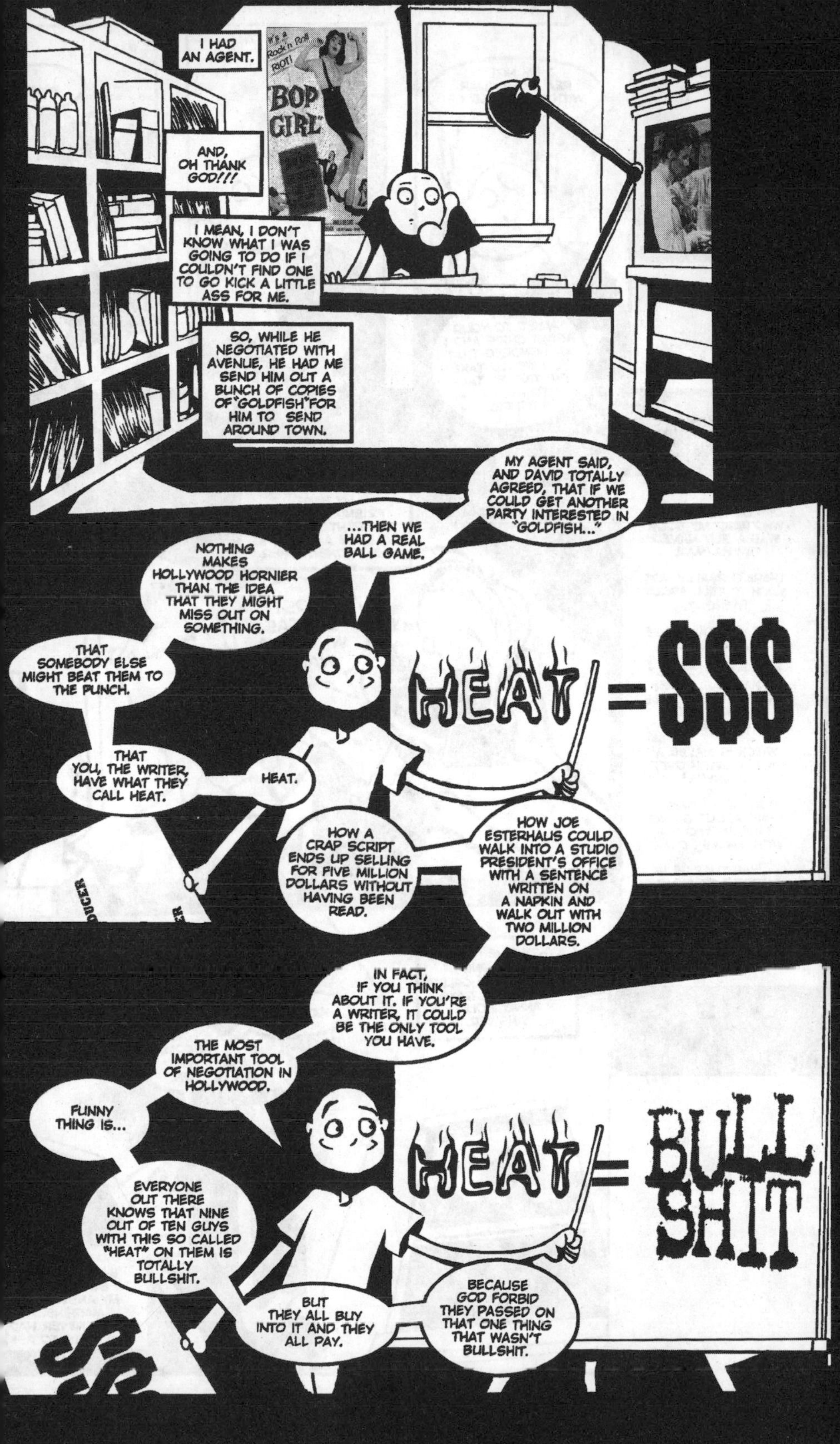

I HAD AN AGENT.
It's a Rock'n Roll RIOT!
BOP GIRL
AND, OH THANK GOD!!!
I MEAN, I DON'T KNOW WHAT I WAS GOING TO DO IF I COULDN'T FIND ONE TO GO KICK A LITTLE ASS FOR ME.
SO, WHILE HE NEGOTIATED WITH AVENUE, HE HAD ME SEND HIM OUT A BUNCH OF COPIES OF "GOLDFISH" FOR HIM TO SEND AROUND TOWN.
MY AGENT SAID, AND DAVID TOTALLY AGREED, THAT IF WE COULD GET ANOTHER PARTY INTERESTED IN "GOLDFISH..."
...THEN WE HAD A REAL BALL GAME.
NOTHING MAKES HOLLYWOOD HORNIER THAN THE IDEA THAT THEY MIGHT MISS OUT ON SOMETHING.
THAT SOMEBODY ELSE MIGHT BEAT THEM TO THE PUNCH.
HEAT = $$$
THAT YOU, THE WRITER, HAVE WHAT THEY CALL HEAT.
HEAT.
HOW A CRAP SCRIPT ENDS UP SELLING FOR FIVE MILLION DOLLARS WITHOUT HAVING BEEN READ.
HOW JOE ESTERHAUS COULD WALK INTO A STUDIO PRESIDENT'S OFFICE WITH A SENTENCE WRITTEN ON A NAPKIN AND WALK OUT WITH TWO MILLION DOLLARS.
IN FACT, IF YOU THINK ABOUT IT. IF YOU'RE A WRITER, IT COULD BE THE ONLY TOOL YOU HAVE.
THE MOST IMPORTANT TOOL OF NEGOTIATION IN HOLLYWOOD.
FUNNY THING IS...
HEAT = BULL SHIT
EVERYONE OUT THERE KNOWS THAT NINE OUT OF TEN GUYS WITH THIS SO CALLED "HEAT" ON THEM IS TOTALLY BULLSHIT.
BUT THEY ALL BUY INTO IT AND THEY ALL PAY.
BECAUSE GOD FORBID THEY PASSED ON THAT ONE THING THAT WASN'T BULLSHIT.

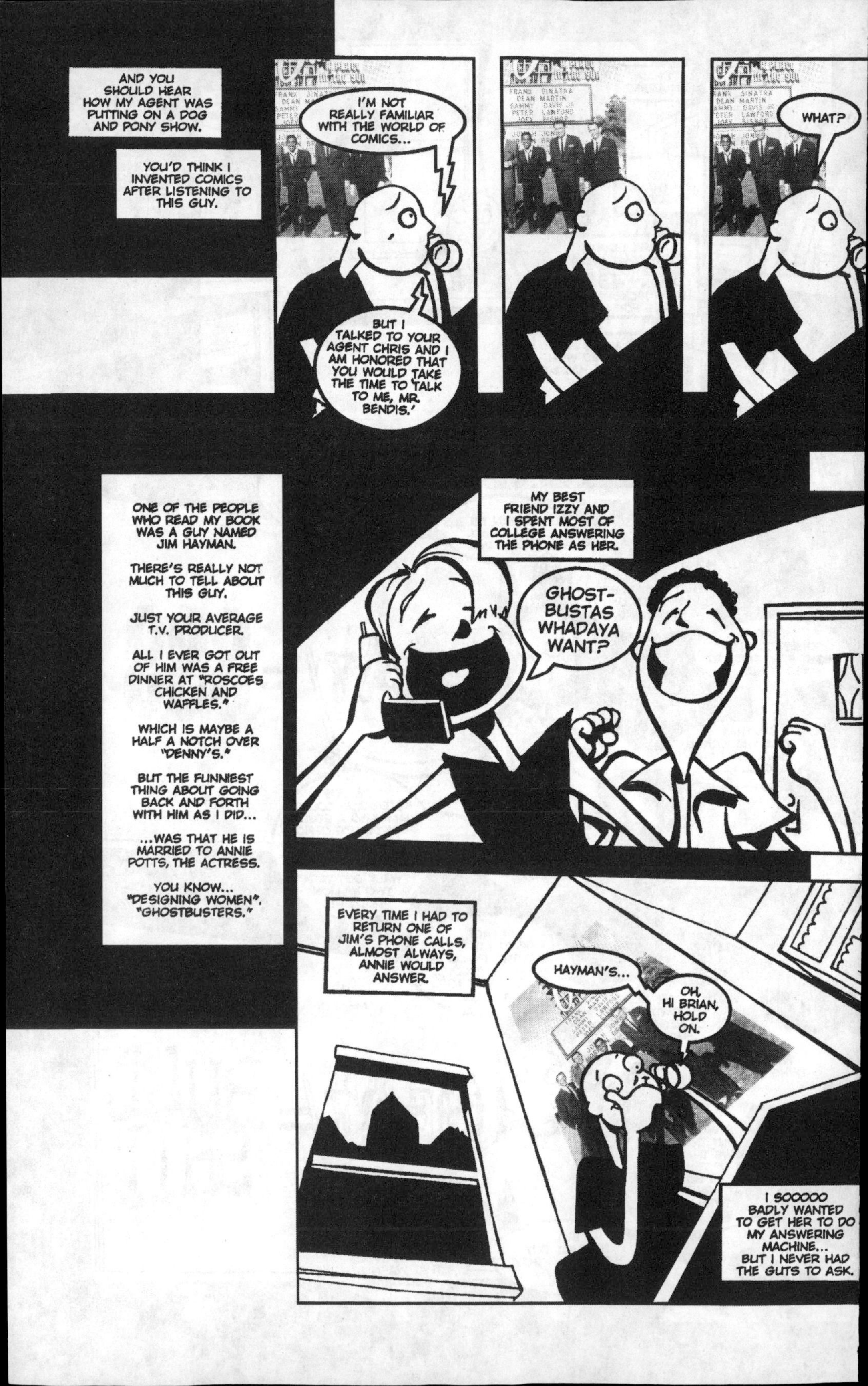
AND YOU SHOULD HEAR HOW MY AGENT WAS PUTTING ON A DOG AND PONY SHOW.
YOU'D THINK I INVENTED COMICS AFTER LISTENING TO THIS GUY.
I'M NOT REALLY FAMILIAR WITH THE WORLD OF COMICS...
BUT I TALKED TO YOUR AGENT CHRIS AND I AM HONORED THAT YOU WOULD TAKE THE TIME TO 'TALK TO ME, MR. BENDIS.'
FRANK SINATRA
DEAN MARTIN
SAMMY DAVIS JR
PETER LAWFORD
JOEY BISHOP
WHAT?
ONE OF THE PEOPLE WHO READ MY BOOK WAS A GUY NAMED JIM HAYMAN.
THERE'S REALLY NOT MUCH TO TELL ABOUT THIS GUY.
JUST YOUR AVERAGE T.V. PRODUCER.
ALL I EVER GOT OUT OF HIM WAS A FREE DINNER AT "ROSCOES CHICKEN AND WAFFLES."
WHICH IS MAYBE A HALF A NOTCH OVER "DENNY'S."
BUT THE FUNNIEST THING ABOUT GOING BACK AND FORTH WITH HIM AS I DID...
...WAS THAT HE IS MARRIED TO ANNIE POTTS, THE ACTRESS.
YOU KNOW... "DESIGNING WOMEN", "GHOSTBUSTERS."
MY BEST FRIEND IZZY AND I SPENT MOST OF COLLEGE ANSWERING THE PHONE AS HER.
GHOST-BUSTAS WHADAYA WANT?
EVERY TIME I HAD TO RETURN ONE OF JIM'S PHONE CALLS, ALMOST ALWAYS, ANNIE WOULD ANSWER.
HAYMAN'S...
OH, HI BRIAN, HOLD ON.
I SOOOOO BADLY WANTED TO GET HER TO DO MY ANSWERING MACHINE... BUT I NEVER HAD THE GUTS TO ASK.

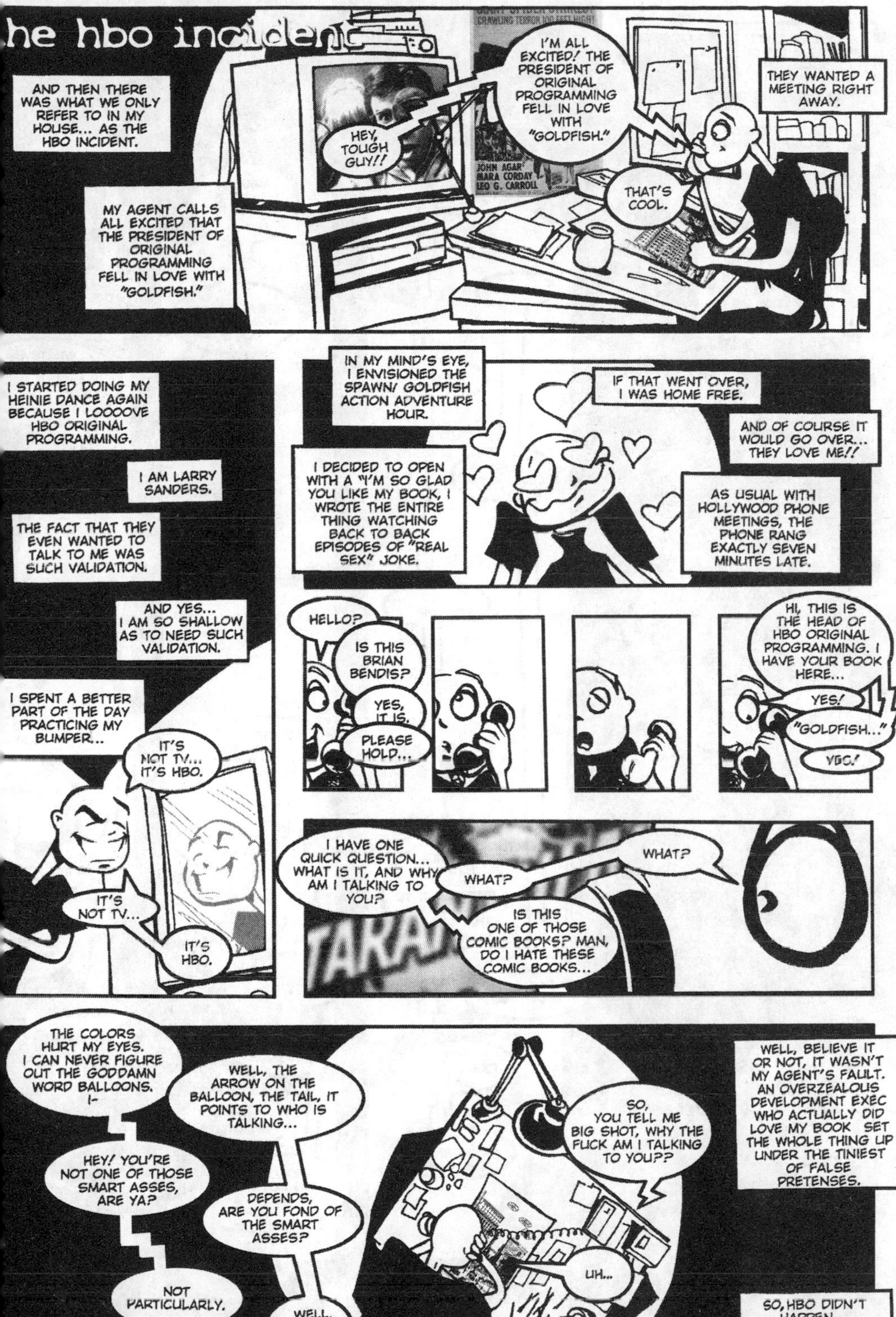
he hbo incident
AND THEN THERE WAS WHAT WE ONLY REFER TO IN MY HOUSE... AS THE HBO INCIDENT.
HEY, TOUGH GUY!!
JOHN AGAR
MARA CORDAY
LEO G. CARROLL
I'M ALL EXCITED! THE PRESIDENT OF ORIGINAL PROGRAMMING FELL IN LOVE WITH "GOLDFISH."
THEY WANTED A MEETING RIGHT AWAY.
THAT'S COOL.
MY AGENT CALLS ALL EXCITED THAT THE PRESIDENT OF ORIGINAL PROGRAMMING FELL IN LOVE WITH "GOLDFISH."
I STARTED DOING MY HEINIE DANCE AGAIN BECAUSE I LOOOOVE HBO ORIGINAL PROGRAMMING.
I AM LARRY SANDERS.
THE FACT THAT THEY EVEN WANTED TO TALK TO ME WAS SUCH VALIDATION.
AND YES... I AM SO SHALLOW AS TO NEED SUCH VALIDATION.
I SPENT A BETTER PART OF THE DAY PRACTICING MY BUMPER...
IT'S NOT TV... IT'S HBO.
IT'S NOT TV...
IT'S HBO.
IN MY MIND'S EYE, I ENVISIONED THE SPAWN/ GOLDFISH ACTION ADVENTURE HOUR.
IF THAT WENT OVER, I WAS HOME FREE.
AND OF COURSE IT WOULD GO OVER... THEY LOVE ME!!
I DECIDED TO OPEN WITH A "I'M SO GLAD YOU LIKE MY BOOK, I WROTE THE ENTIRE THING WATCHING BACK TO BACK EPISODES OF "REAL SEX" JOKE.
AS USUAL WITH HOLLYWOOD PHONE MEETINGS, THE PHONE RANG EXACTLY SEVEN MINUTES LATE.
HELLO?
IS THIS BRIAN BENDIS?
YES, IT IS.
PLEASE HOLD...
HI, THIS IS THE HEAD OF HBO ORIGINAL PROGRAMMING. I HAVE YOUR BOOK HERE...
YES!
"GOLDFISH..."
I HAVE ONE QUICK QUESTION... WHAT IS IT, AND WHY AM I TALKING TO YOU?
WHAT?
WHAT?
IS THIS ONE OF THOSE COMIC BOOKS? MAN, DO I HATE THESE COMIC BOOKS...
THE COLORS HURT MY EYES. I CAN NEVER FIGURE OUT THE GODDAMN WORD BALLOONS. I-
WELL, THE ARROW ON THE BALLOON, THE TAIL, IT POINTS TO WHO IS TALKING...
HEY! YOU'RE NOT ONE OF THOSE SMART ASSES, ARE YA?
DEPENDS, ARE YOU FOND OF THE SMART ASSES?
NOT PARTICULARLY.
WELL, THEN MAYBE...
SO, YOU TELL ME BIG SHOT, WHY THE FUCK AM I TALKING TO YOU??
UH...
WELL, BELIEVE IT OR NOT, IT WASN'T MY AGENT'S FAULT. AN OVERZEALOUS DEVELOPMENT EXEC WHO ACTUALLY DID LOVE MY BOOK SET THE WHOLE THING UP UNDER THE TINIEST OF FALSE PRETENSES.
SO, HBO DIDN'T HAPPEN...

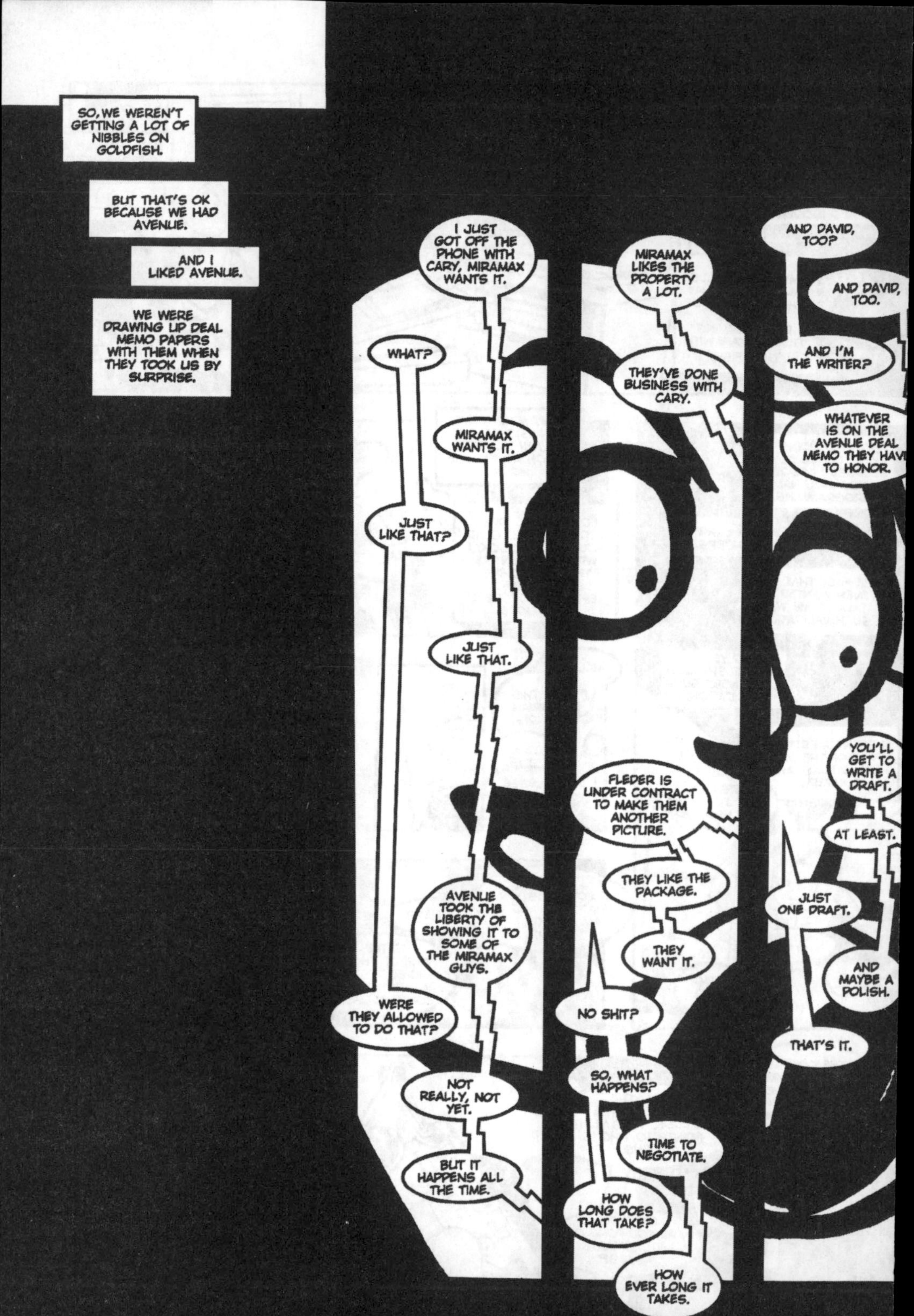
SO, WE WEREN'T GETTING A LOT OF NIBBLES ON GOLDFISH.
BUT THAT'S OK BECAUSE WE HAD AVENUE.
AND I LIKED AVENUE.
WE WERE DRAWING UP DEAL MEMO PAPERS WITH THEM WHEN THEY TOOK US BY SURPRISE.
I JUST GOT OFF THE PHONE WITH CARY, MIRAMAX WANTS IT.
WHAT?
MIRAMAX WANTS IT.
JUST LIKE THAT?
JUST LIKE THAT.
AVENUE TOOK THE LIBERTY OF SHOWING IT TO SOME OF THE MIRAMAX GUYS.
WERE THEY ALLOWED TO DO THAT?
NOT REALLY, NOT YET.
BUT IT HAPPENS ALL THE TIME.
MIRAMAX LIKES THE PROPERTY A LOT.
THEY'VE DONE BUSINESS WITH CARY.
FLEDER IS UNDER CONTRACT TO MAKE THEM ANOTHER PICTURE.
THEY LIKE THE PACKAGE.
THEY WANT IT.
NO SHIT?
SO, WHAT HAPPENS?
TIME TO NEGOTIATE.
HOW LONG DOES THAT TAKE?
HOW EVER LONG IT TAKES.
AND DAVID, TOO?
AND DAVID, TOO.
AND I'M THE WRITER?
WHATEVER IS ON THE AVENUE DEAL MEMO THEY HAV
TO HONOR.
YOU'LL GET TO WRITE A DRAFT.
AT LEAST.
JUST ONE DRAFT.
AND MAYBE A POLISH.
THAT'S IT.

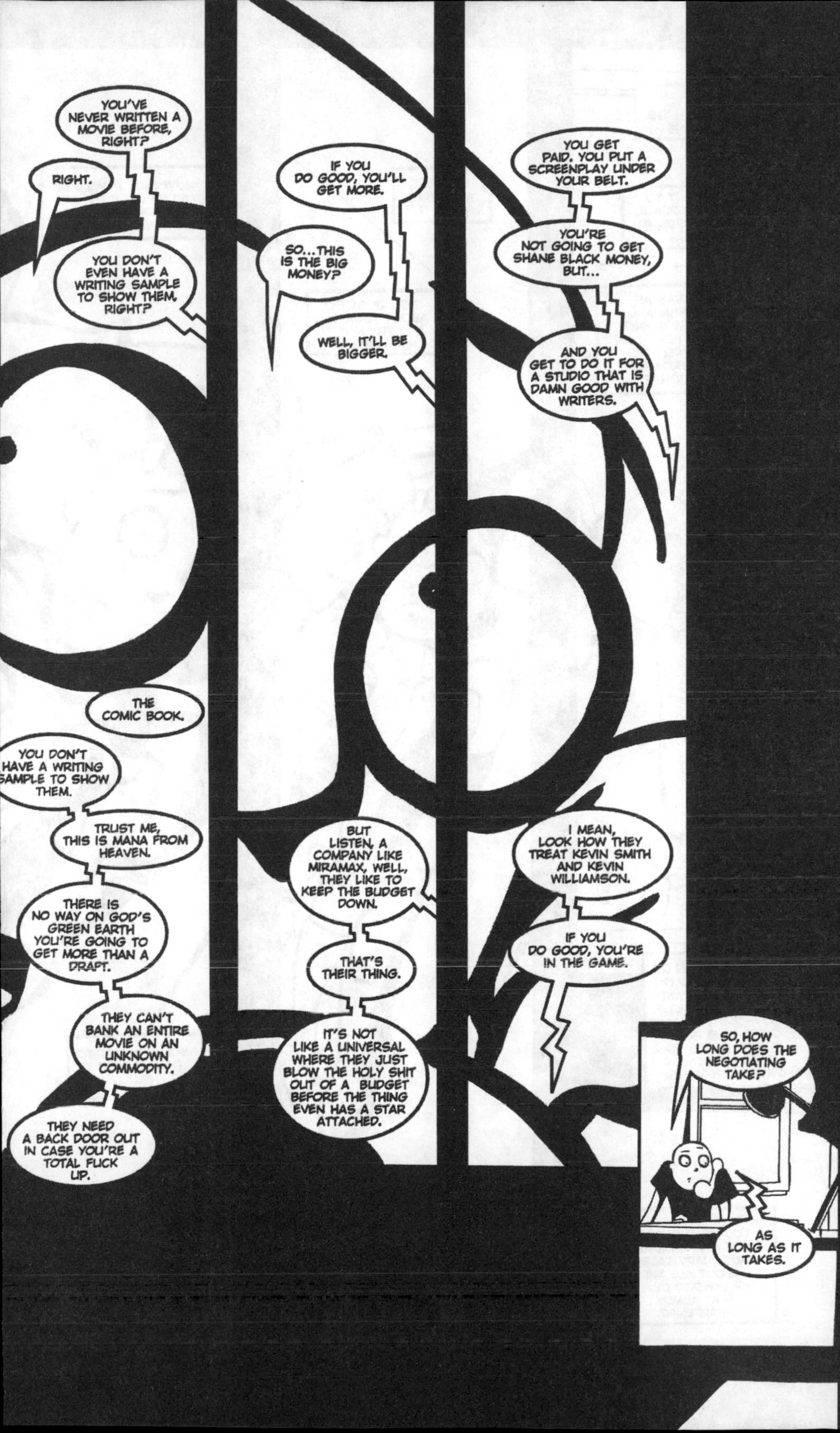
YOU'VE NEVER WRITTEN A MOVIE BEFORE, RIGHT?
RIGHT.
YOU DON'T EVEN HAVE A WRITING SAMPLE TO SHOW THEM, RIGHT?
IF YOU DO GOOD, YOU'LL GET MORE.
SO...THIS IS THE BIG MONEY?
WELL, IT'LL BE BIGGER.
YOU GET PAID. YOU PUT A SCREENPLAY UNDER YOUR BELT.
YOU'RE NOT GOING TO GET SHANE BLACK MONEY, BUT...
AND YOU GET TO DO IT FOR A STUDIO THAT IS DAMN GOOD WITH WRITERS.
THE COMIC BOOK.
YOU DON'T HAVE A WRITING SAMPLE TO SHOW THEM.
TRUST ME, THIS IS MANA FROM HEAVEN.
THERE IS NO WAY ON GOD'S GREEN EARTH YOU'RE GOING TO GET MORE THAN A DRAFT.
THEY CAN'T BANK AN ENTIRE MOVIE ON AN UNKNOWN COMMODITY.
THEY NEED A BACK DOOR OUT IN CASE YOU'RE A TOTAL FUCK UP.
BUT LISTEN, A COMPANY LIKE MIRAMAX, WELL, THEY LIKE TO KEEP THE BUDGET DOWN.
THAT'S THEIR THING.
IT'S NOT LIKE A UNIVERSAL WHERE THEY JUST BLOW THE HOLY SHIT OUT OF A BUDGET BEFORE THE THING EVEN HAS A STAR ATTACHED.
I MEAN, LOOK HOW THEY TREAT KEVIN SMITH AND KEVIN WILLIAMSON.
IF YOU DO GOOD, YOU'RE IN THE GAME.
SO, HOW LONG DOES THE NEGOTIATING TAKE?
AS LONG AS IT TAKES.

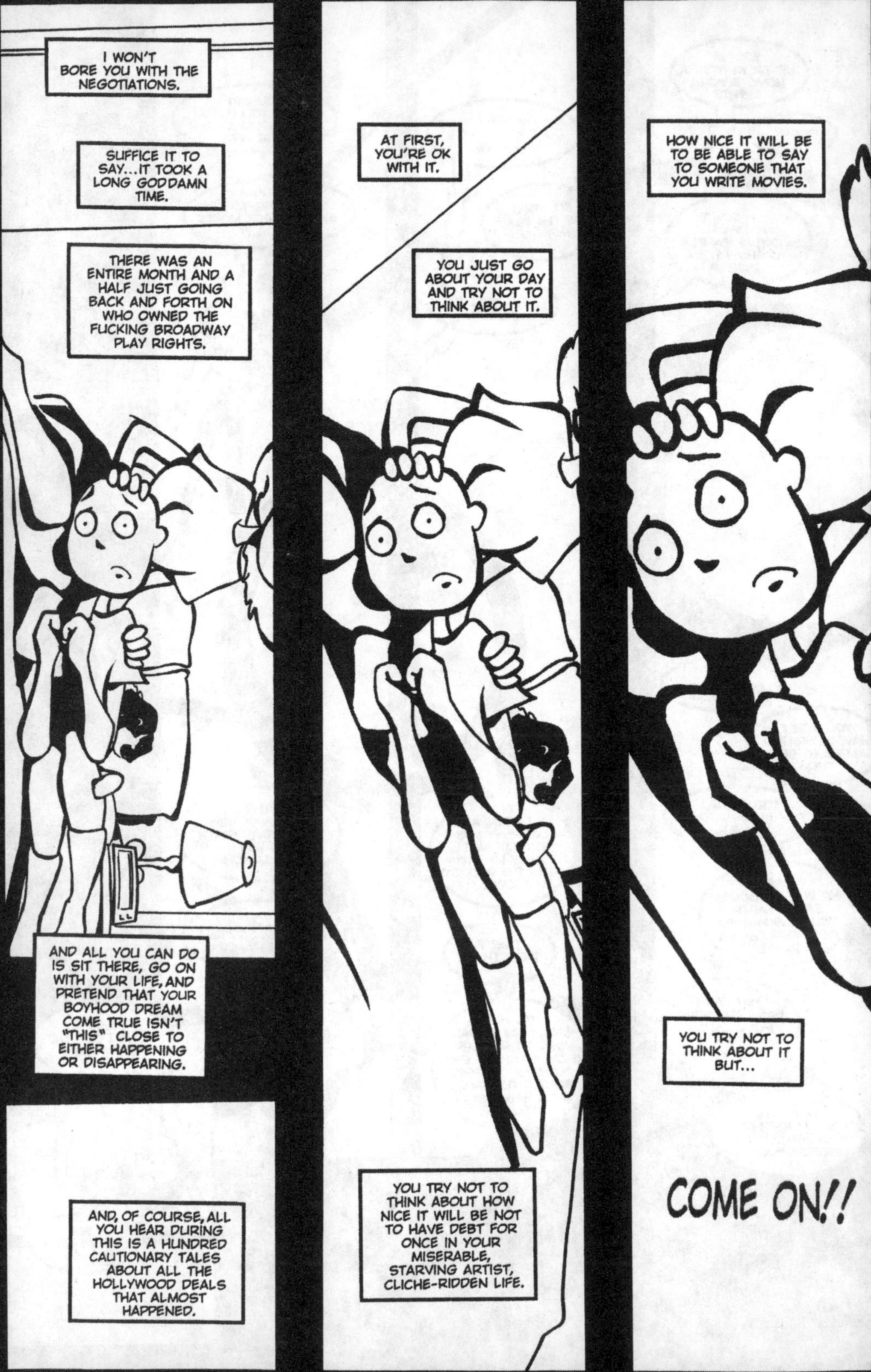

I WON'T BORE YOU WITH THE NEGOTIATIONS.
SUFFICE IT TO SAY...IT TOOK A LONG GODDAMN TIME.
THERE WAS AN ENTIRE MONTH AND A HALF JUST GOING BACK AND FORTH ON WHO OWNED THE FUCKING BROADWAY PLAY RIGHTS.
AND ALL YOU CAN DO IS SIT THERE, GO ON WITH YOUR LIFE, AND PRETEND THAT YOUR BOYHOOD DREAM COME TRUE ISN'T "THIS" CLOSE TO EITHER HAPPENING OR DISAPPEARING.
AND, OF COURSE, ALL YOU HEAR DURING THIS IS A HUNDRED CAUTIONARY TALES ABOUT ALL THE HOLLYWOOD DEALS THAT ALMOST HAPPENED.
AT FIRST, YOU'RE OK WITH IT.
YOU JUST GO ABOUT YOUR DAY AND TRY NOT TO THINK ABOUT IT.
YOU TRY NOT TO THINK ABOUT HOW NICE IT WILL BE NOT TO HAVE DEBT FOR ONCE IN YOUR MISERABLE, STARVING ARTIST, CLICHE-RIDDEN LIFE.
HOW NICE IT WILL BE TO BE ABLE TO SAY TO SOMEONE THAT YOU WRITE MOVIES.
YOU TRY NOT TO THINK ABOUT IT BUT...
COME ON!!

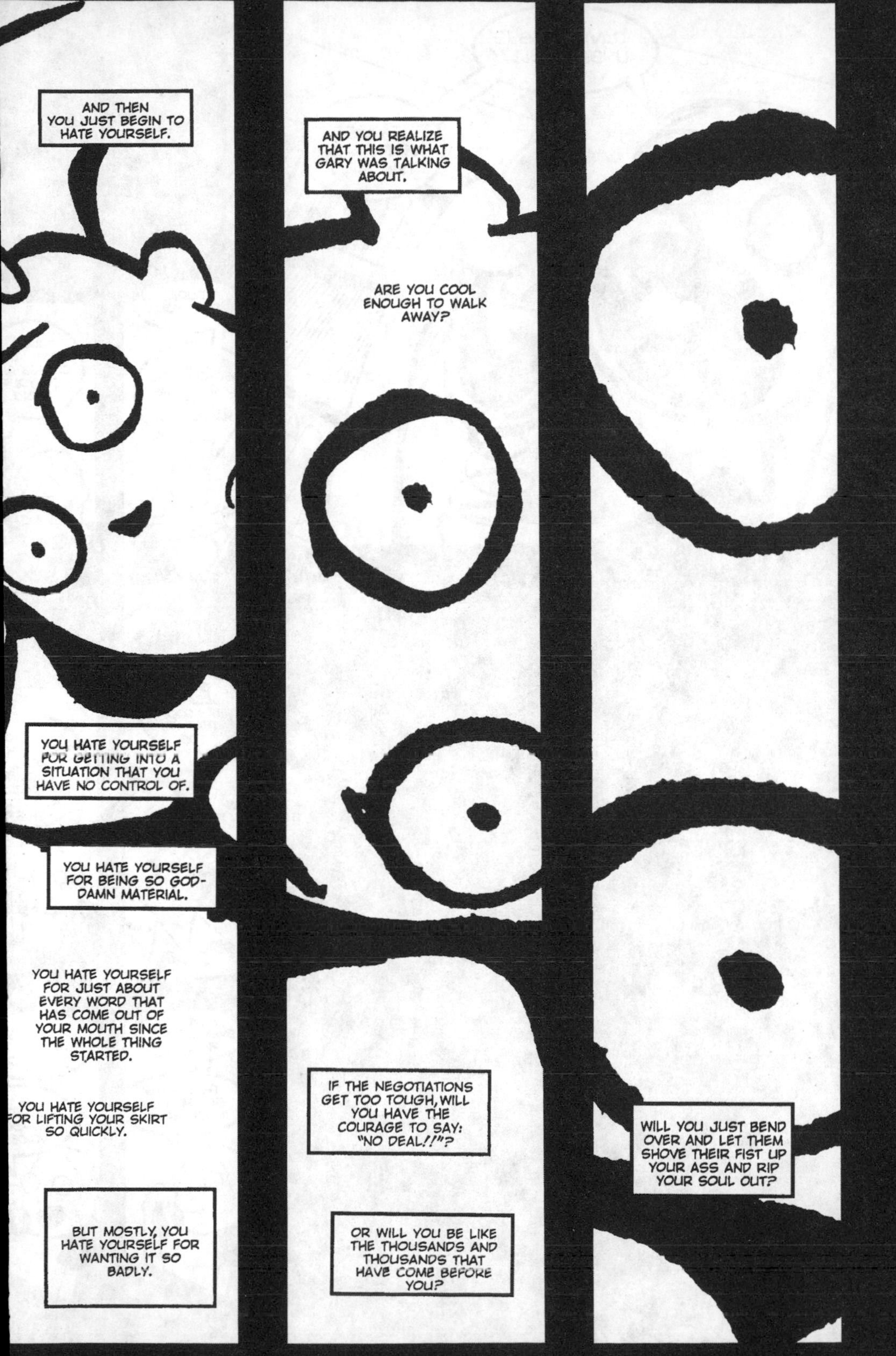
AND THEN YOU JUST BEGIN TO HATE YOURSELF.
YOU HATE YOURSELF FOR GETTING INTO A SITUATION THAT YOU HAVE NO CONTROL OF.
YOU HATE YOURSELF FOR BEING SO GOD-DAMN MATERIAL.
YOU HATE YOURSELF FOR JUST ABOUT EVERY WORD THAT HAS COME OUT OF YOUR MOUTH SINCE THE WHOLE THING STARTED.
YOU HATE YOURSELF FOR LIFTING YOUR SKIRT SO QUICKLY.
BUT MOSTLY, YOU HATE YOURSELF FOR WANTING IT SO BADLY.
AND YOU REALIZE THAT THIS IS WHAT GARY WAS TALKING ABOUT.
ARE YOU COOL ENOUGH TO WALK AWAY?
IF THE NEGOTIATIONS GET TOO TOUGH, WILL YOU HAVE THE COURAGE TO SAY: "NO DEAL!!"?
OR WILL YOU BE LIKE THE THOUSANDS AND THOUSANDS THAT HAVE COME BEFORE YOU?
WILL YOU JUST BEND OVER AND LET THEM SHOVE THEIR FIST UP YOUR ASS AND RIP YOUR SOUL OUT?

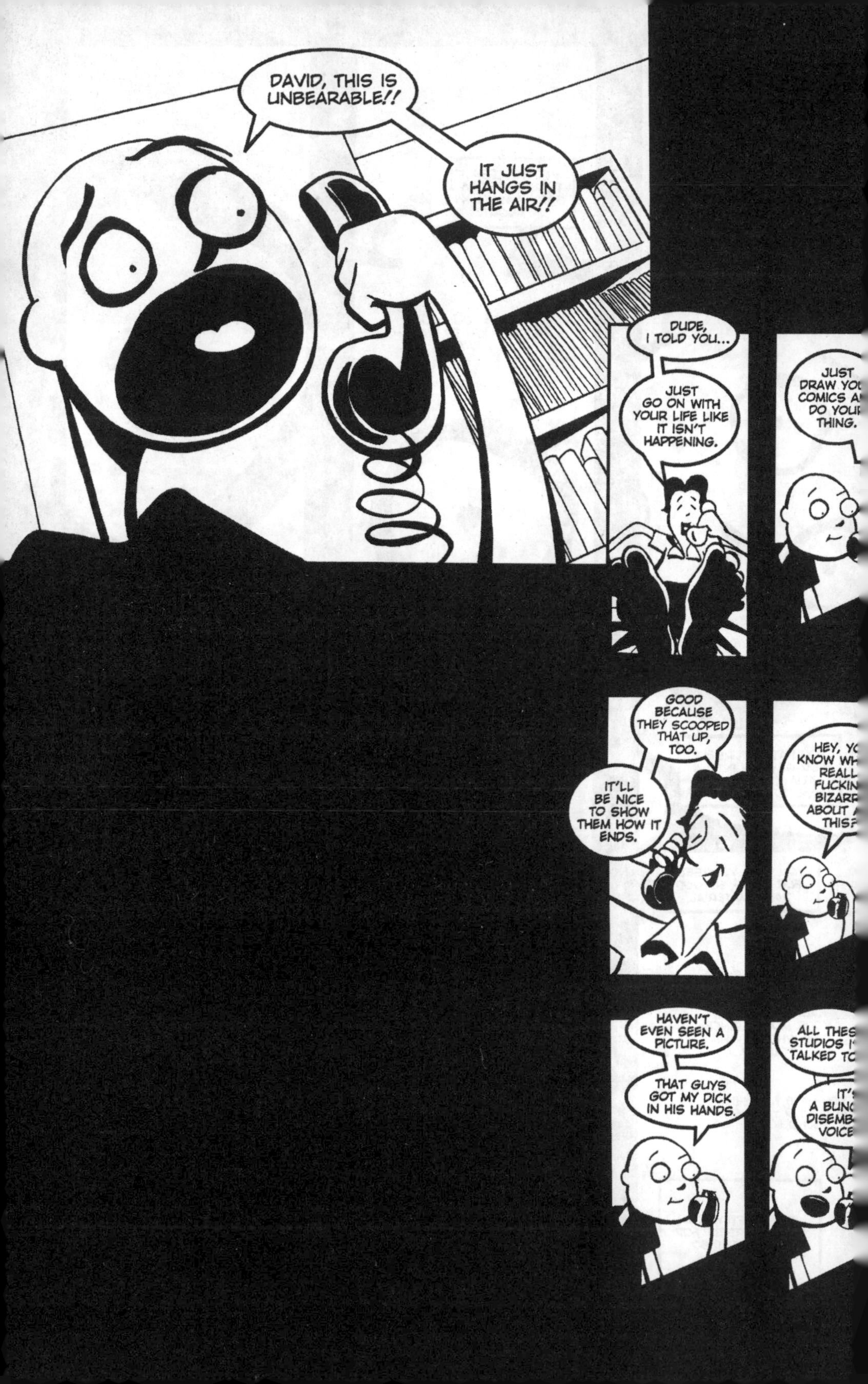
DAVID, THIS IS UNBEARABLE!!
IT JUST HANGS IN THE AIR!!
DUDE, I TOLD YOU...
JUST GO ON WITH YOUR LIFE LIKE IT ISN'T HAPPENING.
JUST DRAW YO COMICS A DO YOUR THING.
GOOD BECAUSE THEY SCOOPED THAT UP, TOO.
IT'LL BE NICE TO SHOW THEM HOW IT ENDS.
HEY, Y KNOW WH REALL FUCKIN BIZARR ABOUT THIS?
HAVEN'T EVEN SEEN A PICTURE.
THAT GUYS GOT MY DICK IN HIS HANDS.
ALL THES STUDIOS I TALKED T
IT' A BUN DISEMB VOICE

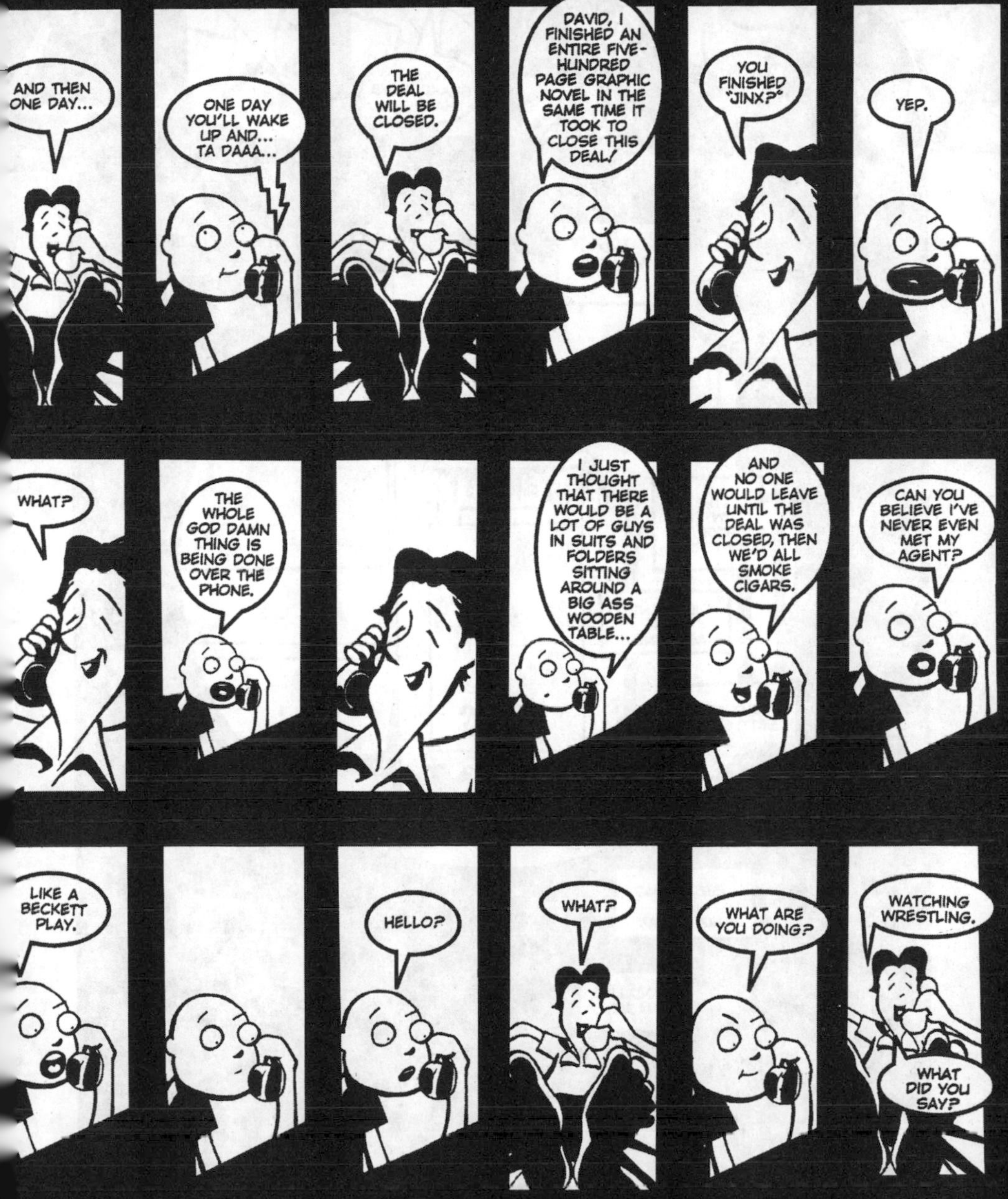
AND THEN ONE DAY...
ONE DAY YOU'LL WAKE UP AND... TA DAAA...
THE DEAL WILL BE CLOSED.
DAVID, I FINISHED AN ENTIRE FIVE-HUNDRED PAGE GRAPHIC NOVEL IN THE SAME TIME IT TOOK TO CLOSE THIS DEAL!
YOU FINISHED "JINX?"
YEP.
WHAT?
THE WHOLE GOD DAMN THING IS BEING DONE OVER THE PHONE.
I JUST THOUGHT THAT THERE WOULD BE A LOT OF GUYS IN SUITS AND FOLDERS SITTING AROUND A BIG ASS WOODEN TABLE...
AND NO ONE WOULD LEAVE UNTIL THE DEAL WAS CLOSED, THEN WE'D ALL SMOKE CIGARS.
CAN YOU BELIEVE I'VE NEVER EVEN MET MY AGENT?
LIKE A BECKETT PLAY.
HELLO?
WHAT?
WHAT ARE YOU DOING?
WATCHING WRESTLING.
WHAT DID YOU SAY?

NEVERMIND,
LISTEN...

I
TOLD YOU...

AFTER WE
CLOSE THIS
DEAL AND YOU
KICK ASS ON
THE SCRIPT-

-AS
WE BOTH
KNOW YOU
WILL-

YOU'RE
GOING TO
COME BACK
OUT HERE.

PEOPLE ARE
GOING TO
WANT TO MEET
YOU.

YOU'LL DO
THE MEET AND
GREET

YOU'LL
SHAKE SOME
HANDS...

YOU'LL GET
SOME FREE
MEALS.

I DO
LIKE FREE
MEALS...

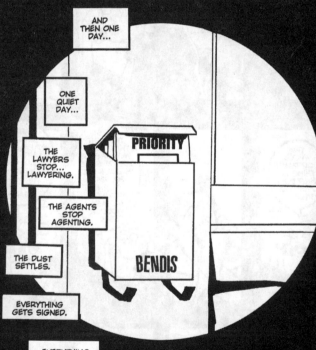
AND
THEN ONE
DAY...

ONE
QUIET
DAY...

THE
LAWYERS
STOP...
LAWYERING.

THE AGENTS
STOP
AGENTING.

THE DUST
SETTLES.

EVERYTHING
GETS SIGNED.

EVERYTHING
GETS
NOTARIZED.

AND LIKE
MAGIC...

PRIORITY

BENDIS

THE CHECK
COMES.

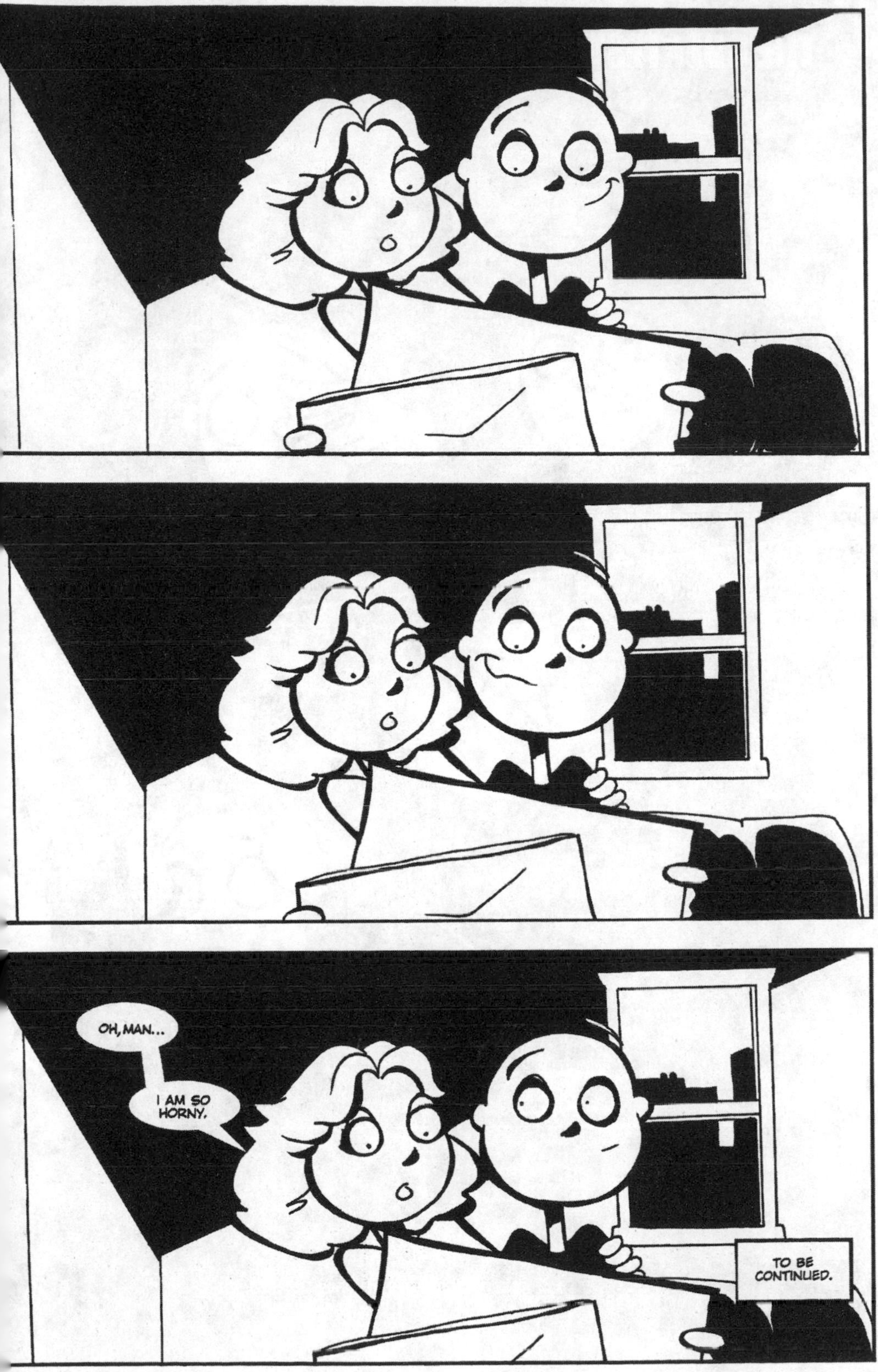
OH, MAN...
I AM SO HORNY.
TO BE CONTINUED.

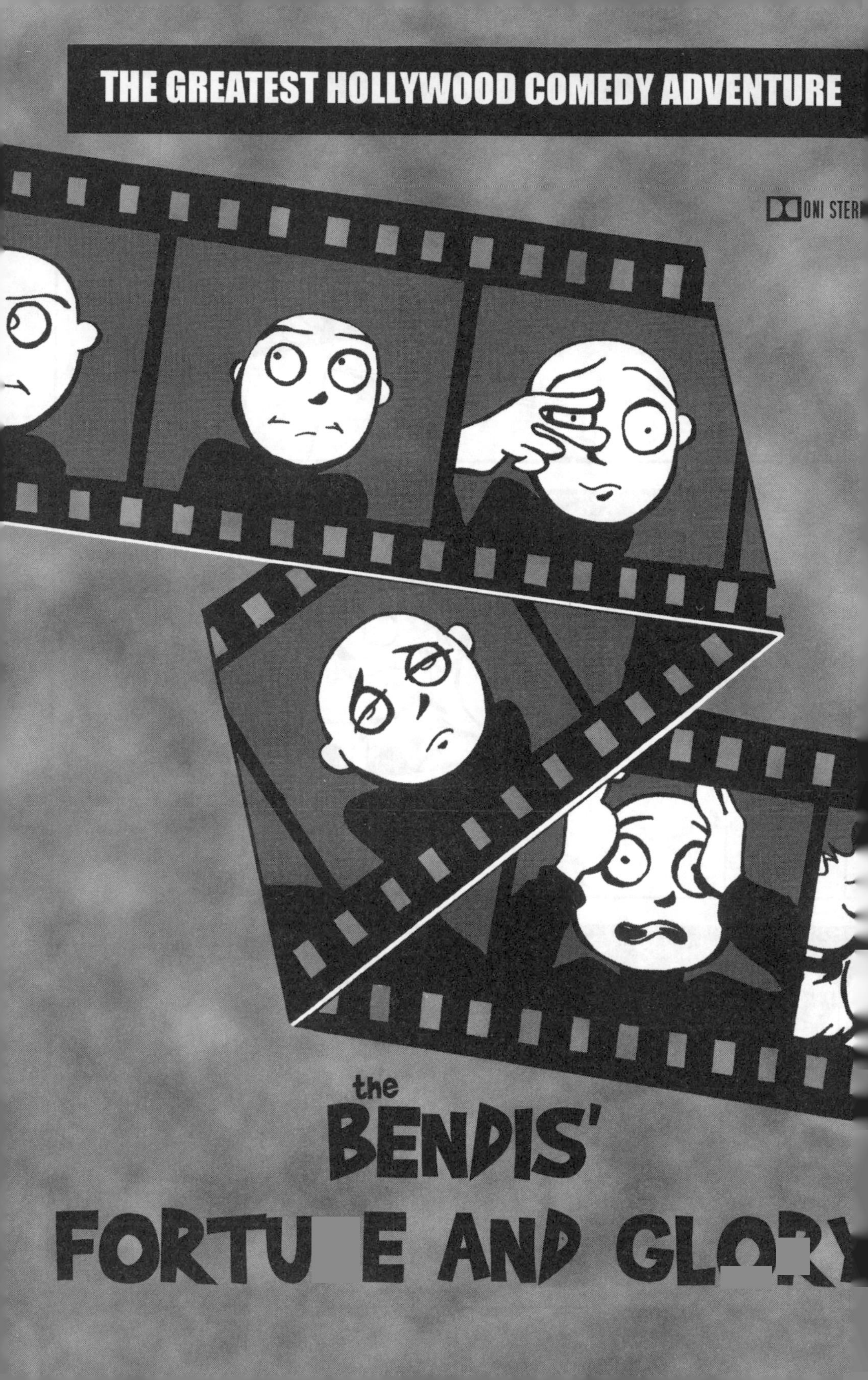
THE GREATEST HOLLYWOOD COMEDY ADVENTURE
the
BENDIS'
FORTU E AND GLO Y

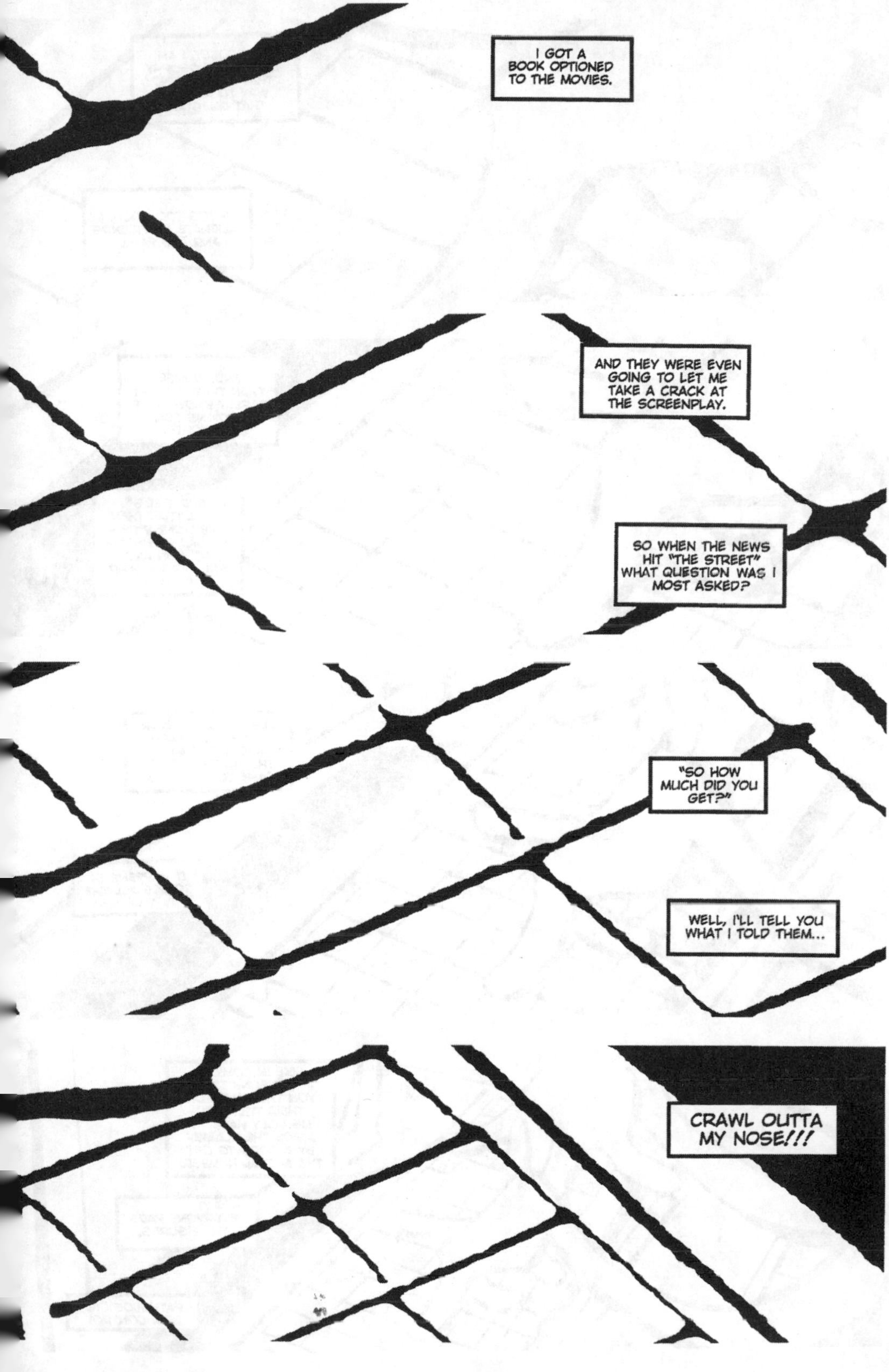
I GOT A BOOK OPTIONED TO THE MOVIES.
AND THEY WERE EVEN GOING TO LET ME TAKE A CRACK AT THE SCREENPLAY.
SO WHEN THE NEWS HIT "THE STREET" WHAT QUESTION WAS I MOST ASKED?
"SO HOW MUCH DID YOU GET?"
WELL, I'LL TELL YOU WHAT I TOLD THEM...
CRAWL OUTTA MY NOSE!!!

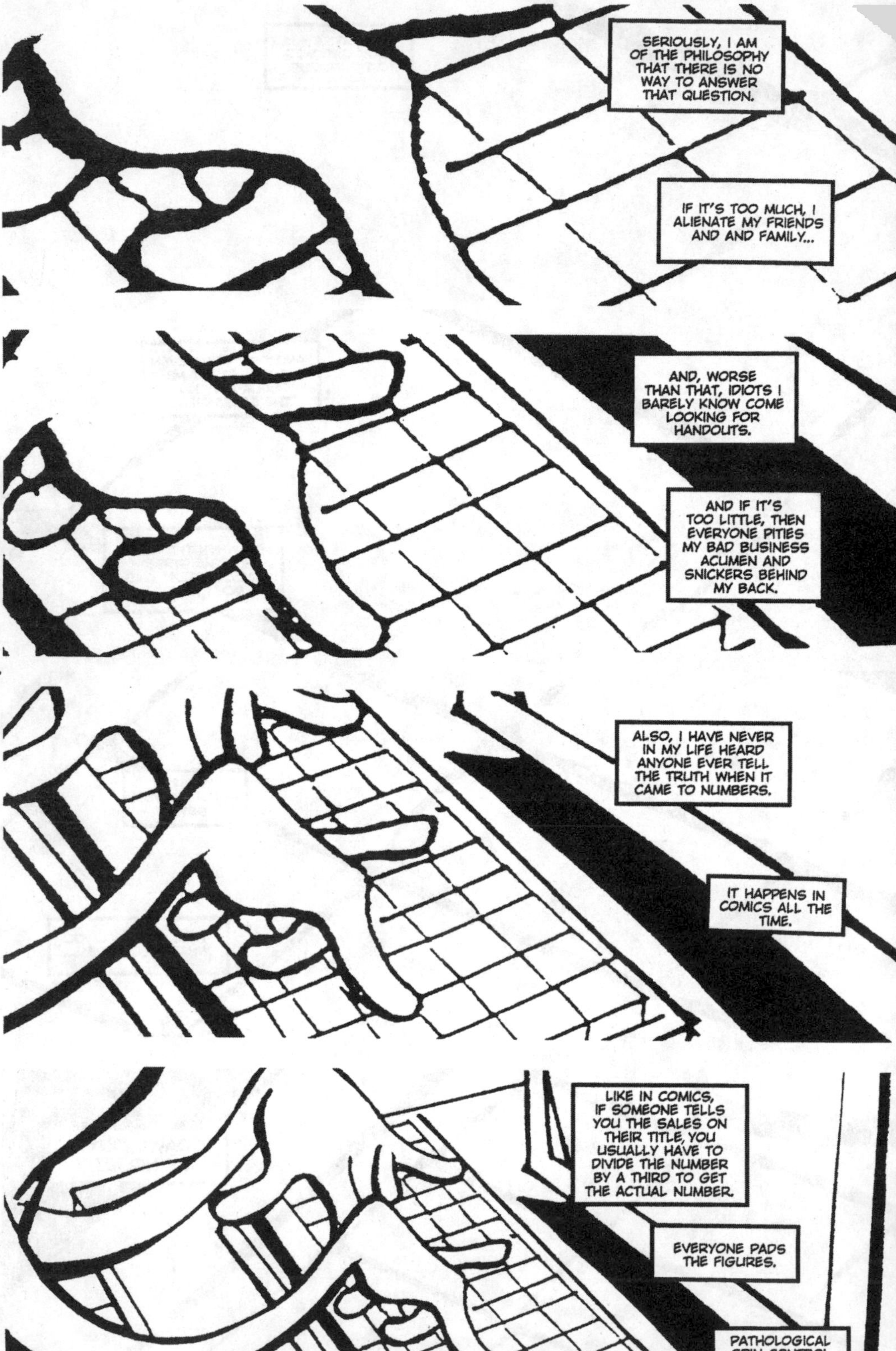
SERIOUSLY, I AM OF THE PHILOSOPHY THAT THERE IS NO WAY TO ANSWER THAT QUESTION.
IF IT'S TOO MUCH, I ALIENATE MY FRIENDS AND AND FAMILY...
AND, WORSE THAN THAT, IDIOTS I BARELY KNOW COME LOOKING FOR HANDOUTS.
AND IF IT'S TOO LITTLE, THEN EVERYONE PITIES MY BAD BUSINESS ACUMEN AND SNICKERS BEHIND MY BACK.
ALSO, I HAVE NEVER IN MY LIFE HEARD ANYONE EVER TELL THE TRUTH WHEN IT CAME TO NUMBERS.
IT HAPPENS IN COMICS ALL THE TIME.
LIKE IN COMICS, IF SOMEONE TELLS YOU THE SALES ON THEIR TITLE, YOU USUALLY HAVE TO DIVIDE THE NUMBER BY A THIRD TO GET THE ACTUAL NUMBER.
EVERYONE PADS THE FIGURES.
PATHOLOGICAL SPIN CONTROL.

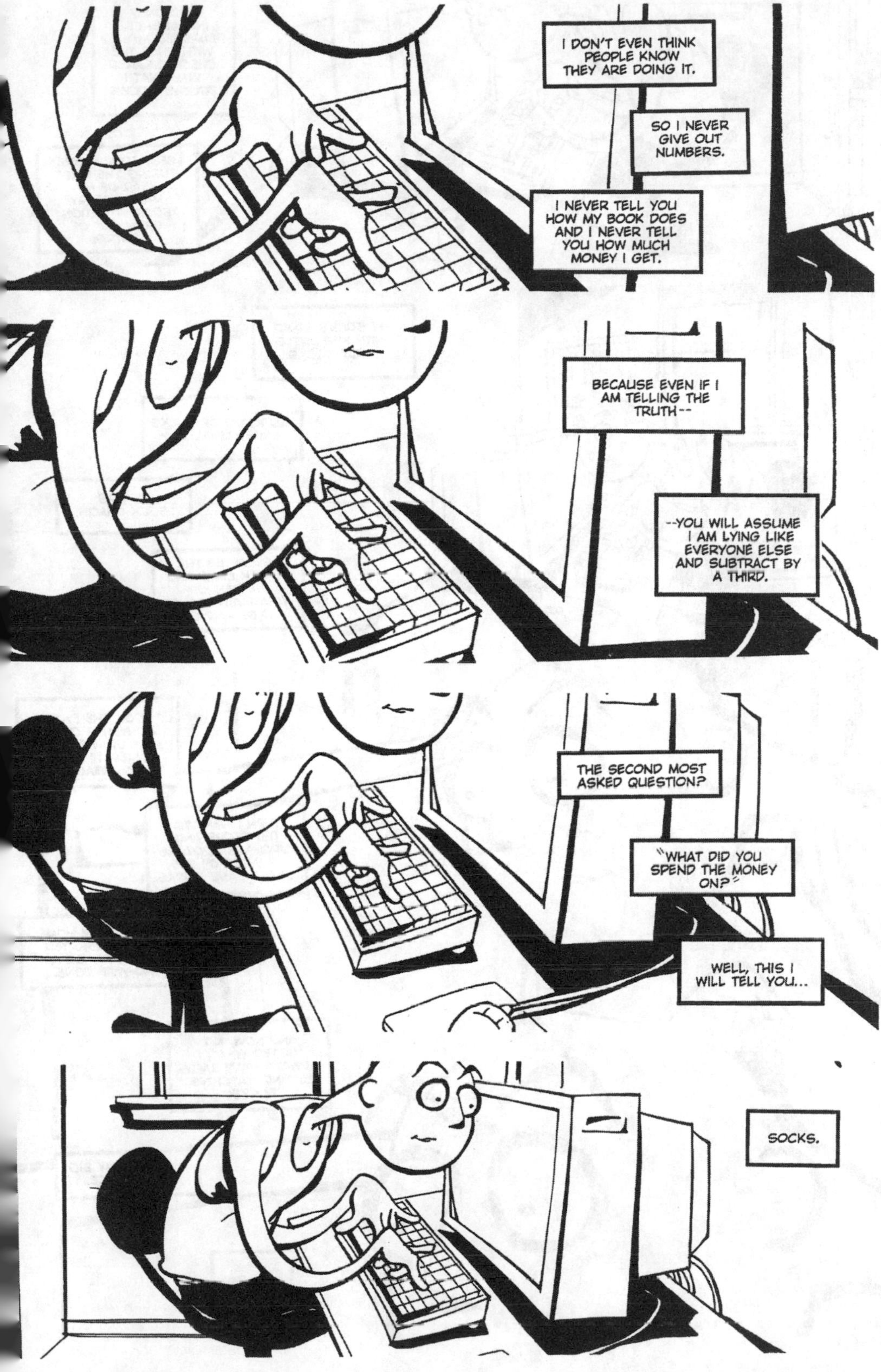
I DON'T EVEN THINK PEOPLE KNOW THEY ARE DOING IT.
SO I NEVER GIVE OUT NUMBERS.
I NEVER TELL YOU HOW MY BOOK DOES AND I NEVER TELL YOU HOW MUCH MONEY I GET.
BECAUSE EVEN IF I AM TELLING THE TRUTH--
--YOU WILL ASSUME I AM LYING LIKE EVERYONE ELSE AND SUBTRACT BY A THIRD.
THE SECOND MOST ASKED QUESTION?
"WHAT DID YOU SPEND THE MONEY ON?"
WELL, THIS I WILL TELL YOU...
SOCKS.

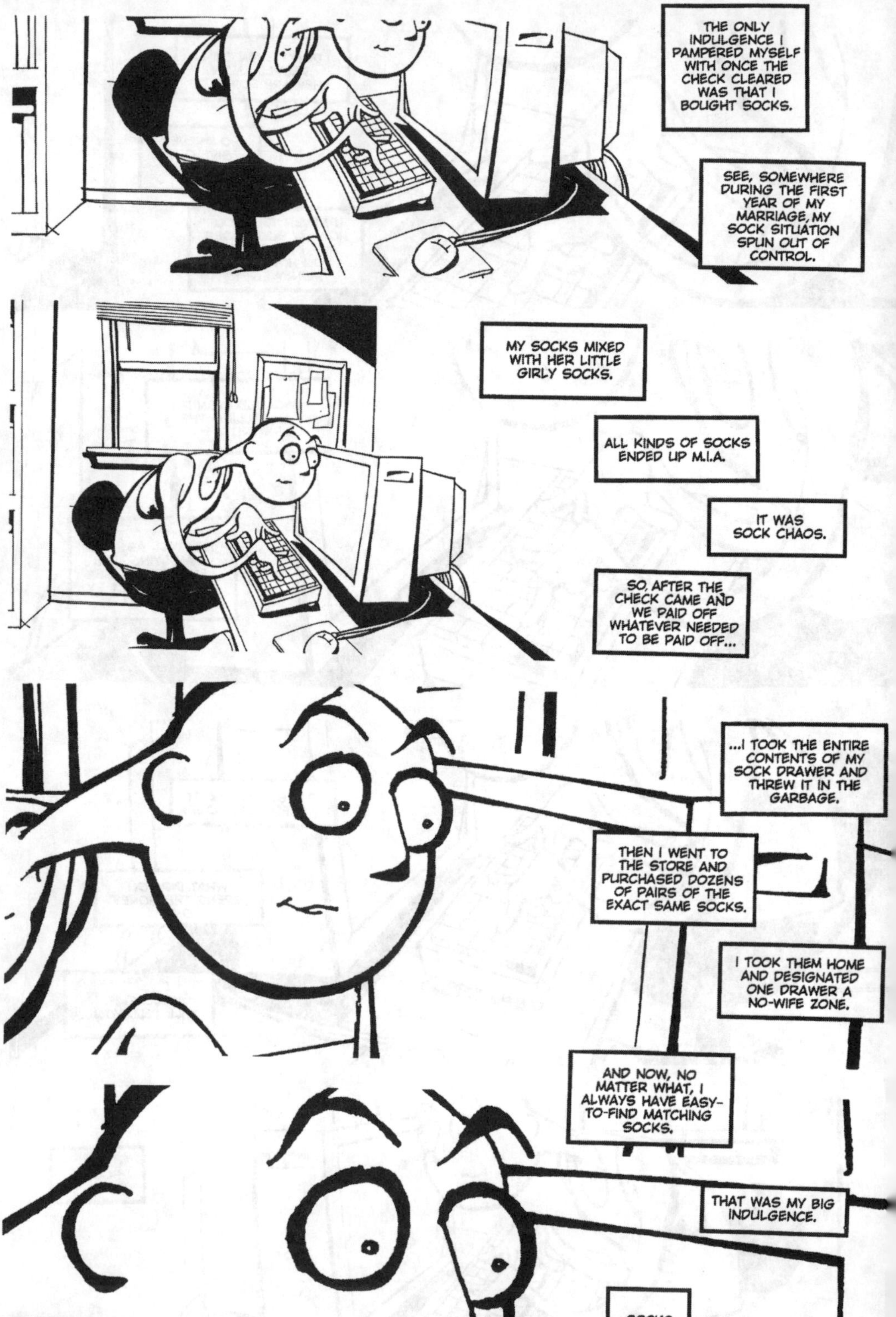
THE ONLY INDULGENCE I PAMPERED MYSELF WITH ONCE THE CHECK CLEARED WAS THAT I BOUGHT SOCKS.
SEE, SOMEWHERE DURING THE FIRST YEAR OF MY MARRIAGE, MY SOCK SITUATION SPUN OUT OF CONTROL.
MY SOCKS MIXED WITH HER LITTLE GIRLY SOCKS.
ALL KINDS OF SOCKS ENDED UP M.I.A.
IT WAS SOCK CHAOS.
SO, AFTER THE CHECK CAME AND WE PAID OFF WHATEVER NEEDED TO BE PAID OFF...
...I TOOK THE ENTIRE CONTENTS OF MY SOCK DRAWER AND THREW IT IN THE GARBAGE.
THEN I WENT TO THE STORE AND PURCHASED DOZENS OF PAIRS OF THE EXACT SAME SOCKS.
I TOOK THEM HOME AND DESIGNATED ONE DRAWER A NO-WIFE ZONE.
AND NOW, NO MATTER WHAT, I ALWAYS HAVE EASY-TO-FIND MATCHING SOCKS.
THAT WAS MY BIG INDULGENCE.
SOCKS.

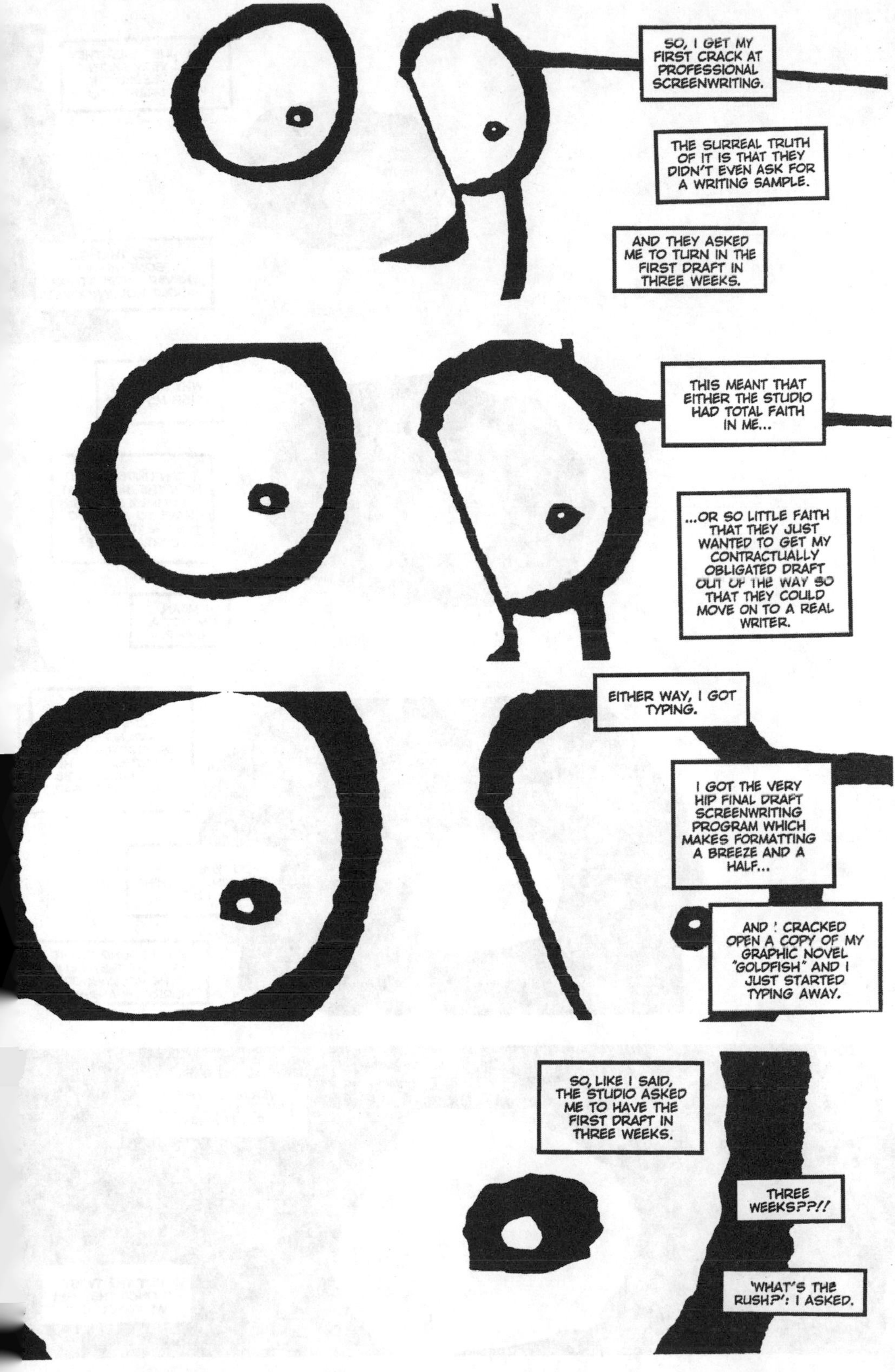
SO, I GET MY FIRST CRACK AT PROFESSIONAL SCREENWRITING.
THE SURREAL TRUTH OF IT IS THAT THEY DIDN'T EVEN ASK FOR A WRITING SAMPLE.
AND THEY ASKED ME TO TURN IN THE FIRST DRAFT IN THREE WEEKS.
THIS MEANT THAT EITHER THE STUDIO HAD TOTAL FAITH IN ME...
...OR SO LITTLE FAITH THAT THEY JUST WANTED TO GET MY CONTRACTUALLY OBLIGATED DRAFT OUT OF THE WAY SO THAT THEY COULD MOVE ON TO A REAL WRITER.
EITHER WAY, I GOT TYPING.
I GOT THE VERY HIP FINAL DRAFT SCREENWRITING PROGRAM WHICH MAKES FORMATTING A BREEZE AND A HALF...
AND I CRACKED OPEN A COPY OF MY GRAPHIC NOVEL "GOLDFISH" AND I JUST STARTED TYPING AWAY.
SO, LIKE I SAID, THE STUDIO ASKED ME TO HAVE THE FIRST DRAFT IN THREE WEEKS.
THREE WEEKS??!!
'WHAT'S THE RUSH?': I ASKED.

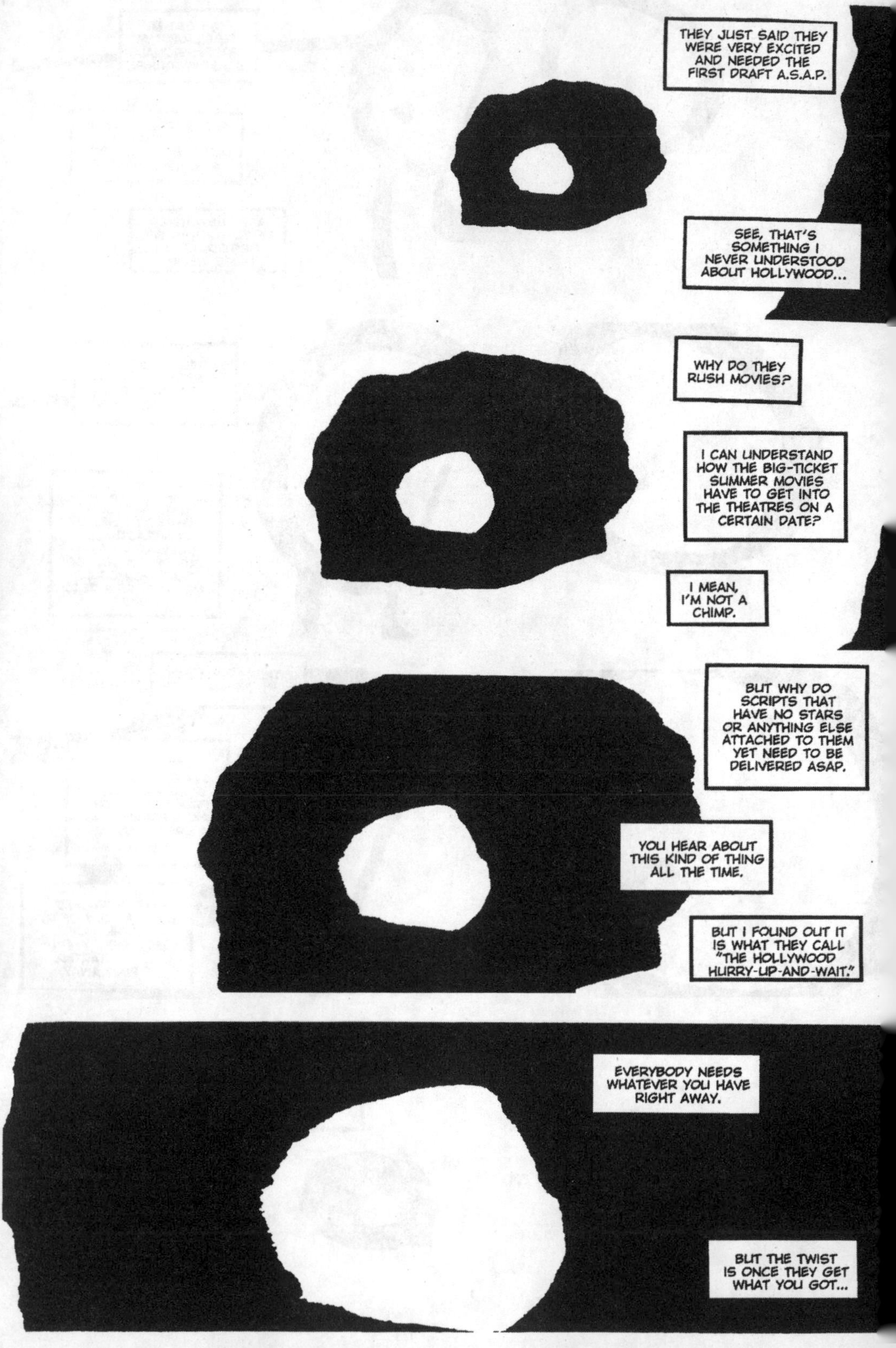
THEY JUST SAID THEY WERE VERY EXCITED AND NEEDED THE FIRST DRAFT A.S.A.P.
SEE, THAT'S SOMETHING I NEVER UNDERSTOOD ABOUT HOLLYWOOD...
WHY DO THEY RUSH MOVIES?
I CAN UNDERSTAND HOW THE BIG-TICKET SUMMER MOVIES HAVE TO GET INTO THE THEATRES ON A CERTAIN DATE?
I MEAN, I'M NOT A CHIMP.
BUT WHY DO SCRIPTS THAT HAVE NO STARS OR ANYTHING ELSE ATTACHED TO THEM YET NEED TO BE DELIVERED ASAP.
YOU HEAR ABOUT THIS KIND OF THING ALL THE TIME.
BUT I FOUND OUT IT IS WHAT THEY CALL "THE HOLLYWOOD HURRY-UP-AND-WAIT."
EVERYBODY NEEDS WHATEVER YOU HAVE RIGHT AWAY.
BUT THE TWIST IS ONCE THEY GET WHAT YOU GOT...

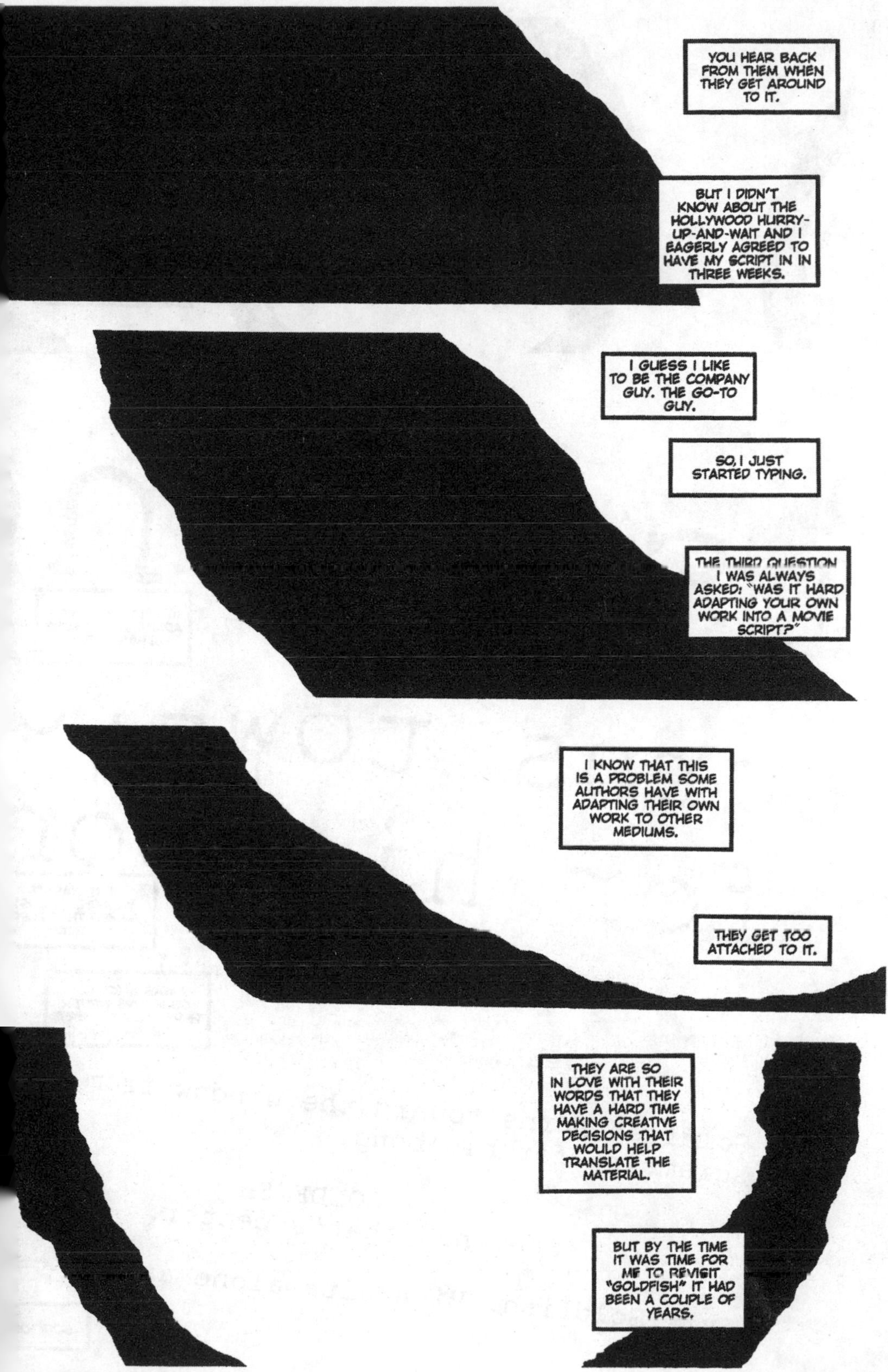
YOU HEAR BACK FROM THEM WHEN THEY GET AROUND TO IT.
BUT I DIDN'T KNOW ABOUT THE HOLLYWOOD HURRY-UP-AND-WAIT AND I EAGERLY AGREED TO HAVE MY SCRIPT IN IN THREE WEEKS.
I GUESS I LIKE TO BE THE COMPANY GUY. THE GO-TO GUY.
SO, I JUST STARTED TYPING.
THE THIRD QUESTION I WAS ALWAYS ASKED: "WAS IT HARD ADAPTING YOUR OWN WORK INTO A MOVIE SCRIPT?"
I KNOW THAT THIS IS A PROBLEM SOME AUTHORS HAVE WITH ADAPTING THEIR OWN WORK TO OTHER MEDIUMS.
THEY GET TOO ATTACHED TO IT.
THEY ARE SO IN LOVE WITH THEIR WORDS THAT THEY HAVE A HARD TIME MAKING CREATIVE DECISIONS THAT WOULD HELP TRANSLATE THE MATERIAL.
BUT BY THE TIME IT WAS TIME FOR ME TO REVISIT "GOLDFISH" IT HAD BEEN A COUPLE OF YEARS.

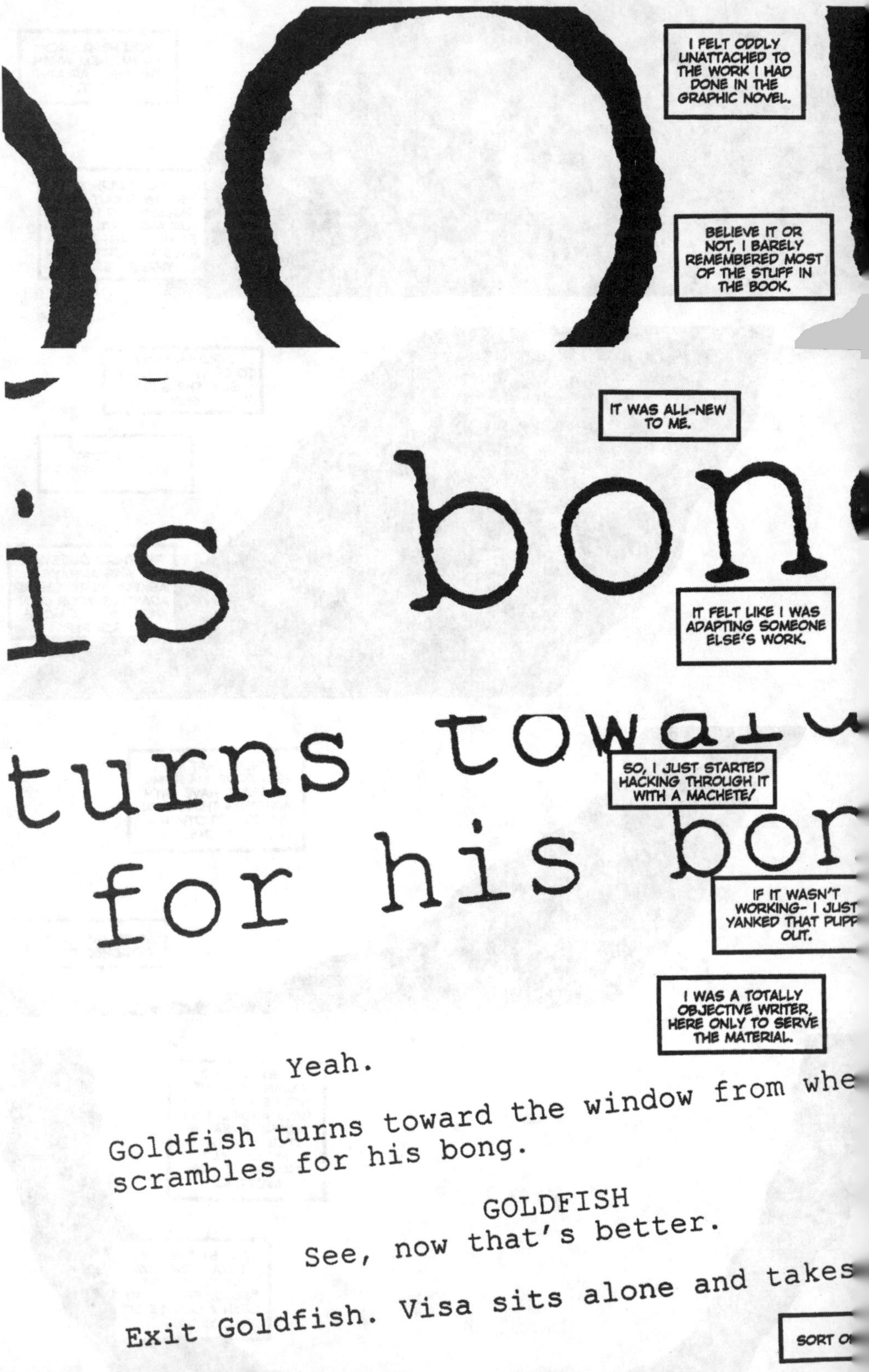
I FELT ODDLY UNATTACHED TO THE WORK I HAD DONE IN THE GRAPHIC NOVEL.
BELIEVE IT OR NOT, I BARELY REMEMBERED MOST OF THE STUFF IN THE BOOK.
IT WAS ALL-NEW TO ME.
is bon
IT FELT LIKE I WAS ADAPTING SOMEONE ELSE'S WORK.
turns tow
SO, I JUST STARTED HACKING THROUGH IT WITH A MACHETE!
for his bon
IF IT WASN'T WORKING- I JUST YANKED THAT PUPP OUT.
I WAS A TOTALLY OBJECTIVE WRITER, HERE ONLY TO SERVE THE MATERIAL.
Yeah.
Goldfish turns toward the window from whe
scrambles for his bong.
GOLDFISH
See, now that's better.
Exit Goldfish. Visa sits alone and takes
SORT O

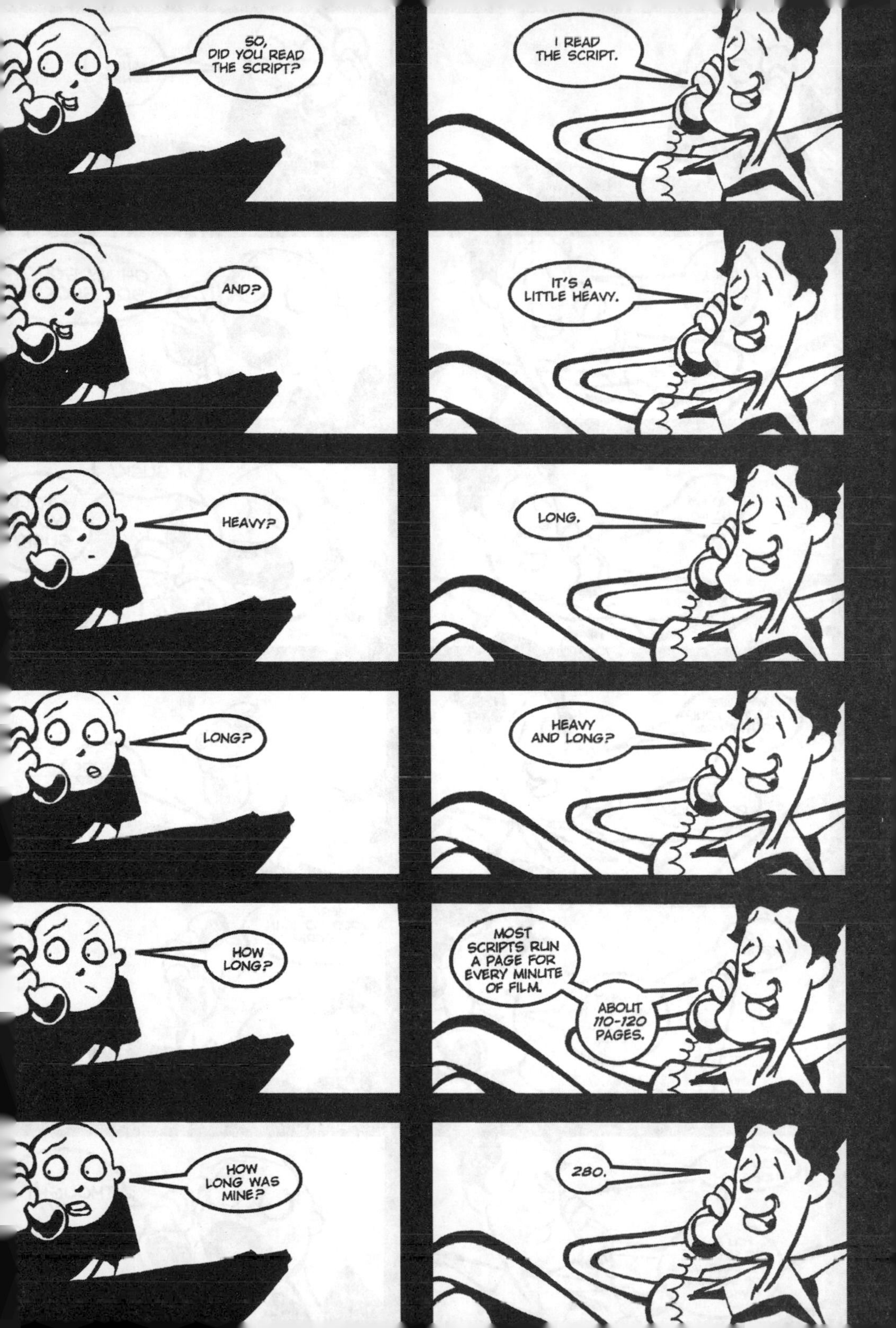
SO, DID YOU READ THE SCRIPT?
I READ THE SCRIPT.
AND?
IT'S A LITTLE HEAVY.
HEAVY?
LONG.
LONG?
HEAVY AND LONG?
HOW LONG?
MOST SCRIPTS RUN A PAGE FOR EVERY MINUTE OF FILM.
ABOUT 110-120 PAGES.
HOW LONG WAS MINE?
280.

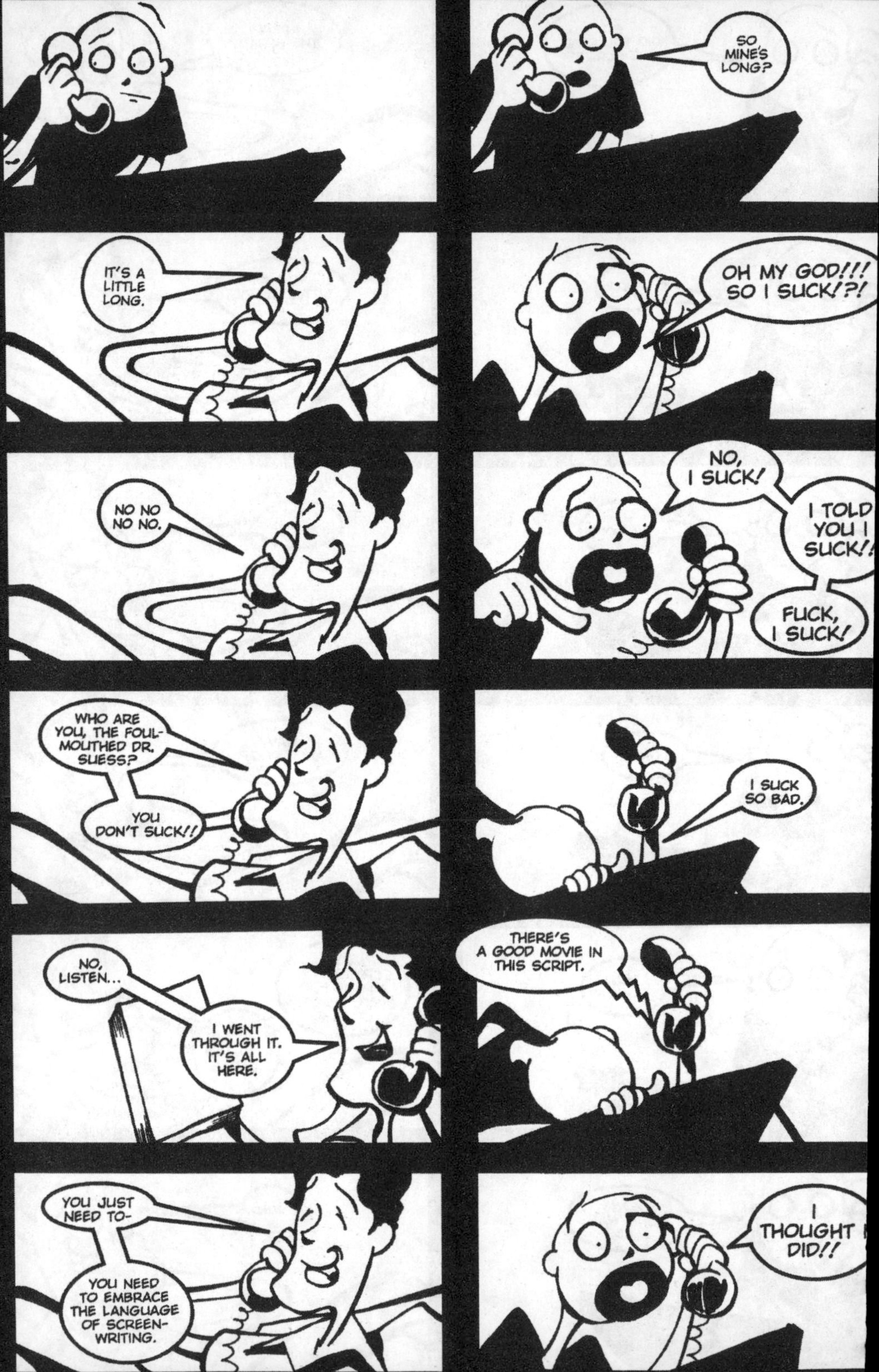
SO MINE'S LONG?
IT'S A LITTLE LONG.
OH MY GOD!!! SO I SUCK!?!
NO NO NO NO.
NO, I SUCK!
I TOLD YOU I SUCK!!
FUCK, I SUCK!
WHO ARE YOU, THE FOUL-MOUTHED DR. SUESS?
YOU DON'T SUCK!!
I SUCK SO BAD.
NO, LISTEN...
I WENT THROUGH IT. IT'S ALL HERE.
THERE'S A GOOD MOVIE IN THIS SCRIPT.
YOU JUST NEED TO-
YOU NEED TO EMBRACE THE LANGUAGE OF SCREEN-WRITING.
I THOUGHT I DID!!

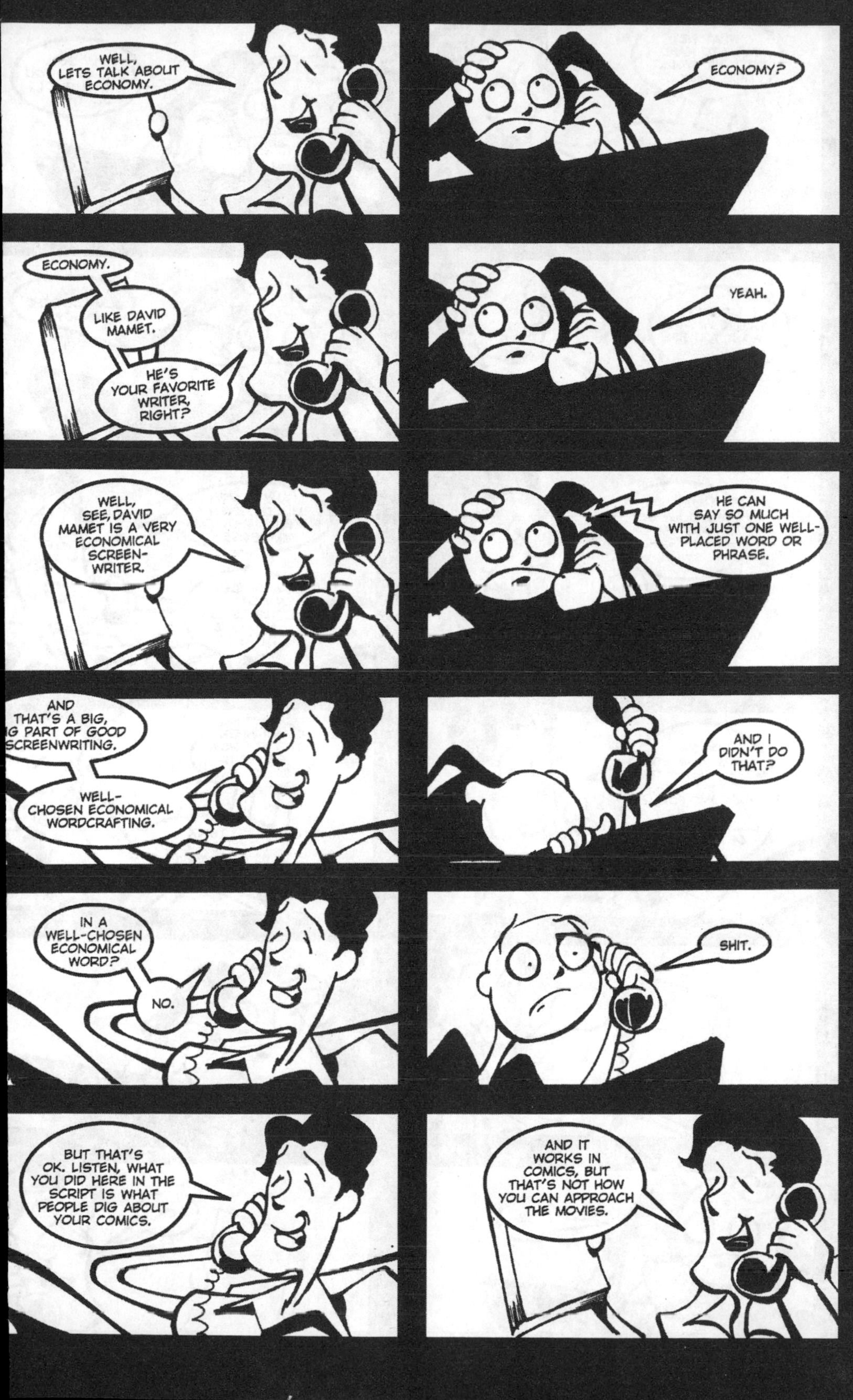
WELL, LETS TALK ABOUT ECONOMY.
ECONOMY?
ECONOMY.
LIKE DAVID MAMET.
HE'S YOUR FAVORITE WRITER, RIGHT?
YEAH.
WELL, SEE, DAVID MAMET IS A VERY ECONOMICAL SCREEN-WRITER.
HE CAN SAY SO MUCH WITH JUST ONE WELL-PLACED WORD OR PHRASE.
AND THAT'S A BIG, G PART OF GOOD SCREENWRITING.
WELL-CHOSEN ECONOMICAL WORDCRAFTING.
AND I DIDN'T DO THAT?
IN A WELL-CHOSEN ECONOMICAL WORD?
NO.
SHIT.
BUT THAT'S OK. LISTEN, WHAT YOU DID HERE IN THE SCRIPT IS WHAT PEOPLE DIG ABOUT YOUR COMICS.
AND IT WORKS IN COMICS, BUT THAT'S NOT HOW YOU CAN APPROACH THE MOVIES.

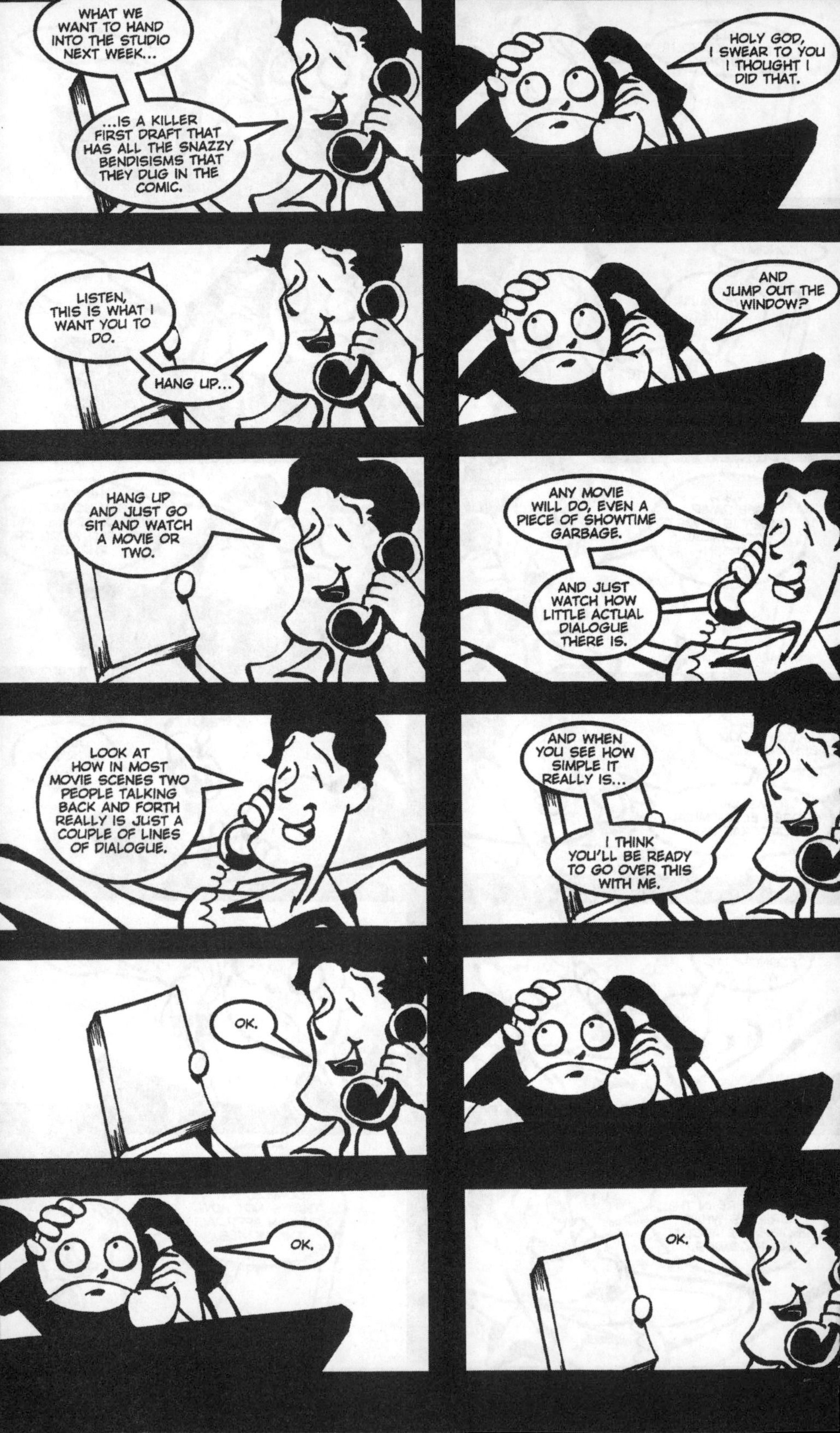
WHAT WE WANT TO HAND INTO THE STUDIO NEXT WEEK...
...IS A KILLER FIRST DRAFT THAT HAS ALL THE SNAZZY BENDISISMS THAT THEY DUG IN THE COMIC.
HOLY GOD, I SWEAR TO YOU I THOUGHT I DID THAT.
LISTEN, THIS IS WHAT I WANT YOU TO DO.
HANG UP...
AND JUMP OUT THE WINDOW?
HANG UP AND JUST GO SIT AND WATCH A MOVIE OR TWO.
ANY MOVIE WILL DO, EVEN A PIECE OF SHOWTIME GARBAGE.
AND JUST WATCH HOW LITTLE ACTUAL DIALOGUE THERE IS.
LOOK AT HOW IN MOST MOVIE SCENES TWO PEOPLE TALKING BACK AND FORTH REALLY IS JUST A COUPLE OF LINES OF DIALOGUE.
AND WHEN YOU SEE HOW SIMPLE IT REALLY IS...
I THINK YOU'LL BE READY TO GO OVER THIS WITH ME.
OK.
OK.
OK.

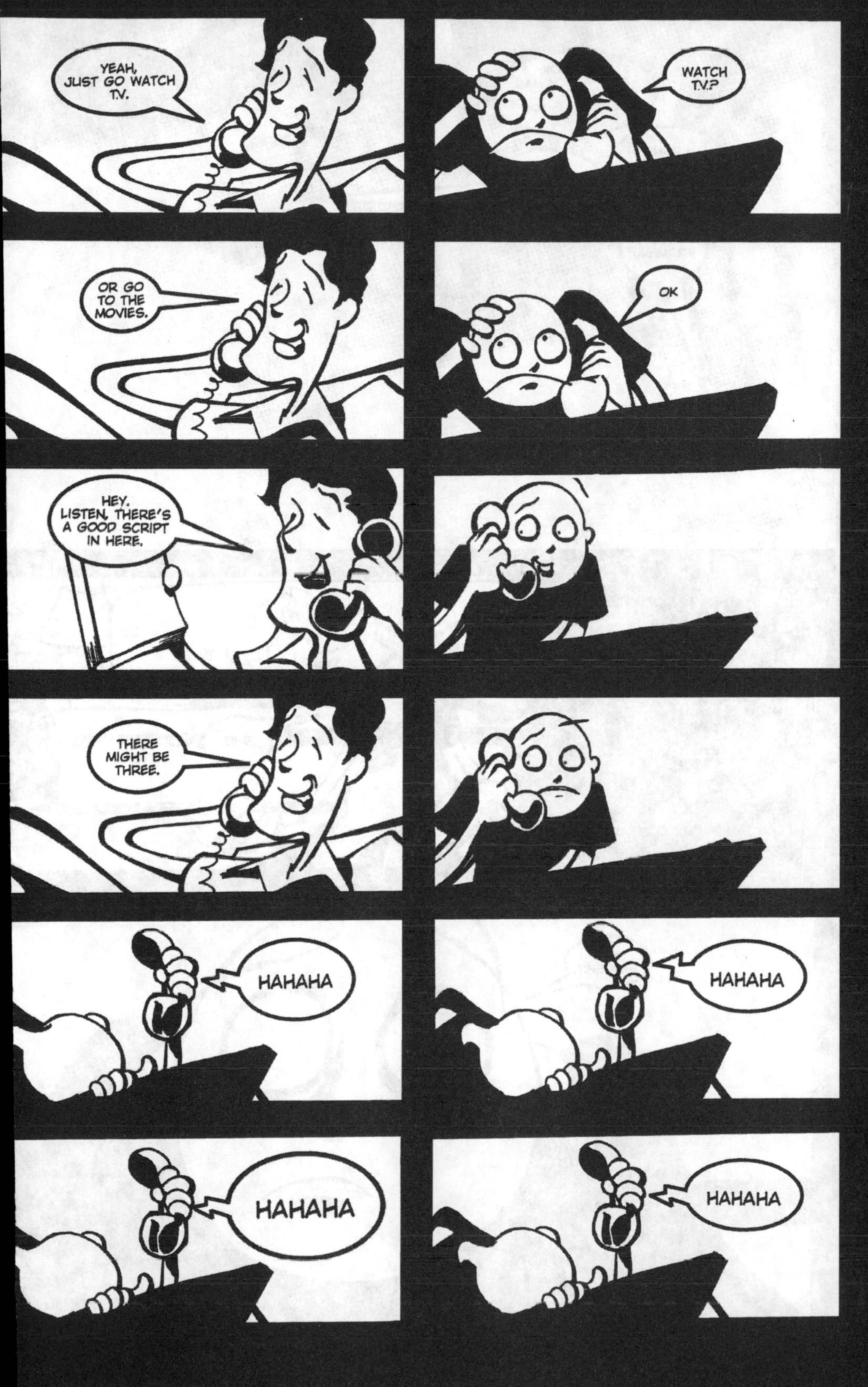
YEAH, JUST GO WATCH T.V.
WATCH T.V.?
OR GO TO THE MOVIES.
OK
HEY. LISTEN, THERE'S A GOOD SCRIPT IN HERE.
THERE MIGHT BE THREE.
HAHAHA
HAHAHA
HAHAHA
HAHAHA

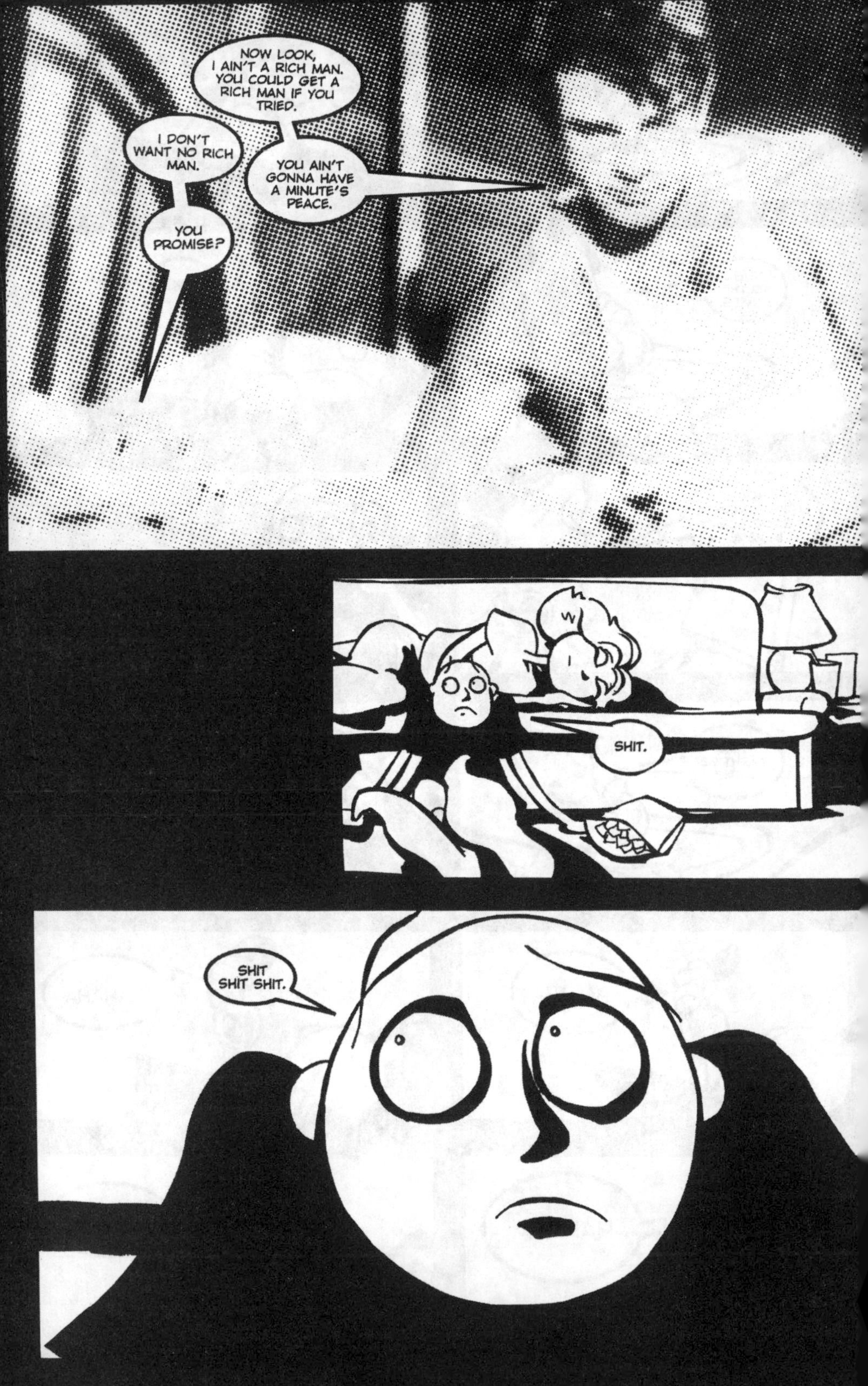
NOW LOOK, I AIN'T A RICH MAN. YOU COULD GET A RICH MAN IF YOU TRIED.
I DON'T WANT NO RICH MAN.
YOU AIN'T GONNA HAVE A MINUTE'S PEACE.
YOU PROMISE?
SHIT.
SHIT SHIT SHIT.

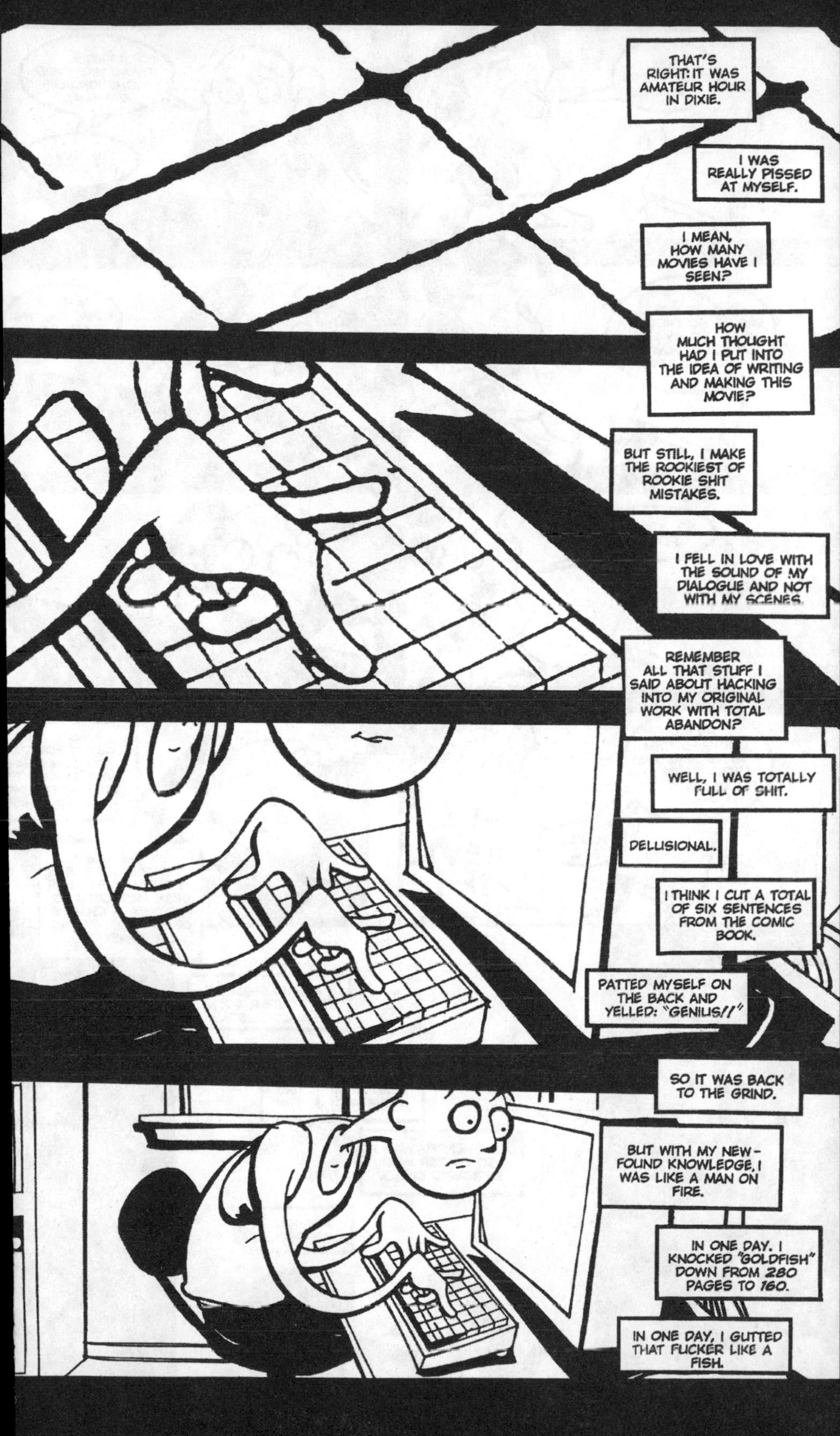
THAT'S RIGHT: IT WAS AMATEUR HOUR IN DIXIE.
I WAS REALLY PISSED AT MYSELF.
I MEAN, HOW MANY MOVIES HAVE I SEEN?
HOW MUCH THOUGHT HAD I PUT INTO THE IDEA OF WRITING AND MAKING THIS MOVIE?
BUT STILL, I MAKE THE ROOKIEST OF ROOKIE SHIT MISTAKES.
I FELL IN LOVE WITH THE SOUND OF MY DIALOGUE AND NOT WITH MY SCENES.
REMEMBER ALL THAT STUFF I SAID ABOUT HACKING INTO MY ORIGINAL WORK WITH TOTAL ABANDON?
WELL, I WAS TOTALLY FULL OF SHIT.
DELUSIONAL.
I THINK I CUT A TOTAL OF SIX SENTENCES FROM THE COMIC BOOK.
PATTED MYSELF ON THE BACK AND YELLED: "GENIUS!!"
SO IT WAS BACK TO THE GRIND.
BUT WITH MY NEW-FOUND KNOWLEDGE, I WAS LIKE A MAN ON FIRE.
IN ONE DAY. I KNOCKED "GOLDFISH" DOWN FROM 280 PAGES TO 160.
IN ONE DAY, I GUTTED THAT FUCKER LIKE A FISH.

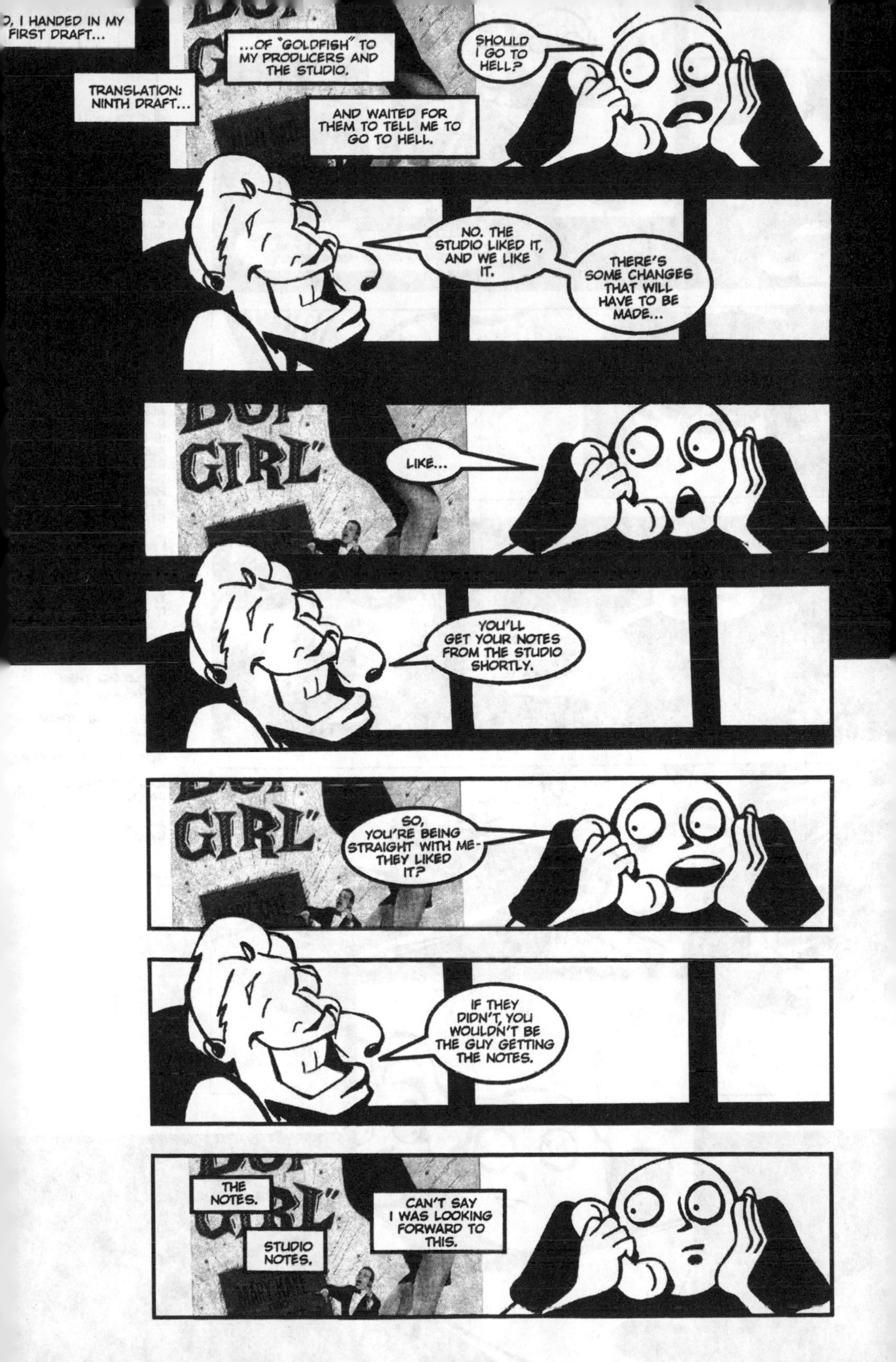

O, I HANDED IN MY FIRST DRAFT...
TRANSLATION: NINTH DRAFT...
...OF "GOLDFISH" TO MY PRODUCERS AND THE STUDIO.
AND WAITED FOR THEM TO TELL ME TO GO TO HELL.
SHOULD I GO TO HELL?
NO. THE STUDIO LIKED IT, AND WE LIKE IT.
THERE'S SOME CHANGES THAT WILL HAVE TO BE MADE...
GIRL"
LIKE...
YOU'LL GET YOUR NOTES FROM THE STUDIO SHORTLY.
GIRL"
SO, YOU'RE BEING STRAIGHT WITH ME- THEY LIKED IT?
IF THEY DIDN'T, YOU WOULDN'T BE THE GUY GETTING THE NOTES.
THE NOTES.
STUDIO NOTES.
CAN'T SAY I WAS LOOKING FORWARD TO THIS.

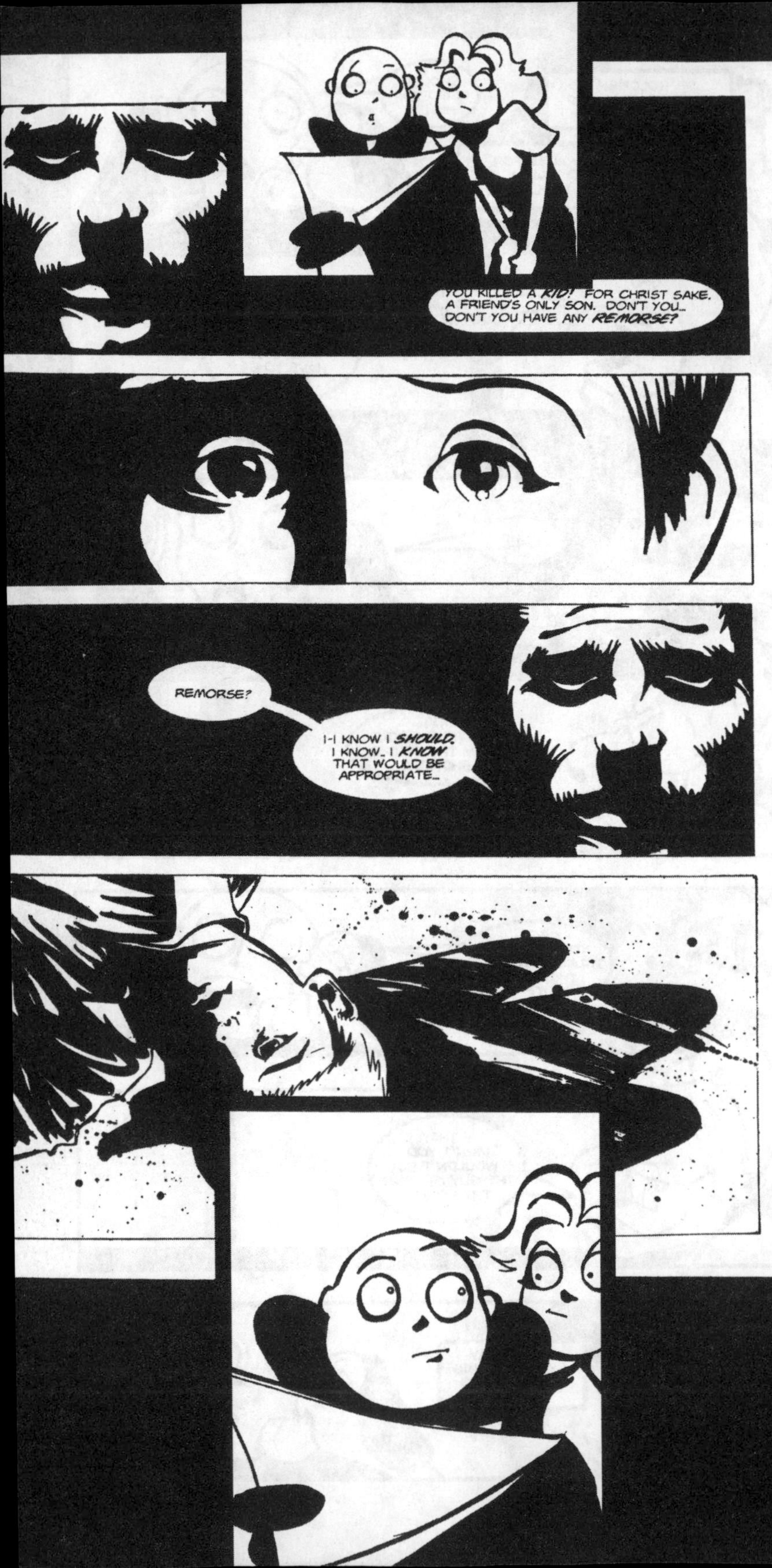
YOU KILLED A *KID!* FOR CHRIST SAKE. A FRIEND'S ONLY SON. DON'T YOU.. DON'T YOU HAVE ANY *REMORSE?*
REMORSE?
I-I KNOW I *SHOULD.* I KNOW.. I *KNOW* THAT WOULD BE APPROPRIATE..

BUT TO MY SURPRISE...

THE NOTES MADE A LOT OF SENSE.

THE BIG PLOT CONCERN WAS THAT I KILLED GOLDFISH'S KID AT THE END OF THE THIRD ACT.

LIKE I DID IN THE BOOK.

THEY EXPLAINED THAT KILLING THE KID BEFORE GOLDFISH GETS TO HIM WORKS IN BOOK FORM...

BUT IN MOVIE FORM, ALL YOU ACCOMPLISH BY KILLING THE KID IS DENYING THE AUDIENCE THE MAGIC REUNION MOMENT YOU'VE BEEN PROMISING THEM SINCE THE FILM STARTED.

I HAD TO SAY THAT THIS MADE DAMN GOOD SENSE.

THEY ALSO THOUGHT IT WOULDN'T KILL ME TO SHAVE TEN PAGES OFF IT. AT *119,* IT CAME IN A LITTLE LONG.

LITTLE DID THEY KNOW...

SO, I DID ANOTHER POLISH...

GOT ANOTHER CHECK...

AND EVERYBODY INVOLVED SEEMED TO BE ABLE TO SMILE AND LOOK ME IN THE EYE.

AFTER MY MEETING WITH THE NEW YORK GUYS I STARTED RECEIVING INVITATIONS TO ALL THE BIG HOLLYWOOD PREMIERES AND PARTIES THAT THE STUDIO HOSTED.

I WAS INVITED TO THE PREMIERES OF "SCREAM 2," "HOLLOWEEN H20," AND "GOOD WILL HUNTING."

I ALWAYS GOT THE INVITATION LIKE FOUR DAYS BEFORE THE EVENT.

SO, EVEN IF I WAS DYING TO GO, IT WOULD HAVE BEEN ONE HUGE EXPENSIVE PAIN IN THE ASS JUST TO SEE JAIMIE LEE CURTIS OUTRUN FATHER TIME BEFORE EVERYBODY ELSE.

SO, I FORWARDED THE INVITES TO MARC ANDREYKO, WHO I HAD STARTED WORKING ON "TORSO" WITH.

MARC WAS A FELLOW CLEVELANDER WHO HAD HEAD OUT WEST TO SEEK HIS FORTUNE.

AND HE WAS DOING PRETTY WELL.

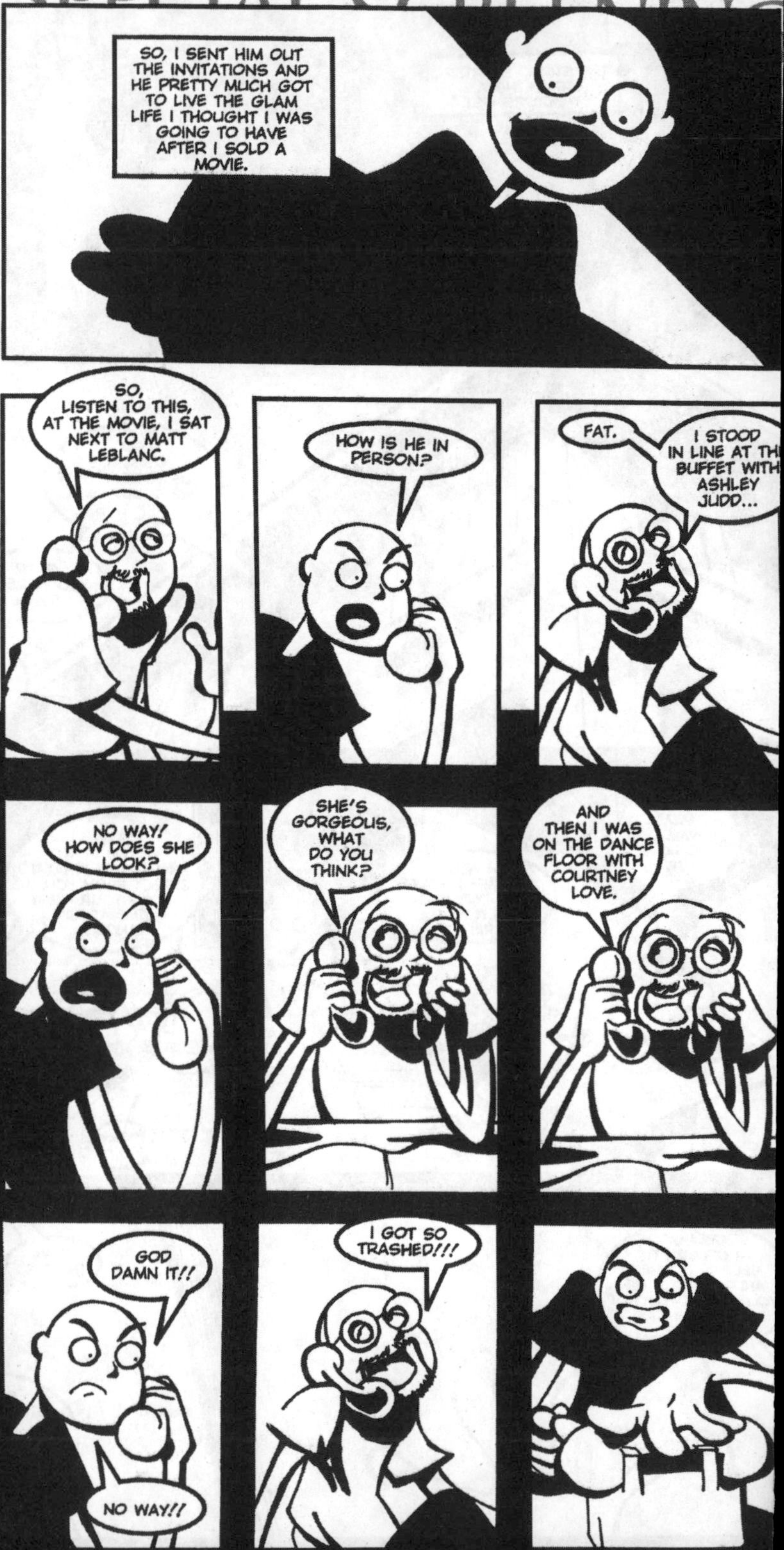

SO, I SENT HIM OUT THE INVITATIONS AND HE PRETTY MUCH GOT TO LIVE THE GLAM LIFE I THOUGHT I WAS GOING TO HAVE AFTER I SOLD A MOVIE.
SO, LISTEN TO THIS, AT THE MOVIE, I SAT NEXT TO MATT LEBLANC.
HOW IS HE IN PERSON?
FAT.
I STOOD IN LINE AT TH BUFFET WITH ASHLEY JUDD...
NO WAY! HOW DOES SHE LOOK?
SHE'S GORGEOUS, WHAT DO YOU THINK?
AND THEN I WAS ON THE DANCE FLOOR WITH COURTNEY LOVE.
GOD DAMN IT!!
NO WAY!!
I GOT SO TRASHED!!!

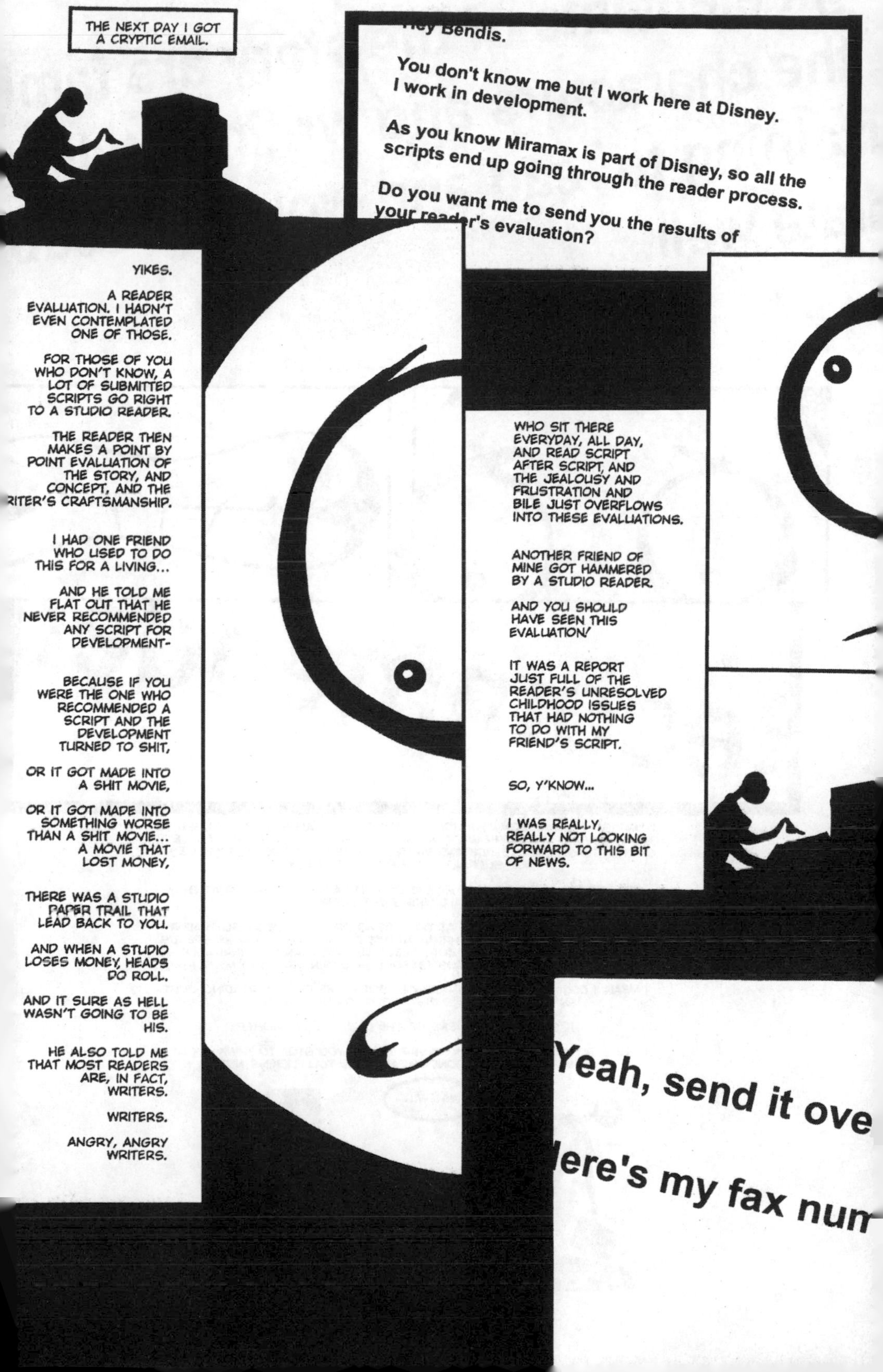
THE NEXT DAY I GOT A CRYPTIC EMAIL.
Hey Bendis.
You don't know me but I work here at Disney. I work in development.
As you know Miramax is part of Disney, so all the scripts end up going through the reader process.
Do you want me to send you the results of your reader's evaluation?
YIKES.
A READER EVALUATION. I HADN'T EVEN CONTEMPLATED ONE OF THOSE.
FOR THOSE OF YOU WHO DON'T KNOW, A LOT OF SUBMITTED SCRIPTS GO RIGHT TO A STUDIO READER.
THE READER THEN MAKES A POINT BY POINT EVALUATION OF THE STORY, AND CONCEPT, AND THE RITER'S CRAFTSMANSHIP.
I HAD ONE FRIEND WHO USED TO DO THIS FOR A LIVING...
AND HE TOLD ME FLAT OUT THAT HE NEVER RECOMMENDED ANY SCRIPT FOR DEVELOPMENT-
BECAUSE IF YOU WERE THE ONE WHO RECOMMENDED A SCRIPT AND THE DEVELOPMENT TURNED TO SHIT,
OR IT GOT MADE INTO A SHIT MOVIE,
OR IT GOT MADE INTO SOMETHING WORSE THAN A SHIT MOVIE... A MOVIE THAT LOST MONEY,
THERE WAS A STUDIO PAPER TRAIL THAT LEAD BACK TO YOU.
AND WHEN A STUDIO LOSES MONEY, HEADS DO ROLL.
AND IT SURE AS HELL WASN'T GOING TO BE HIS.
HE ALSO TOLD ME THAT MOST READERS ARE, IN FACT, WRITERS.
WRITERS.
ANGRY, ANGRY WRITERS.
WHO SIT THERE EVERYDAY, ALL DAY, AND READ SCRIPT AFTER SCRIPT, AND THE JEALOUSY AND FRUSTRATION AND BILE JUST OVERFLOWS INTO THESE EVALUATIONS.
ANOTHER FRIEND OF MINE GOT HAMMERED BY A STUDIO READER.
AND YOU SHOULD HAVE SEEN THIS EVALUATION!
IT WAS A REPORT JUST FULL OF THE READER'S UNRESOLVED CHILDHOOD ISSUES THAT HAD NOTHING TO DO WITH MY FRIEND'S SCRIPT.
SO, Y'KNOW...
I WAS REALLY, REALLY NOT LOOKING FORWARD TO THIS BIT OF NEWS.
Yeah, send it ove
ere's my fax num

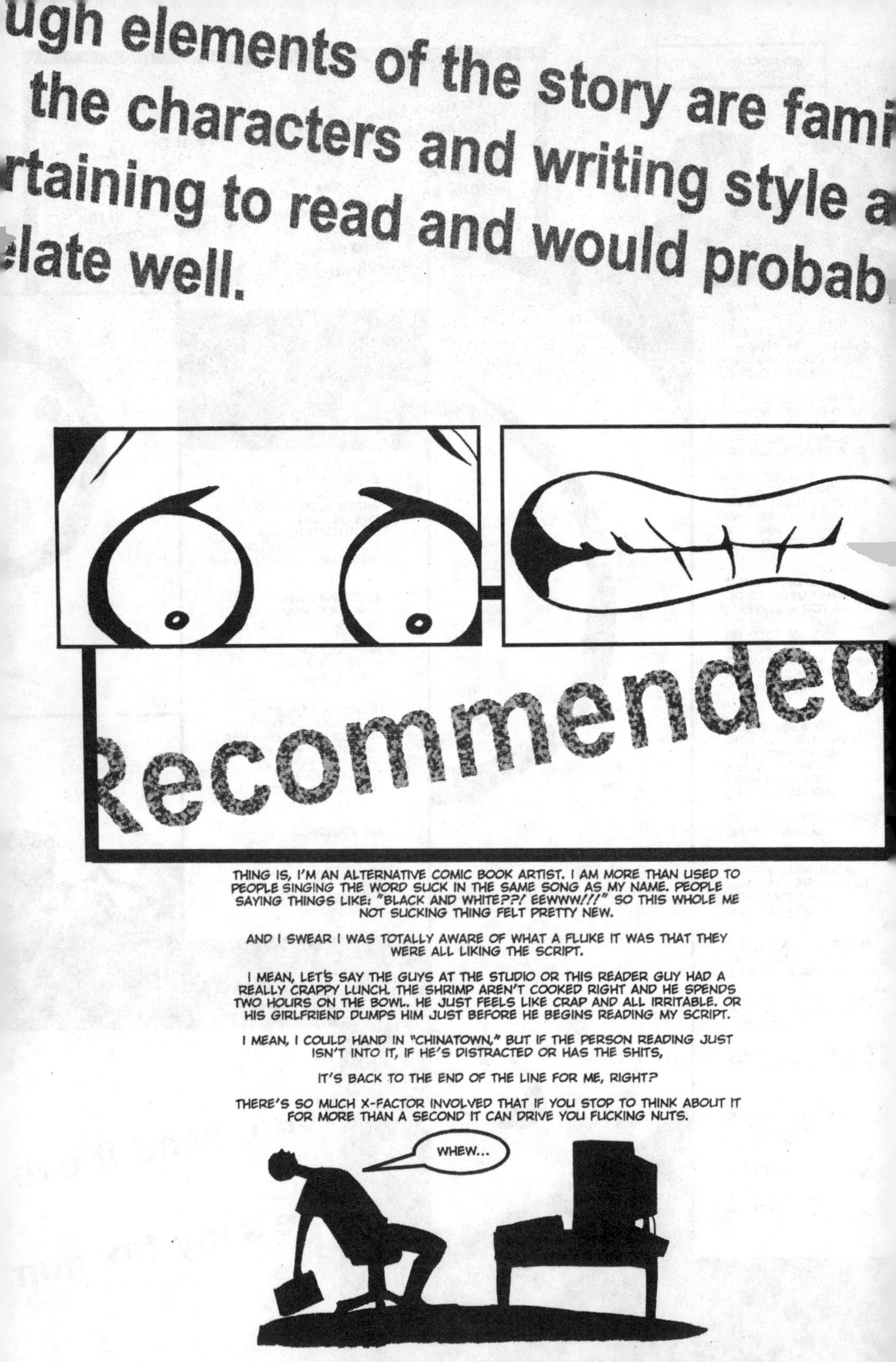
ugh elements of the story are fami
the characters and writing style a
rtaining to read and would probab
late well.
Recommended
THING IS, I'M AN ALTERNATIVE COMIC BOOK ARTIST. I AM MORE THAN USED TO PEOPLE SINGING THE WORD SUCK IN THE SAME SONG AS MY NAME. PEOPLE SAYING THINGS LIKE: "BLACK AND WHITE??! EEWWW!!!" SO THIS WHOLE ME NOT SUCKING THING FELT PRETTY NEW.
AND I SWEAR I WAS TOTALLY AWARE OF WHAT A FLUKE IT WAS THAT THEY WERE ALL LIKING THE SCRIPT.
I MEAN, LET'S SAY THE GUYS AT THE STUDIO OR THIS READER GUY HAD A REALLY CRAPPY LUNCH. THE SHRIMP AREN'T COOKED RIGHT AND HE SPENDS TWO HOURS ON THE BOWL. HE JUST FEELS LIKE CRAP AND ALL IRRITABLE. OR HIS GIRLFRIEND DUMPS HIM JUST BEFORE HE BEGINS READING MY SCRIPT.
I MEAN, I COULD HAND IN "CHINATOWN," BUT IF THE PERSON READING JUST ISN'T INTO IT, IF HE'S DISTRACTED OR HAS THE SHITS,
IT'S BACK TO THE END OF THE LINE FOR ME, RIGHT?
THERE'S SO MUCH X-FACTOR INVOLVED THAT IF YOU STOP TO THINK ABOUT IT FOR MORE THAN A SECOND IT CAN DRIVE YOU FUCKING NUTS.
WHEW...

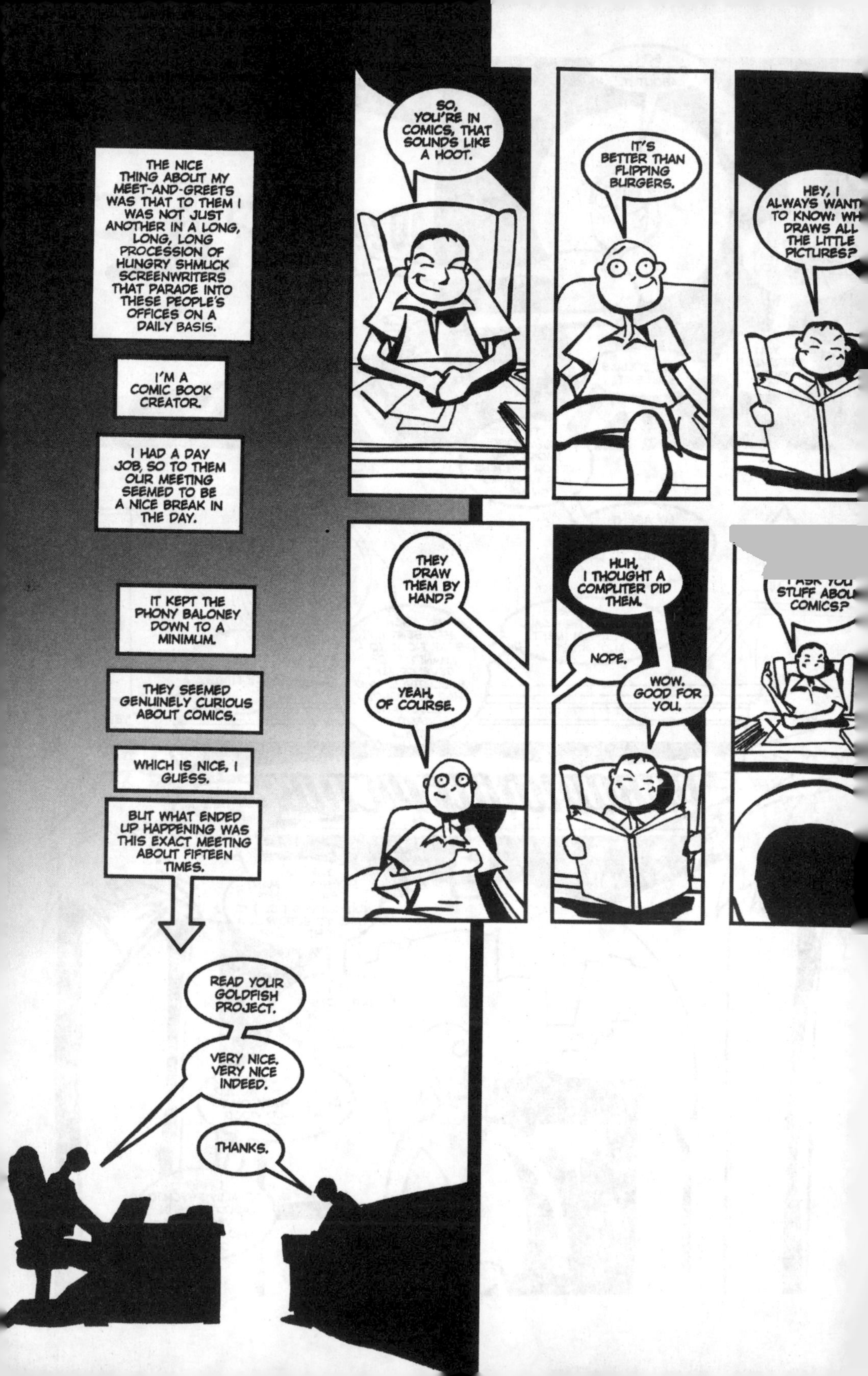

THE NICE THING ABOUT MY MEET-AND-GREETS WAS THAT TO THEM I WAS NOT JUST ANOTHER IN A LONG, LONG, LONG PROCESSION OF HUNGRY SHMUCK SCREENWRITERS THAT PARADE INTO THESE PEOPLE'S OFFICES ON A DAILY BASIS.
I'M A COMIC BOOK CREATOR.
I HAD A DAY JOB, SO TO THEM OUR MEETING SEEMED TO BE A NICE BREAK IN THE DAY.
SO, YOU'RE IN COMICS, THAT SOUNDS LIKE A HOOT.
IT'S BETTER THAN FLIPPING BURGERS.
HEY, I ALWAYS WANT TO KNOW: WH DRAWS ALL THE LITTLE PICTURES?
IT KEPT THE PHONY BALONEY DOWN TO A MINIMUM.
THEY SEEMED GENUINELY CURIOUS ABOUT COMICS.
WHICH IS NICE, I GUESS.
THEY DRAW THEM BY HAND?
YEAH, OF COURSE.
HUH, I THOUGHT A COMPUTER DID THEM.
NOPE.
WOW. GOOD FOR YOU.
STUFF ABOU COMICS?
BUT WHAT ENDED UP HAPPENING WAS THIS EXACT MEETING ABOUT FIFTEEN TIMES.
READ YOUR GOLDFISH PROJECT.
VERY NICE. VERY NICE INDEED.
THANKS.

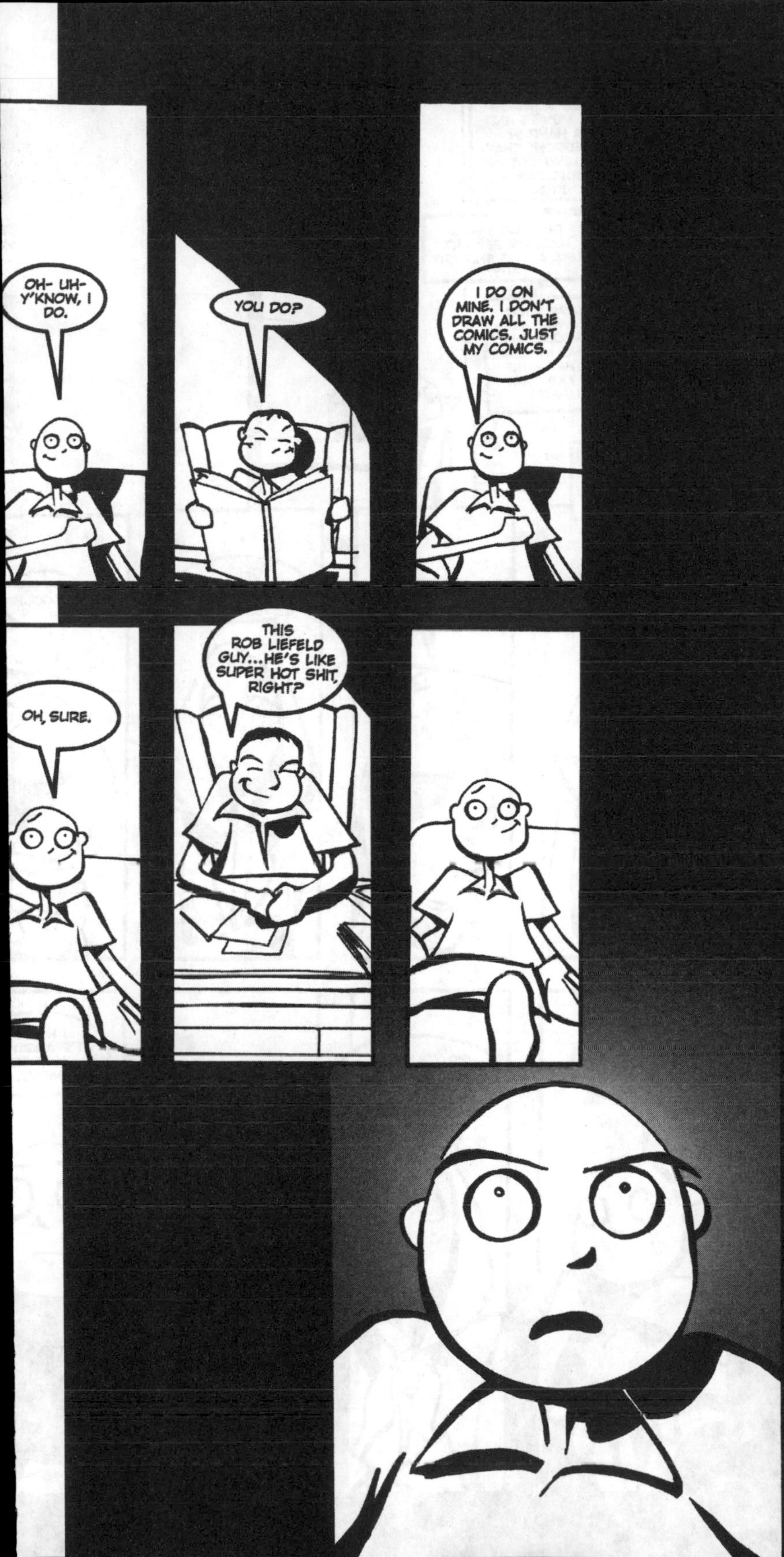
OH- UH- Y'KNOW, I DO.
YOU DO?
I DO ON MINE. I DON'T DRAW ALL THE COMICS. JUST MY COMICS.
OH, SURE.
THIS ROB LIEFELD GUY...HE'S LIKE SUPER HOT SHIT, RIGHT?

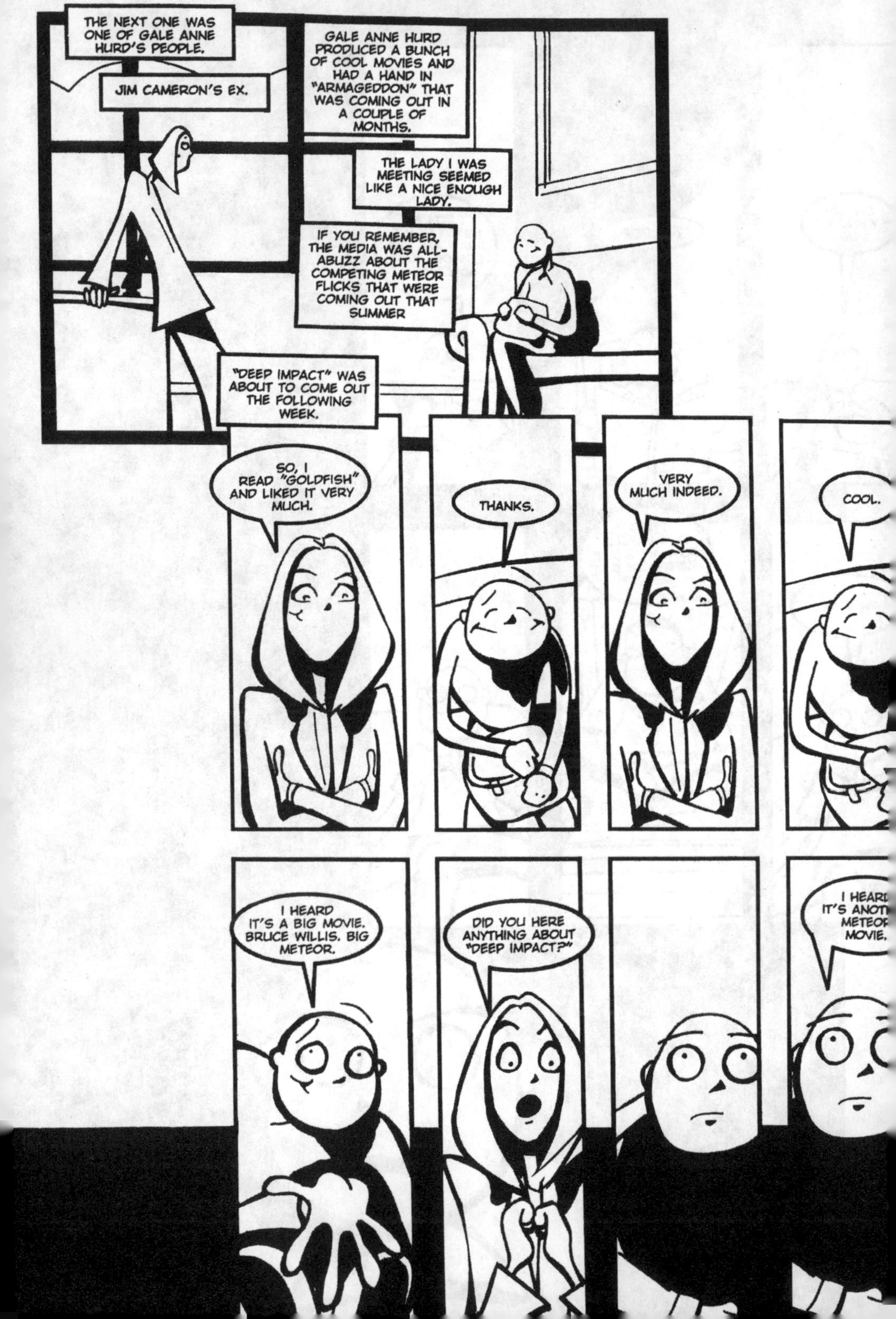
THE NEXT ONE WAS ONE OF GALE ANNE HURD'S PEOPLE.
JIM CAMERON'S EX.
GALE ANNE HURD PRODUCED A BUNCH OF COOL MOVIES AND HAD A HAND IN "ARMAGEDDON" THAT WAS COMING OUT IN A COUPLE OF MONTHS.
THE LADY I WAS MEETING SEEMED LIKE A NICE ENOUGH LADY.
IF YOU REMEMBER, THE MEDIA WAS ALL-ABUZZ ABOUT THE COMPETING METEOR FLICKS THAT WERE COMING OUT THAT SUMMER
"DEEP IMPACT" WAS ABOUT TO COME OUT THE FOLLOWING WEEK.
SO, I READ "GOLDFISH" AND LIKED IT VERY MUCH.
THANKS.
VERY MUCH INDEED.
COOL.
I HEARD IT'S A BIG MOVIE. BRUCE WILLIS. BIG METEOR.
DID YOU HERE ANYTHING ABOUT "DEEP IMPACT?"

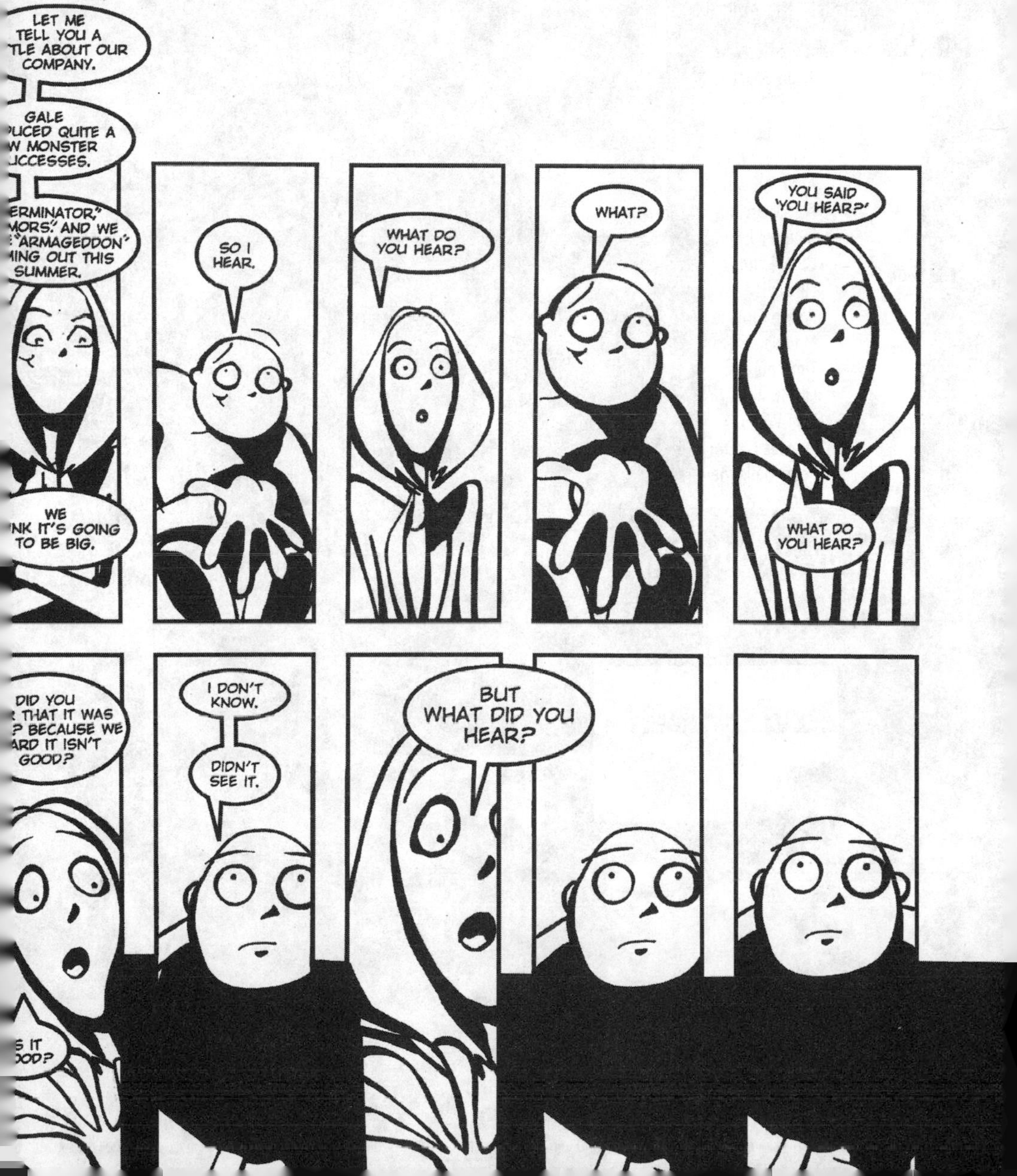
LET ME TELL YOU A TLE ABOUT OUR COMPANY.
GALE UCED QUITE A W MONSTER UCCESSES.
ERMINATOR," MORS." AND WE E "ARMAGEDDON" MING OUT THIS SUMMER.
WE NK IT'S GOING TO BE BIG.
SO I HEAR.
WHAT DO YOU HEAR?
WHAT?
YOU SAID 'YOU HEAR?'
WHAT DO YOU HEAR?
DID YOU R THAT IT WAS ? BECAUSE WE ARD IT ISN'T GOOD?
S IT OOD?
I DON'T KNOW.
DIDN'T SEE IT.
BUT WHAT DID YOU HEAR?

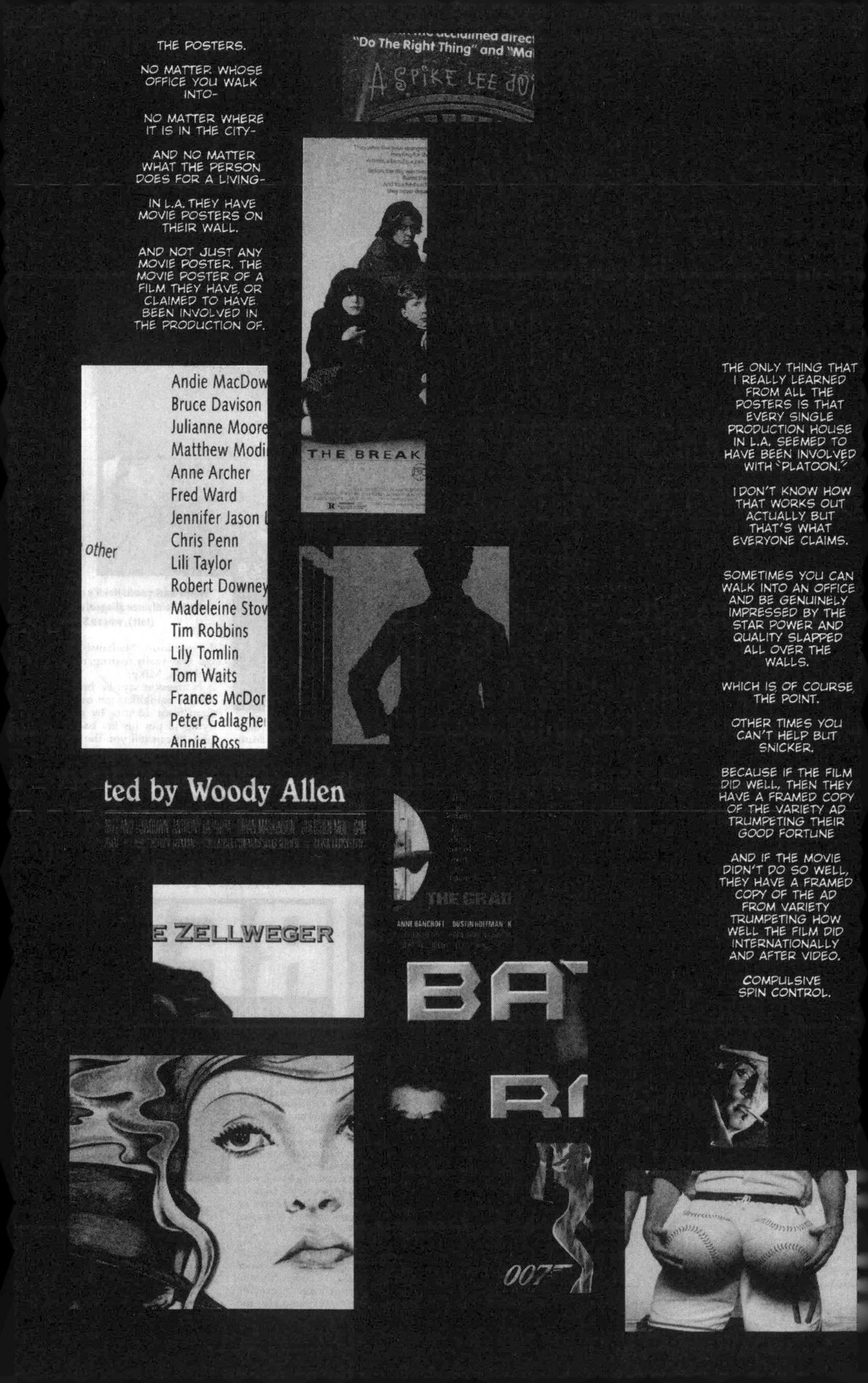

THE POSTERS.

NO MATTER WHOSE
OFFICE YOU WALK
INTO–

NO MATTER WHERE
IT IS IN THE CITY–

AND NO MATTER
WHAT THE PERSON
DOES FOR A LIVING–

IN L.A. THEY HAVE
MOVIE POSTERS ON
THEIR WALL.

AND NOT JUST ANY
MOVIE POSTER. THE
MOVIE POSTER OF A
FILM THEY HAVE, OR
CLAIMED TO HAVE
BEEN INVOLVED IN
THE PRODUCTION OF.

Andie MacDow
Bruce Davison
Julianne Moore
Matthew Modi
Anne Archer
Fred Ward
Jennifer Jason L
Chris Penn
Lili Taylor
Robert Downey
Madeleine Stov
Tim Robbins
Lily Tomlin
Tom Waits
Frances McDor
Peter Gallaghe
Annie Ross

other

THE BREAK

ted by Woody Allen

THE GRAD

ANNE BANCROFT DUSTIN HOFFMAN K

E ZELLWEGER

BA
R

007

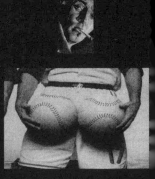

"Do The Right Thing" and "Ma

A SPIKE LEE JO

THE ONLY THING THAT
I REALLY LEARNED
FROM ALL THE
POSTERS IS THAT
EVERY SINGLE
PRODUCTION HOUSE
IN L.A. SEEMED TO
HAVE BEEN INVOLVED
WITH "PLATOON."

I DON'T KNOW HOW
THAT WORKS OUT
ACTUALLY BUT
THAT'S WHAT
EVERYONE CLAIMS.

SOMETIMES YOU CAN
WALK INTO AN OFFICE
AND BE GENUINELY
IMPRESSED BY THE
STAR POWER AND
QUALITY SLAPPED
ALL OVER THE
WALLS.

WHICH IS OF COURSE,
THE POINT.

OTHER TIMES YOU
CAN'T HELP BUT
SNICKER.

BECAUSE IF THE FILM
DID WELL, THEN THEY
HAVE A FRAMED COPY
OF THE VARIETY AD
TRUMPETING THEIR
GOOD FORTUNE

AND IF THE MOVIE
DIDN'T DO SO WELL,
THEY HAVE A FRAMED
COPY OF THE AD
FROM VARIETY
TRUMPETING HOW
WELL THE FILM DID
INTERNATIONALLY
AND AFTER VIDEO.

COMPULSIVE
SPIN CONTROL.

THE SONY LOT IS A PRETTY INTERESTING PLACE.

IT IS A NEW STUDIO LOT AND THEY BUILT IT BIG.

REALLY BIG. GODZILLA BIG.

IN FACT, I WAS THERE THE SUMMER THEY WERE PROMOTING "GODZILLA."

EVERY SQUARE INCH OF THE CITY WAS COVERED IN GIANT "GODZILLA'S FOOT IS BIGGER THAN THIS" SIGNS.

THEY WERE PRETTY MUCH PISSING EVERYONE ELSE IN THE INDUSTRY OFF, AND I THINK THAT'S WHAT THE POINT OF THE SIGNS WERE TO BEGIN WITH.

NOW MOST STUDIOS, WHEN YOU WALK DOWN THE HALLWAYS, TREAT YOU TO THE MOVIE POSTERS OF THIER GREATEST MOMENTS IN MOTION PICTURE HISTORY.

WHEN YOU WALK DOWN THE HALLS AT SONY THEY GLADLY DISPLAY EACH AND EVERY MOVIE POSTER IN THE LIBRARY NO MATTER HOW SHIT ASS BAD THE MOVIE IS.

IN FACT, THERE'S THIS ONE BUILDING THAT IS LITERALLY A WALK OF SHAME.

YOU GET TWO BURT REYNOLDS PICTURES FROM THE MID EIGHTIES, "KRULL," "HARD BODIES," AND AS I WALKED UP TO THE DOOR OF THE OFFICE I HAD THE NEXT MEETING WITH

THERE SHE WAS... "SHEENA, QUEEN OF THE JUNGLE."

ert DE NIRO

There NEVER was a woman like

THRILL CRAZY...
KILL CRAZY...
GUN CRAZY
"GUN CRAZY"
PEGGY CUMMINS
JOHN DALL

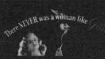

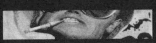

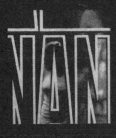

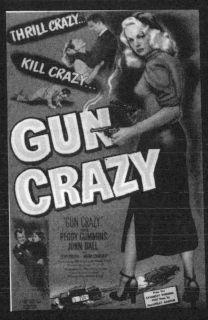

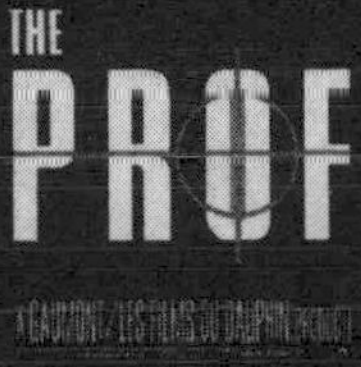

THE
PROF

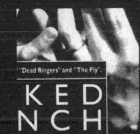

"Dead Ringers" and "The Fly".
KED
NCH
all rational thought.

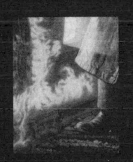

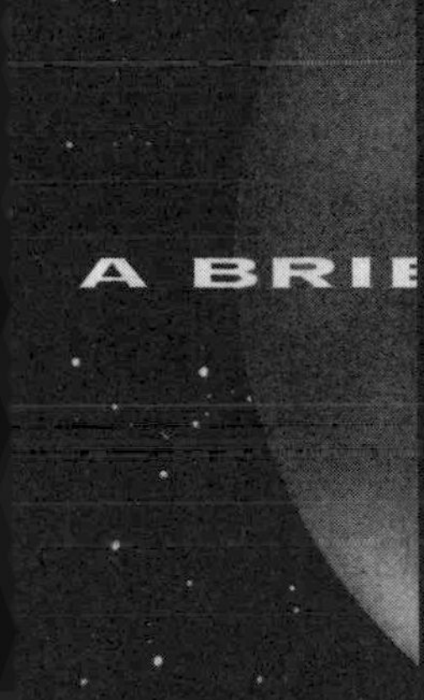

A BRIE

r 24th

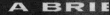

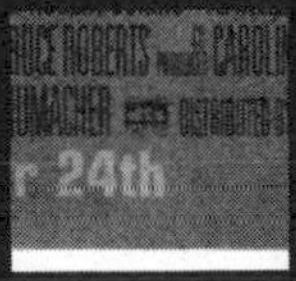

BUT I DIDN'T KNOW THAT THESE WERE JUST RAMDOMLY PLACED POSTERS.

I THOUGHT I WAS LOOKING AT THE PRODUCT OF THE FILM COMPANY I WAS GOING INTO AND I WAS VERY CLOSE TO THROWING UP RIGHT THERE ON THE CARPET.

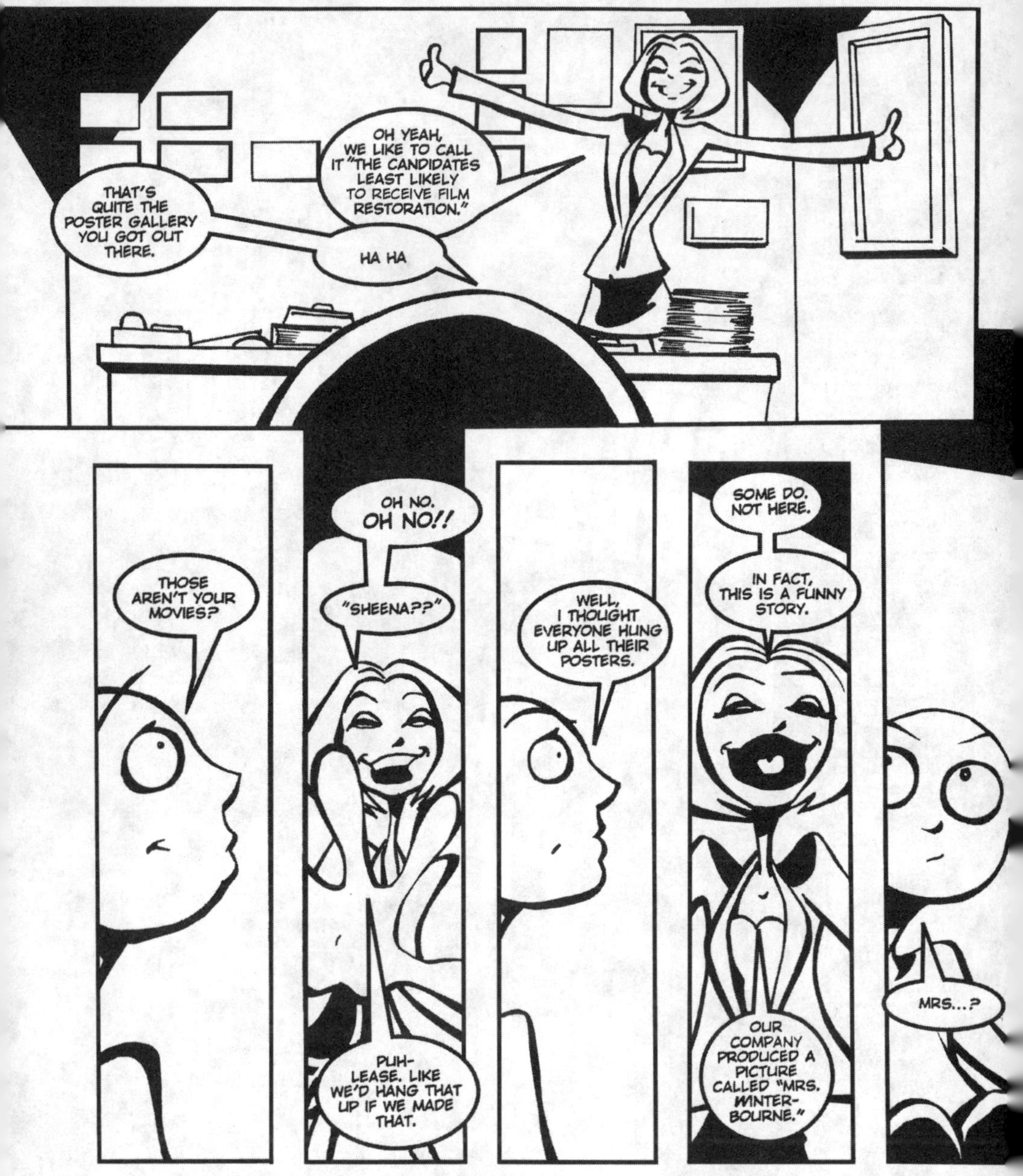
THAT'S QUITE THE POSTER GALLERY YOU GOT OUT THERE.
OH YEAH, WE LIKE TO CALL IT "THE CANDIDATES LEAST LIKELY TO RECEIVE FILM RESTORATION."
HA HA
THOSE AREN'T YOUR MOVIES?
OH NO. OH NO!!
"SHEENA??"
PUH-LEASE. LIKE WE'D HANG THAT UP IF WE MADE THAT.
WELL, I THOUGHT EVERYONE HUNG UP ALL THEIR POSTERS.
SOME DO. NOT HERE.
IN FACT, THIS IS A FUNNY STORY.
OUR COMPANY PRODUCED A PICTURE CALLED "MRS. WINTER-BOURNE."
MRS...?

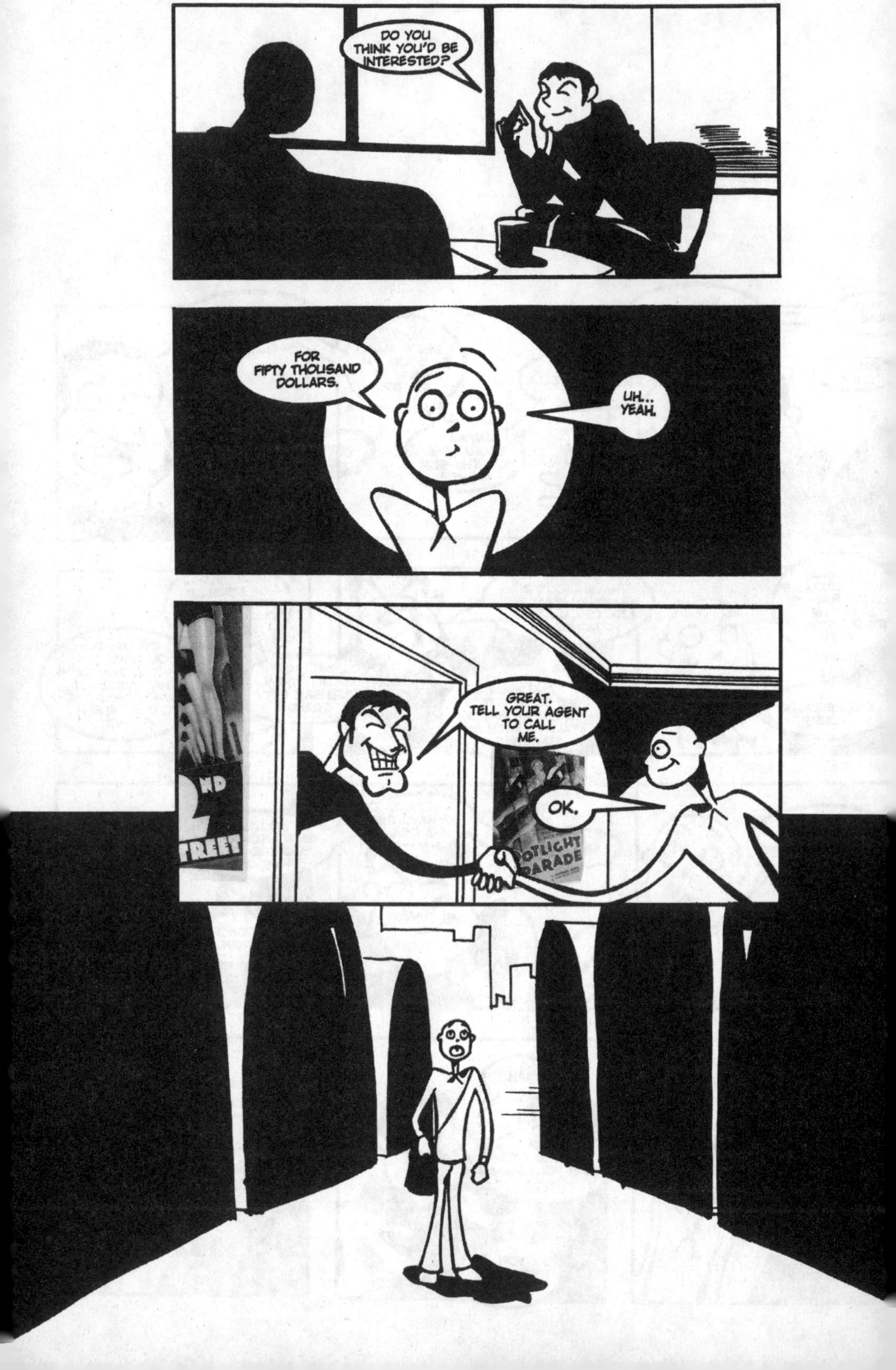
DO YOU THINK YOU'D BE INTERESTED?
FOR FIFTY THOUSAND DOLLARS.
UH... YEAH.
GREAT. TELL YOUR AGENT TO CALL ME.
OK.
2ND STREET
SPOTLIGHT PARADE

YEAH?
HEY,
SO...
SO, THE GUY IS OUT OF HIS FUCKING MIND.
WHAT?
NOT ONLY DOES HE NOT HAVE ACCESS TO THE DISCRETIONARY FUND...
BUT HE HAS NO AUTHORITY TO EVEN MAKE YOU AN OFFER ON SOMETHING IF HE DID.
WHAT?
THE GUY WAS FULL OF SHIT!
THERE'S NO FIFTY THOUSAND DOLLARS TO BE HAD.
THE GUY LIED?
HE TOLD ME RIGHT TO MY FACE TWO MINUTES AGO THAT-

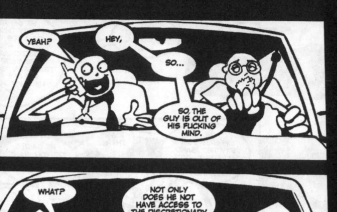

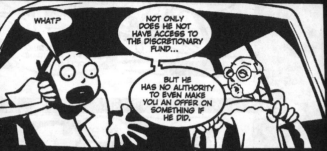

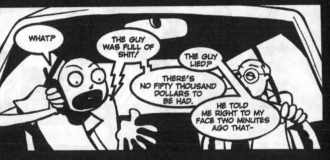

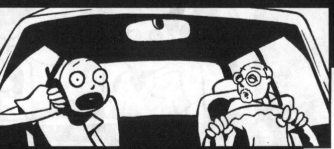

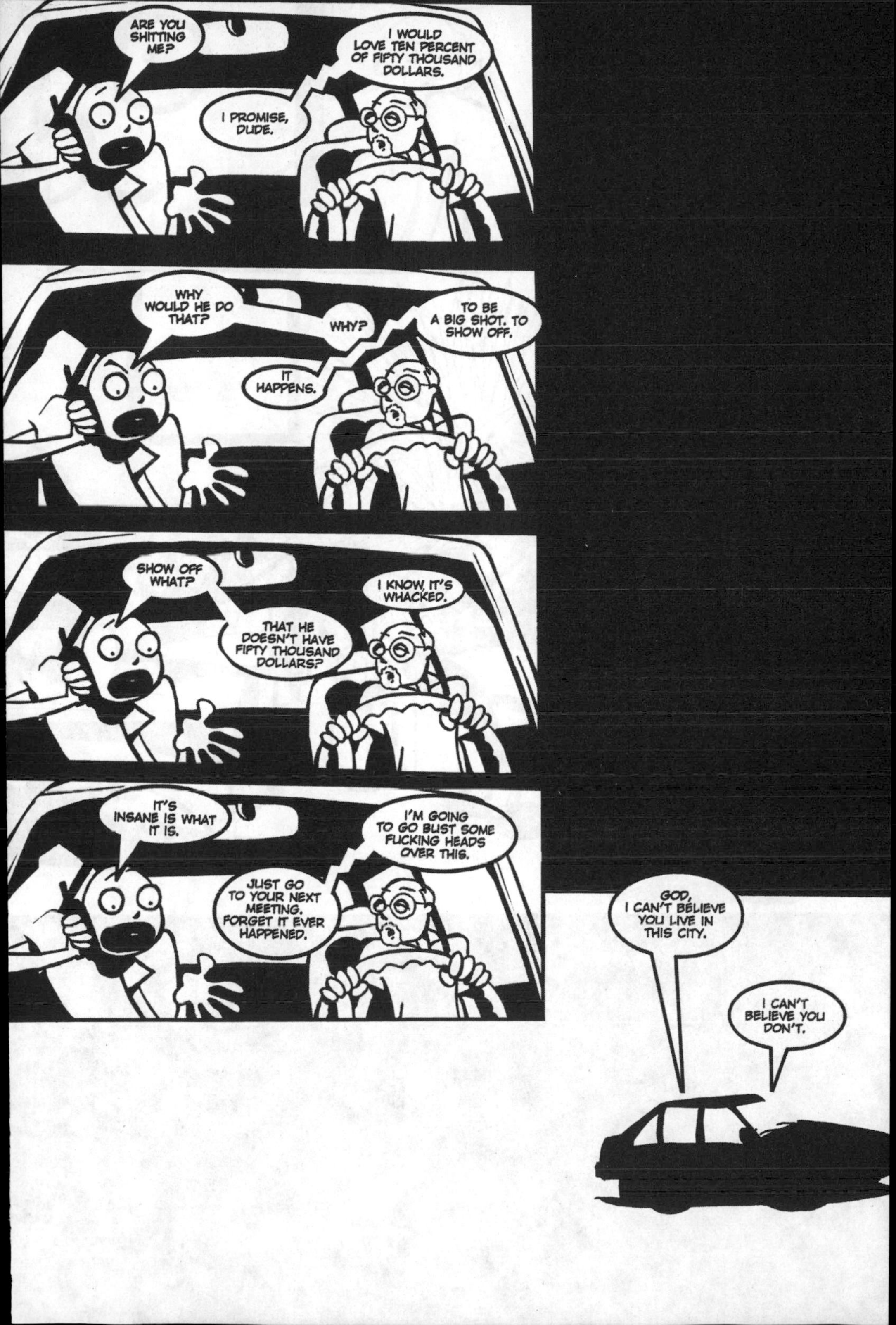
ARE YOU SHITTING ME?
I WOULD LOVE TEN PERCENT OF FIFTY THOUSAND DOLLARS.
I PROMISE, DUDE.
WHY WOULD HE DO THAT?
WHY?
TO BE A BIG SHOT. TO SHOW OFF.
IT HAPPENS.
SHOW OFF WHAT?
THAT HE DOESN'T HAVE FIFTY THOUSAND DOLLARS?
I KNOW, IT'S WHACKED.
IT'S INSANE IS WHAT IT IS.
I'M GOING TO GO BUST SOME FUCKING HEADS OVER THIS.
JUST GO TO YOUR NEXT MEETING. FORGET IT EVER HAPPENED.
GOD, I CAN'T BELIEVE YOU LIVE IN THIS CITY.
I CAN'T BELIEVE YOU DON'T.

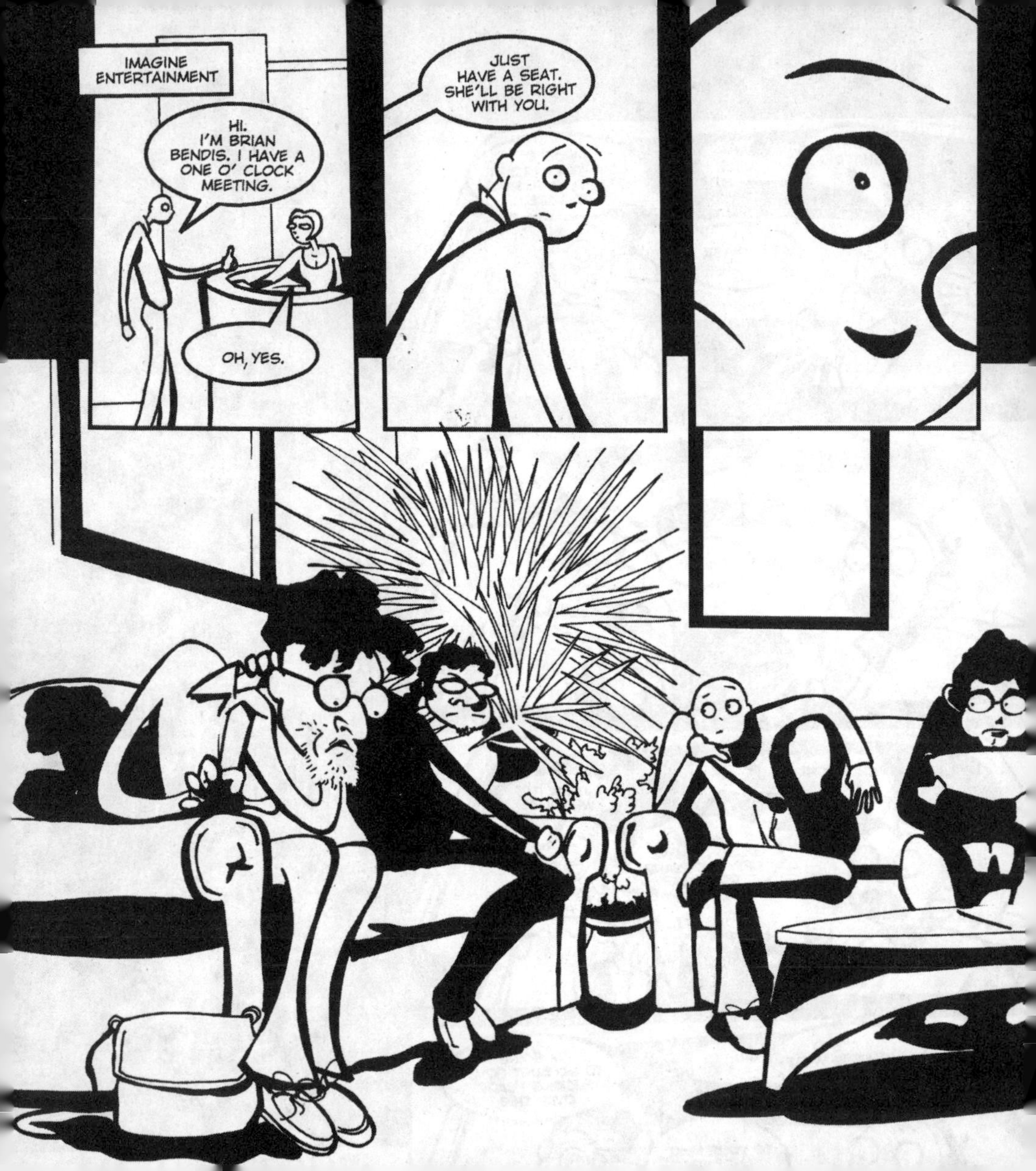
IMAGINE ENTERTAINMENT
HI. I'M BRIAN BENDIS. I HAVE A ONE O' CLOCK MEETING.
OH, YES.
JUST HAVE A SEAT. SHE'LL BE RIGHT WITH YOU.

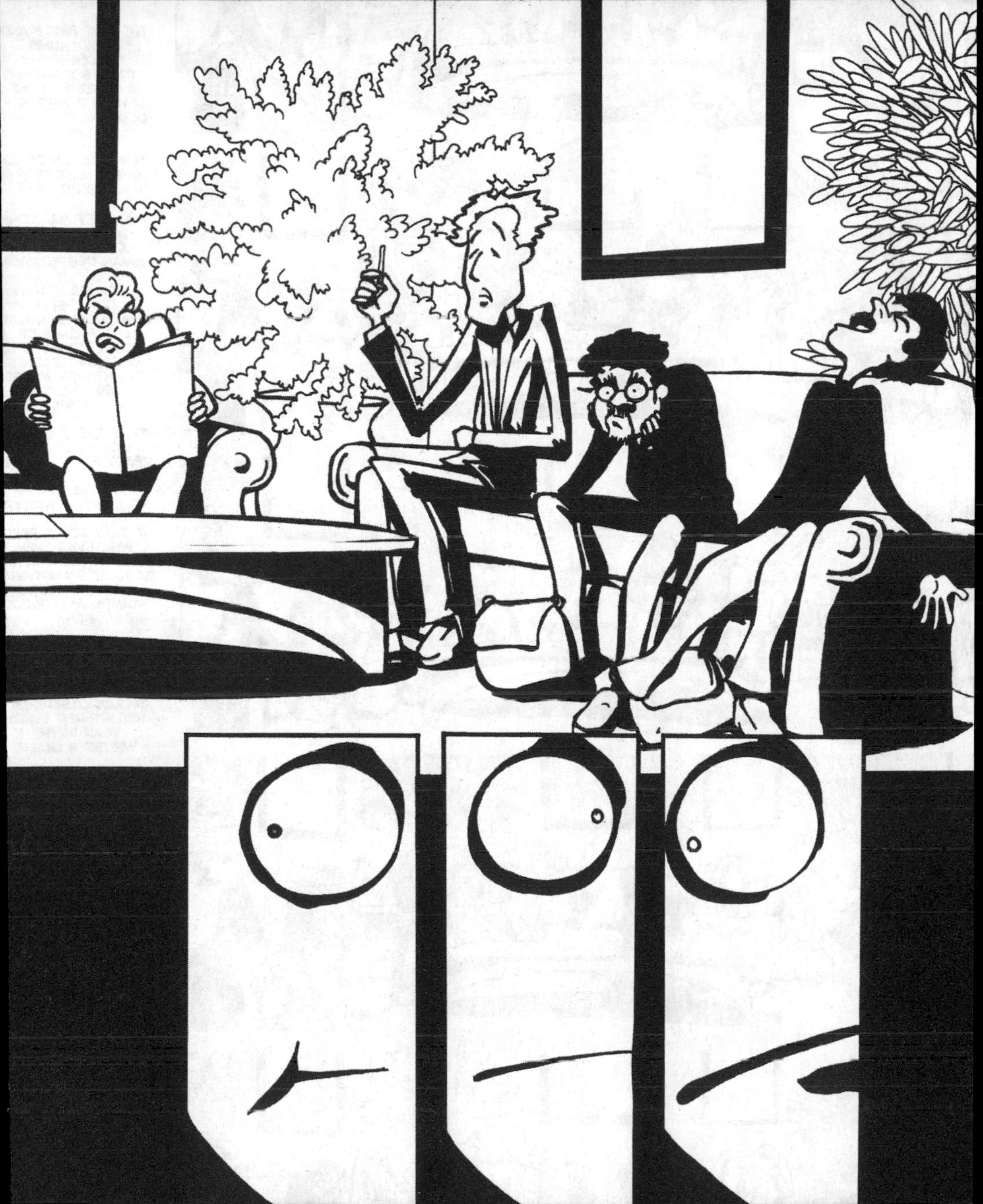

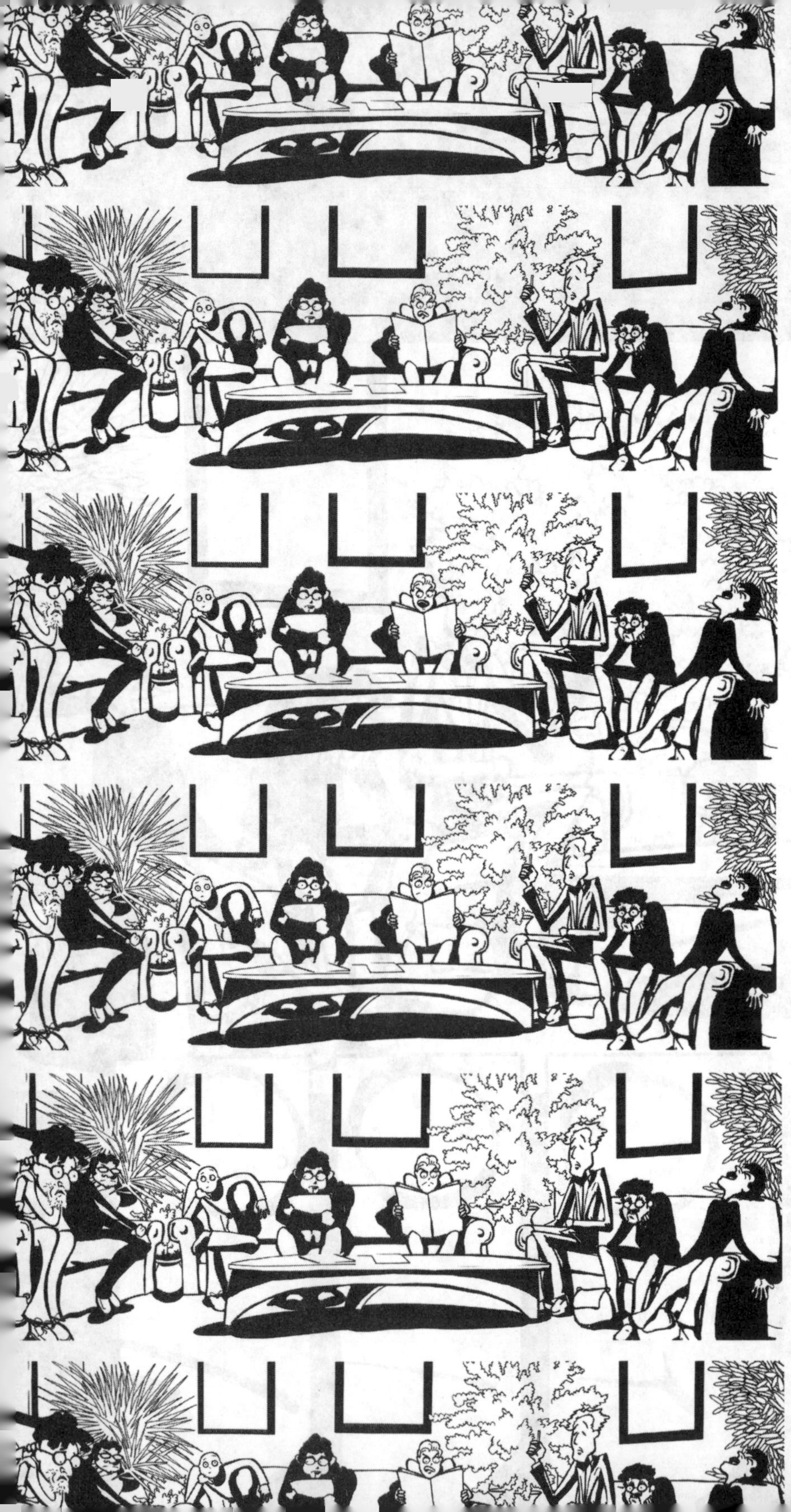

SO, I AM SITTING IN THIS ROOM FILLED WITH THESE GUYS THAT ALL LOOKED LIKE THEY MIGHT BE A COEN BROTHER

YOU KNOW THEY ARE WRITERS BECAUSE THEY ARE THE ONLY PEOPLE IN L.A. THAT DON'T HAVE A TAN, A SHAVE, OR A REASON TO LIVE.

JUST SWEATY, DISHEVELED, CURLY HAIRED GUYS IN SPORTS COATS AND A FIVE A CLOCK SHADOW...

THEY SIT THERE AND THEY THUMB THROUGH THE TRADES CURSING EVERYONE IN THE WORLD WHO IS DOING BETTER THAN THEM.

THEY CLUTCH ONTO THEIR MANDATORY WRITER'S CASE.

AND THEY ALL STINK OF NICOTINE, CAFFEINE, AND HUMAN DESPERATION

BECAUSE IF THEY DON'T SELL WHATEVER IS IN THAT LITTLE CASE OF THEIRS, IT'S BACK TO THE CARPET BARN OR THE KFC OR WHERE-EVER IT IS THEY WORK.

THEY ARE JUST ALL WOUND UP AND READY FOR THE FALL

THIS IS THE LIFE OF HOLLYWOOD WRITER

IF THEY DON'T SELL WHATEVER THEY HAVE IN THEIR LITTLE BAGS, IT'S ANOTHER MONTH OF FOOD STAMPS AND BLOOD BANK

AND I THOUGHT HOW WHACKED IT IS.

THEY SAY THERE ARE *40,000* SCRIPTS REGISTERED EVERY YEAR IN THE WRITER'S GUILD.

THERE ARE ONLY *200-250* MAINSTREAM MOVIES MADE A YEAR, AND HALF OF THOSE ARE FROM PREEXISTING SOURCES.

SO OUT OF THE *40,000* PEOPLE RUNNING AROUND TOWN WITH THEIR LITTLE SCRIPT IN THEIR LITTLE BAG ONLY *100* MIGHT GET TO SELL THEIRS.

IT'S LIKE THE LOTTERY...

ONLY WITH THE ADDED BONUS OF REJECTION AND HUMILIATION.

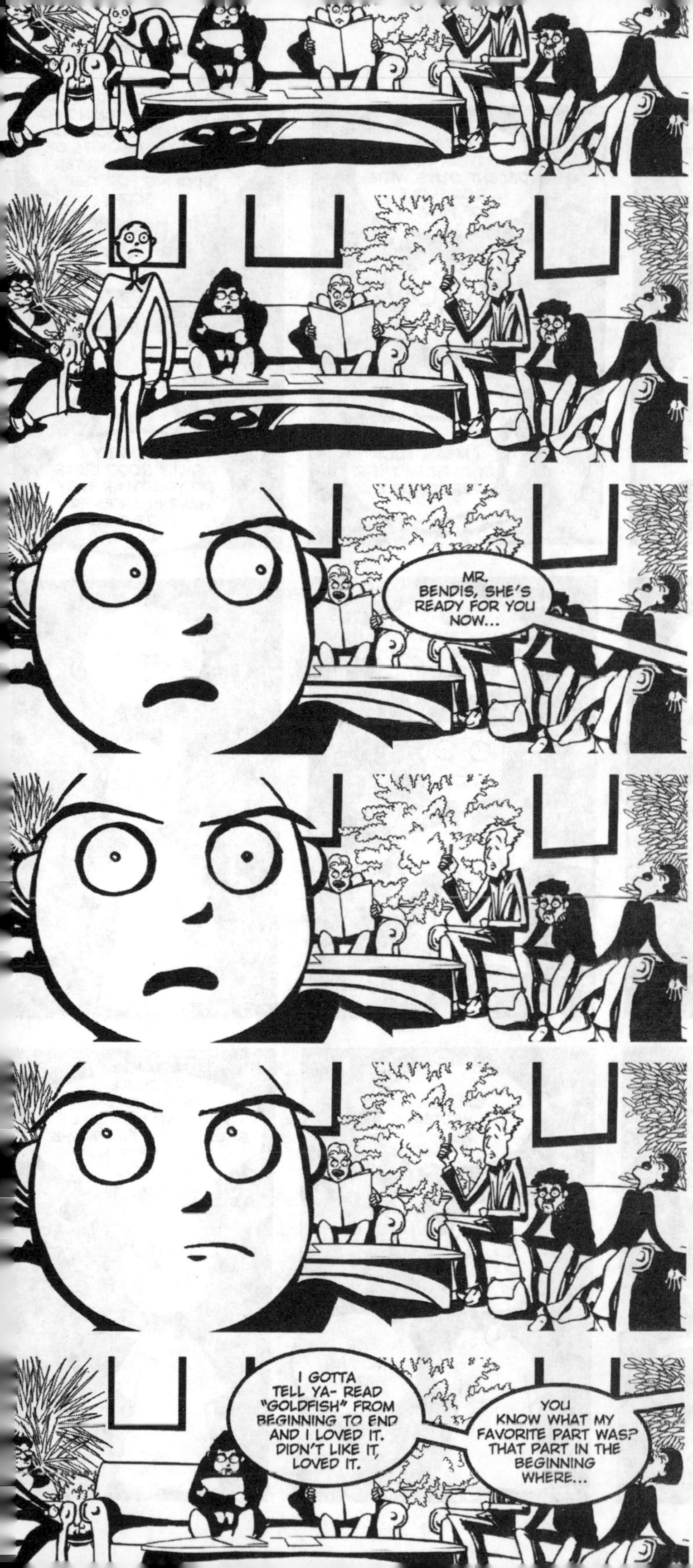
MR. BENDIS, SHE'S READY FOR YOU NOW...
I GOTTA TELL YA- READ "GOLDFISH" FROM BEGINNING TO END AND I LOVED IT. DIDN'T LIKE IT, LOVED IT.
YOU KNOW WHAT MY FAVORITE PART WAS? THAT PART IN THE BEGINNING WHERE...

AND HERE I AM GOING FROM MEETING TO MEETING TO MEET PEOPLE WHO FORGET ME THE SECOND I LEAVE THEIR OFFICE.

AND EVEN IF THEY ARE TOTALLY DAZZLED BY ME, THEY REALLY AREN'T IN ANY POSITION TO DO ANYTHING ABOUT IT.

I'M A COMIC BOOK ARTIST. WHAT AM I DOING HERE WITH THESE GUYS?

I DECIDED IT WAS TIME FOR ME TO GO HOME AND DO SOME WORK.

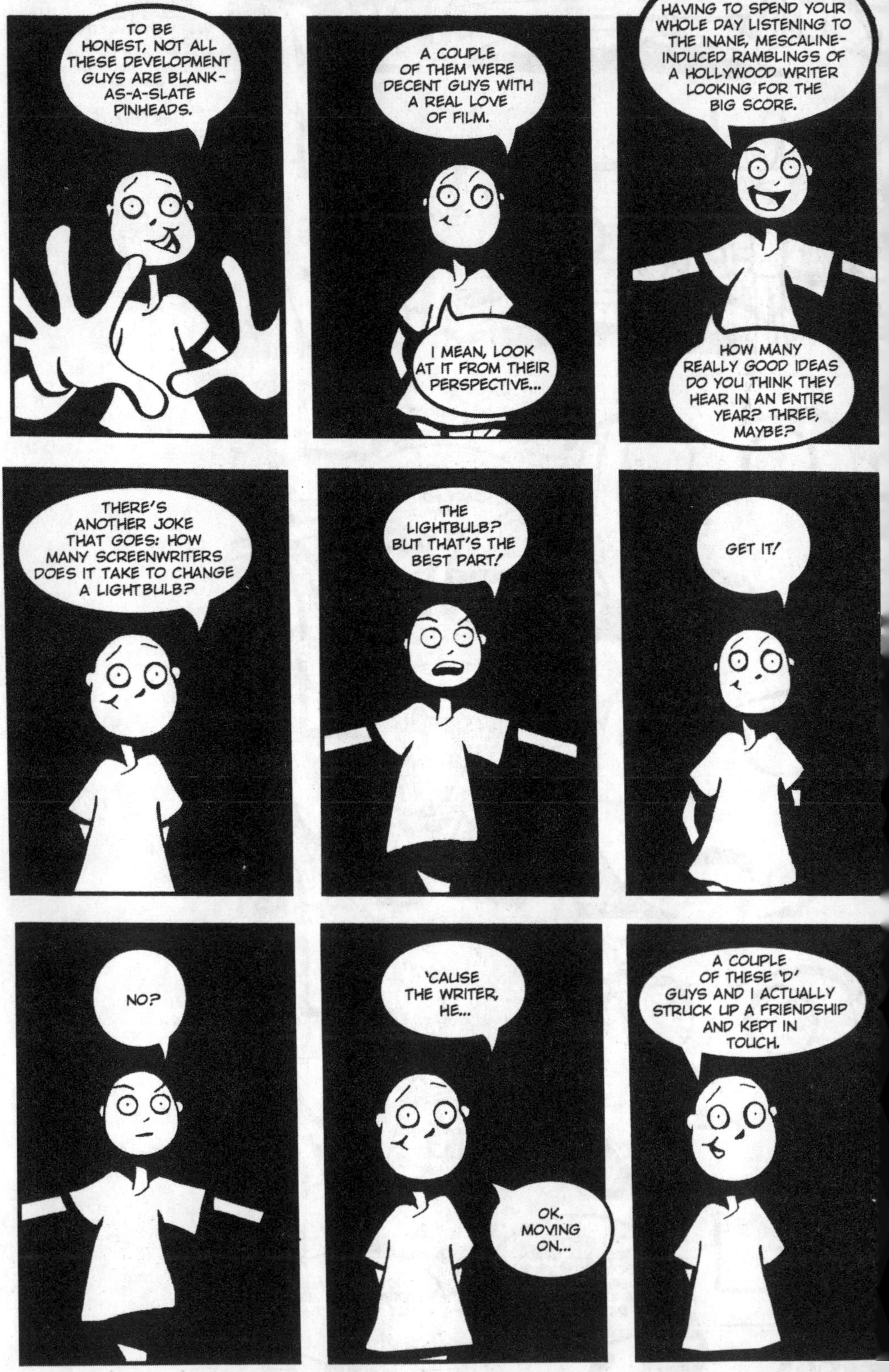
TO BE HONEST, NOT ALL THESE DEVELOPMENT GUYS ARE BLANK-AS-A-SLATE PINHEADS.
A COUPLE OF THEM WERE DECENT GUYS WITH A REAL LOVE OF FILM.
I MEAN, LOOK AT IT FROM THEIR PERSPECTIVE...
IMAGINE HAVING TO SPEND YOUR WHOLE DAY LISTENING TO THE INANE, MESCALINE-INDUCED RAMBLINGS OF A HOLLYWOOD WRITER LOOKING FOR THE BIG SCORE.
HOW MANY REALLY GOOD IDEAS DO YOU THINK THEY HEAR IN AN ENTIRE YEAR? THREE, MAYBE?
THERE'S ANOTHER JOKE THAT GOES: HOW MANY SCREENWRITERS DOES IT TAKE TO CHANGE A LIGHTBULB?
THE LIGHTBULB? BUT THAT'S THE BEST PART!
GET IT!
NO?
'CAUSE THE WRITER, HE...
OK. MOVING ON...
A COUPLE OF THESE 'D' GUYS AND I ACTUALLY STRUCK UP A FRIENDSHIP AND KEPT IN TOUCH.

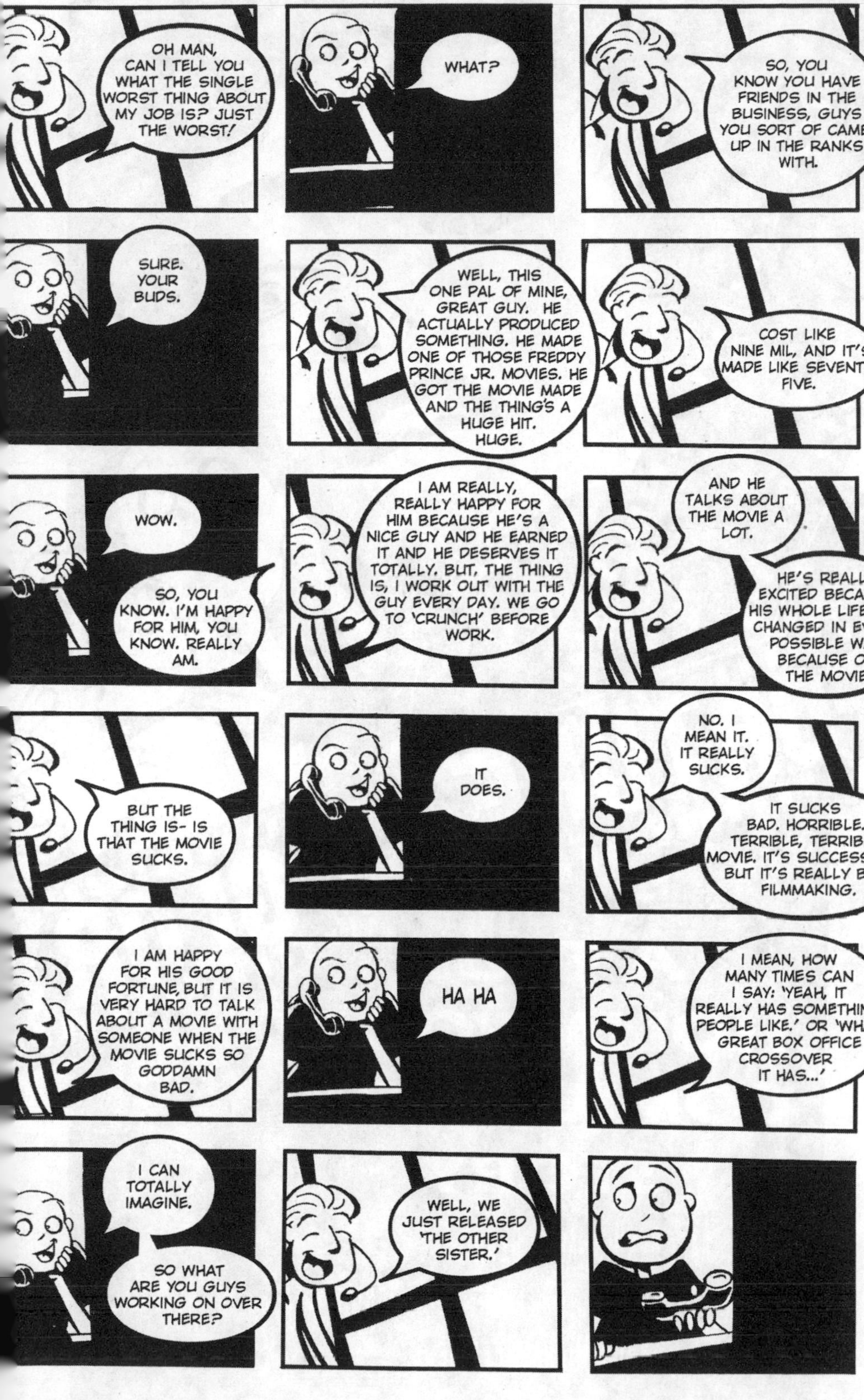
OH MAN, CAN I TELL YOU WHAT THE SINGLE WORST THING ABOUT MY JOB IS? JUST THE WORST!
WHAT?
SO, YOU KNOW YOU HAVE FRIENDS IN THE BUSINESS, GUYS YOU SORT OF CAME UP IN THE RANKS WITH.
SURE. YOUR BUDS.
WELL, THIS ONE PAL OF MINE, GREAT GUY. HE ACTUALLY PRODUCED SOMETHING. HE MADE ONE OF THOSE FREDDY PRINCE JR. MOVIES. HE GOT THE MOVIE MADE AND THE THING'S A HUGE HIT. HUGE.
COST LIKE NINE MIL, AND IT'S MADE LIKE SEVENTY-FIVE.
WOW.
SO, YOU KNOW. I'M HAPPY FOR HIM, YOU KNOW. REALLY AM.
I AM REALLY, REALLY HAPPY FOR HIM BECAUSE HE'S A NICE GUY AND HE EARNED IT AND HE DESERVES IT TOTALLY. BUT, THE THING IS, I WORK OUT WITH THE GUY EVERY DAY. WE GO TO 'CRUNCH' BEFORE WORK.
AND HE TALKS ABOUT THE MOVIE A LOT.
HE'S REALLY EXCITED BECAUSE HIS WHOLE LIFE HAS CHANGED IN EVERY POSSIBLE WAY BECAUSE OF THE MOVIE.
BUT THE THING IS- IS THAT THE MOVIE SUCKS.
IT DOES.
NO. I MEAN IT. IT REALLY SUCKS.
IT SUCKS BAD. HORRIBLE. TERRIBLE, TERRIBLE MOVIE. IT'S SUCCESSFUL- BUT IT'S REALLY BAD FILMMAKING.
I AM HAPPY FOR HIS GOOD FORTUNE, BUT IT IS VERY HARD TO TALK ABOUT A MOVIE WITH SOMEONE WHEN THE MOVIE SUCKS SO GODDAMN BAD.
HA HA
I MEAN, HOW MANY TIMES CAN I SAY: 'YEAH, IT REALLY HAS SOMETHING PEOPLE LIKE.' OR 'WHAT GREAT BOX OFFICE CROSSOVER IT HAS...'
I CAN TOTALLY IMAGINE.
SO WHAT ARE YOU GUYS WORKING ON OVER THERE?
WELL, WE JUST RELEASED 'THE OTHER SISTER.'

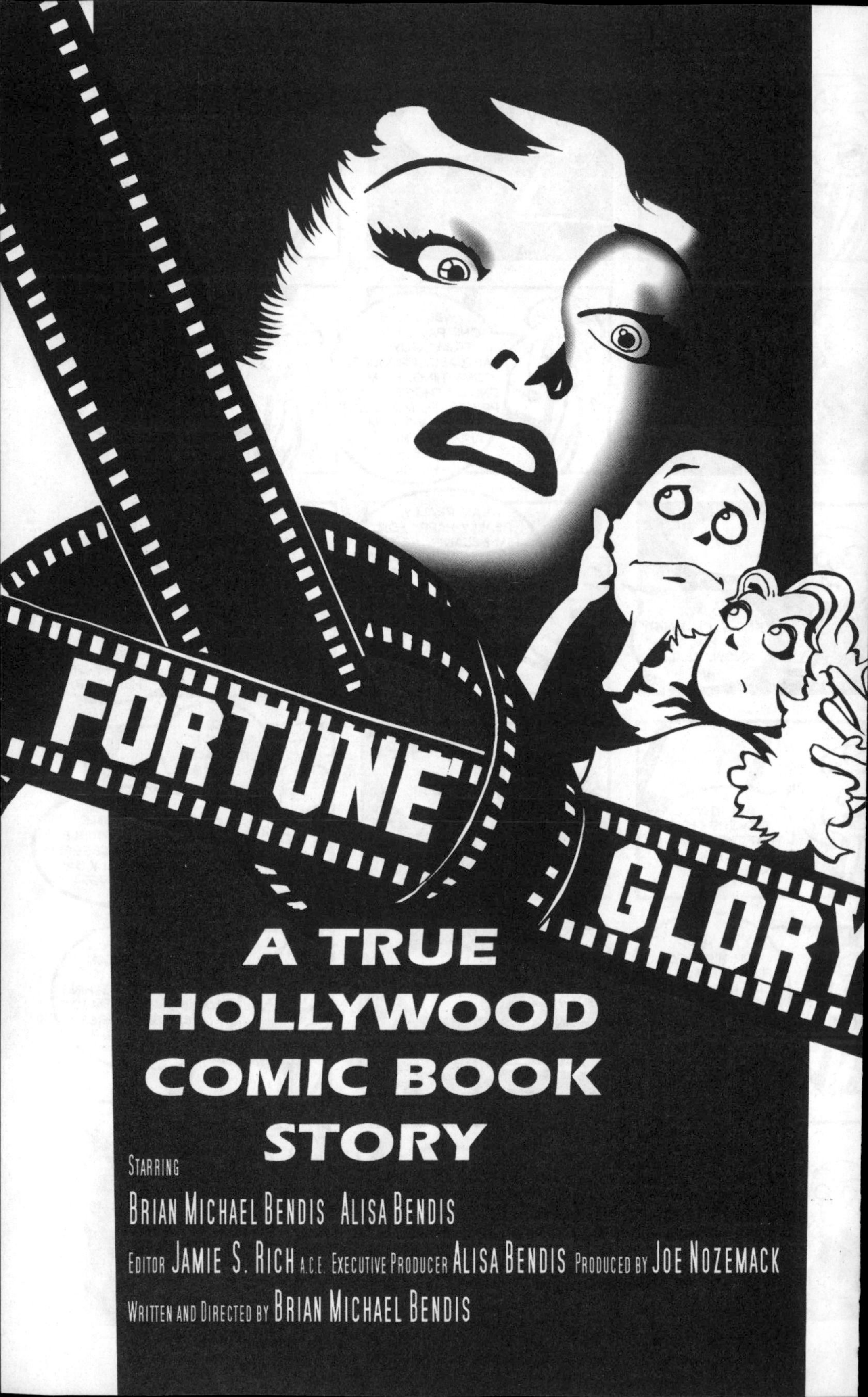
FORTUNE
GLORY
A TRUE
HOLLYWOOD
COMIC BOOK
STORY
STARRING
BRIAN MICHAEL BENDIS ALISA BENDIS
EDITOR JAMIE S. RICH A.C.E. EXECUTIVE PRODUCER ALISA BENDIS PRODUCED BY JOE NOZEMACK
WRITTEN AND DIRECTED BY BRIAN MICHAEL BENDIS

BRIAN MICHAEL BENDIS   ALISA BENDIS

The extraordinary telling of a classic tale.

FORTUNE AND GLORY

A FRANCO ZEFFIRELI FILM

WARNER BROS. AND JINXWORLD ENTERTAINMENT PRESENT
AN ICON PRODUCTION A FRANCO ZEFFIRELLI FILM
BRIAN MICHAEL BENDIS ALISA BENDIS
"FORTUNE AND GLORY"
MARC ANDREYKO DAVID SPREE JUSTIN SILVERA
MUSIC BY ENNIO MORRICONE
ADAPTED FROM THE PLAY BY WILLIAM SHAKESPEARE
SCREENPLAY BY BRIAN MICHAEL BENDIS & FRANCO ZEFFIRELLI
DIRECTED BY FRANCO ZEFFIRELLI

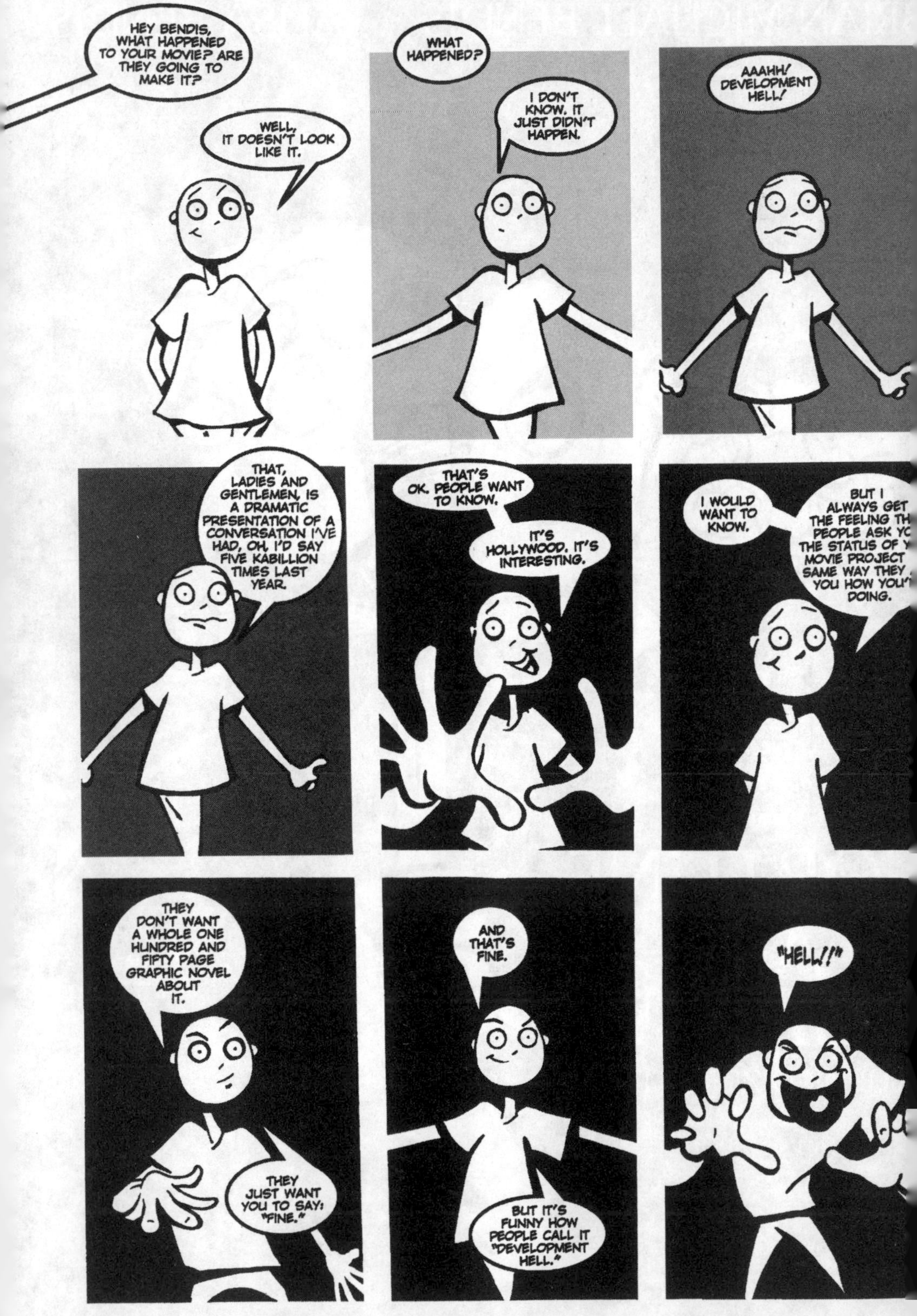

HEY BENDIS, WHAT HAPPENED TO YOUR MOVIE? ARE THEY GOING TO MAKE IT?
WELL, IT DOESN'T LOOK LIKE IT.
WHAT HAPPENED?
I DON'T KNOW. IT JUST DIDN'T HAPPEN.
AAAHH! DEVELOPMENT HELL!
THAT, LADIES AND GENTLEMEN, IS A DRAMATIC PRESENTATION OF A CONVERSATION I'VE HAD, OH, I'D SAY FIVE KABILLION TIMES LAST YEAR.
THAT'S OK. PEOPLE WANT TO KNOW.
IT'S HOLLYWOOD. IT'S INTERESTING.
I WOULD WANT TO KNOW.
BUT I ALWAYS GET THE FEELING TH PEOPLE ASK YO THE STATUS OF Y MOVIE PROJECT SAME WAY THEY YOU HOW YOU' DOING.
THEY DON'T WANT A WHOLE ONE HUNDRED AND FIFTY PAGE GRAPHIC NOVEL ABOUT IT.
THEY JUST WANT YOU TO SAY: "FINE."
AND THAT'S FINE.
BUT IT'S FUNNY HOW PEOPLE CALL IT "DEVELOPMENT HELL."
"HELL!!"

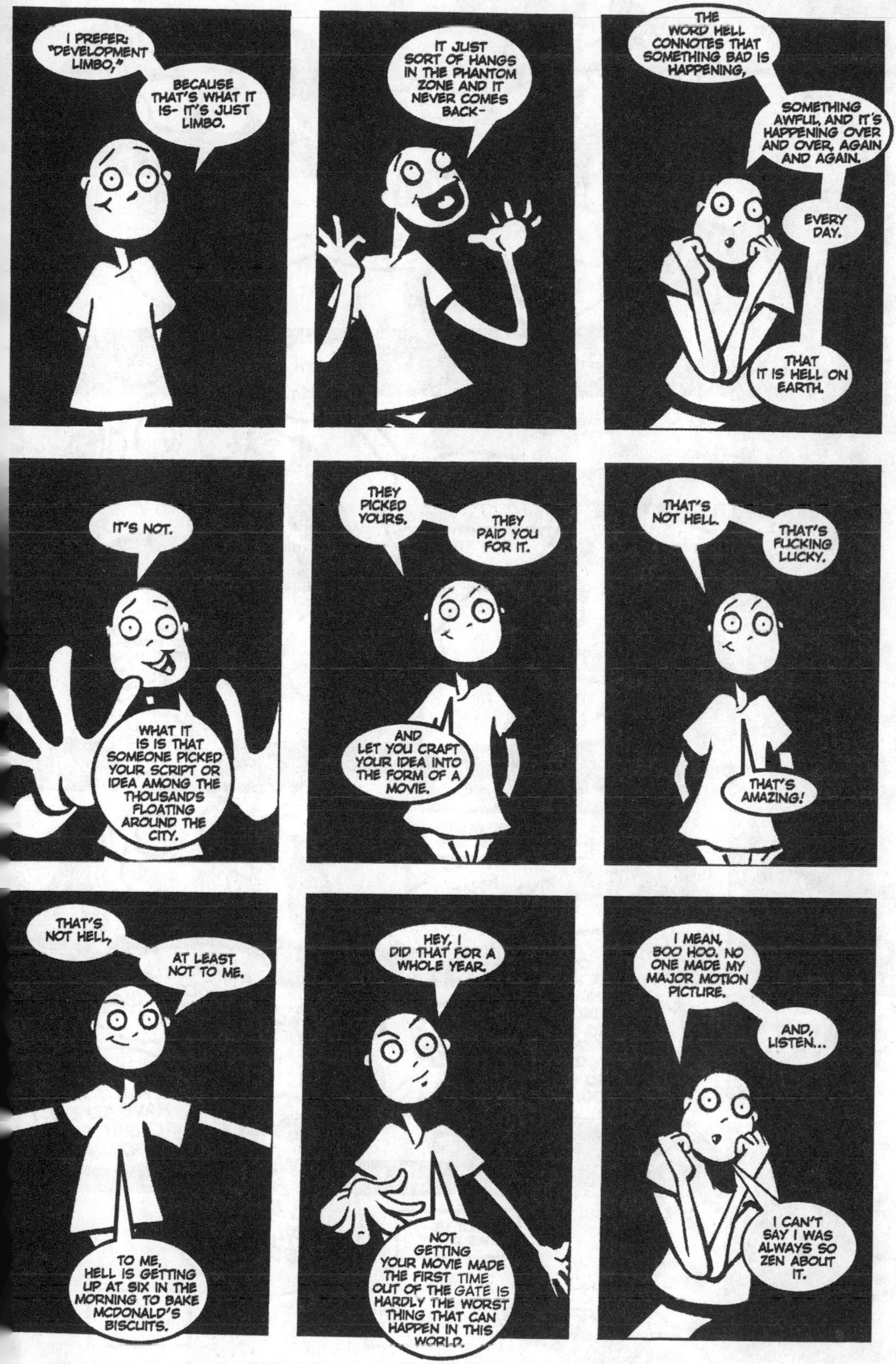
I PREFER: "DEVELOPMENT LIMBO,"
BECAUSE THAT'S WHAT IT IS- IT'S JUST LIMBO.
IT JUST SORT OF HANGS IN THE PHANTOM ZONE AND IT NEVER COMES BACK-
THE WORD HELL CONNOTES THAT SOMETHING BAD IS HAPPENING,
SOMETHING AWFUL, AND IT'S HAPPENING OVER AND OVER, AGAIN AND AGAIN.
EVERY DAY.
THAT IT IS HELL ON EARTH.
IT'S NOT.
WHAT IT IS IS THAT SOMEONE PICKED YOUR SCRIPT OR IDEA AMONG THE THOUSANDS FLOATING AROUND THE CITY.
THEY PICKED YOURS.
THEY PAID YOU FOR IT.
AND LET YOU CRAFT YOUR IDEA INTO THE FORM OF A MOVIE.
THAT'S NOT HELL.
THAT'S FUCKING LUCKY.
THAT'S AMAZING!
THAT'S NOT HELL,
AT LEAST NOT TO ME.
TO ME, HELL IS GETTING UP AT SIX IN THE MORNING TO BAKE MCDONALD'S BISCUITS.
HEY, I DID THAT FOR A WHOLE YEAR.
NOT GETTING YOUR MOVIE MADE THE FIRST TIME OUT OF THE GATE IS HARDLY THE WORST THING THAT CAN HAPPEN IN THIS WORLD.
I MEAN, BOO HOO. NO ONE MADE MY MAJOR MOTION PICTURE.
AND, LISTEN...
I CAN'T SAY I WAS ALWAYS SO ZEN ABOUT IT.

WHILE THE CLOCK WAS TICKING ON MY VIRGIN EXPERIENCE IN HOLLYWOOD.

A DAMN GOOD FRIEND OF MINE, MARC ANDREYKO, CAME OVER FOR WHAT WE NOW REFER TO AS "THE PASSOVER SEDER OF DESTINY!"

MY WIFE AND I LIKE TO TAKE THE JEWISH HOLIDAY OF PASSOVER AND INVITE AS MANY GENTILE FRIENDS AS WE CAN TO THE TRADITIONAL DINNER CEREMONY.

MANY ARE THRILLED TO BE INVITED TO THE NEW EXPERIENCE AND EAGERLY ACCEPT...

...ONLY TO FIND OUT THAT US INVITING THEM TO THE FIVE HOUR DINNER CEREMONY OF READING THE HISTORY OF THE JEWS FROM THE SEDER IS OUR VERSION OF A JEWISH PRACTICAL JOKE.

I MEAN, THE JEWS HAD TO SUFFER THROUGH THE DESERT FOR FORTY DAYS AND FORTY NIGHTS...

WE'RE GOING TO MAKE AS MANY OF YOU SUFFER AS WE CAN GET OUR HANDS ON.

HEE HEE.

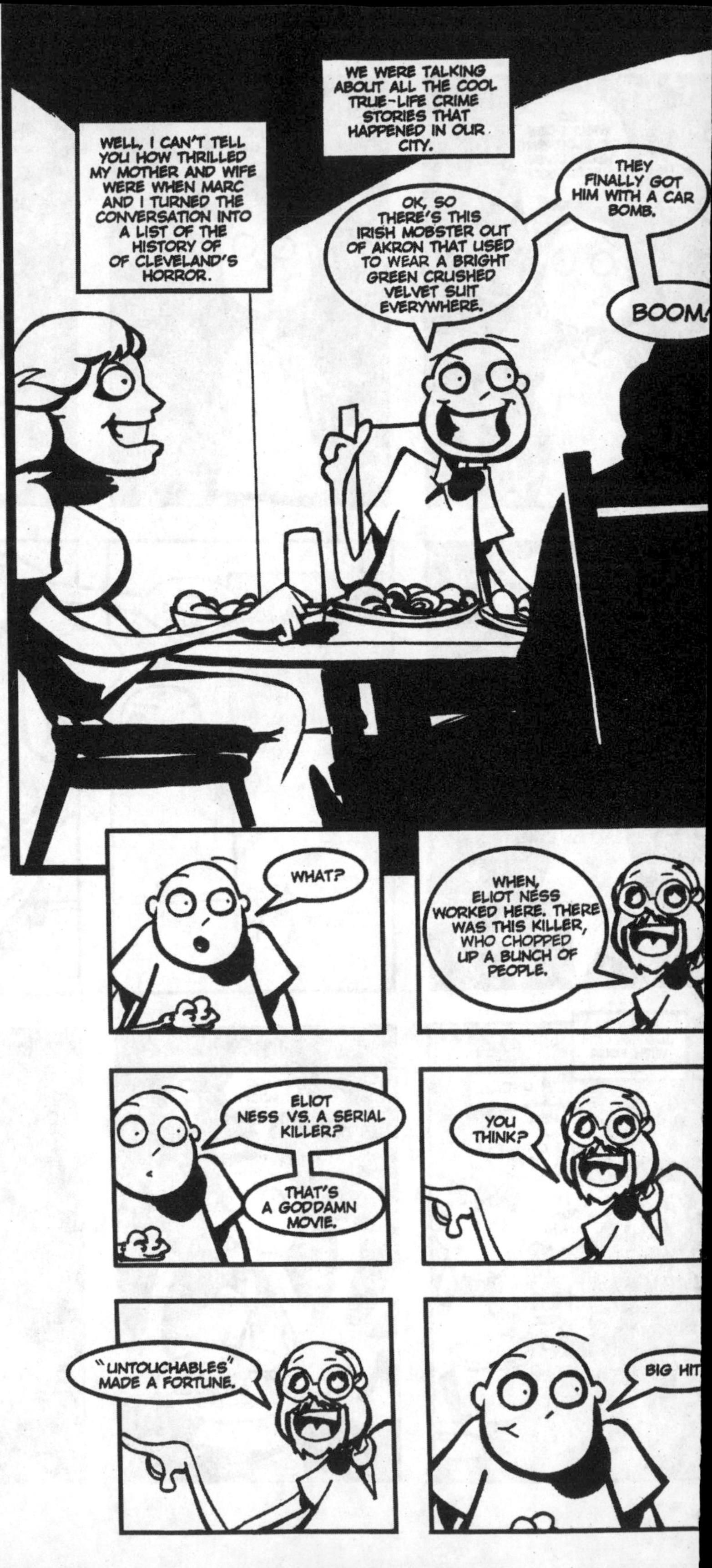

WELL, I CAN'T TELL YOU HOW THRILLED MY MOTHER AND WIFE WERE WHEN MARC AND I TURNED THE CONVERSATION INTO A LIST OF THE HISTORY OF OF CLEVELAND'S HORROR.
WE WERE TALKING ABOUT ALL THE COOL TRUE-LIFE CRIME STORIES THAT HAPPENED IN OUR CITY.
OK, SO THERE'S THIS IRISH MOBSTER OUT OF AKRON THAT USED TO WEAR A BRIGHT GREEN CRUSHED VELVET SUIT EVERYWHERE.
THEY FINALLY GOT HIM WITH A CAR BOMB.
BOOM
WHAT?
WHEN, ELIOT NESS WORKED HERE. THERE WAS THIS KILLER, WHO CHOPPED UP A BUNCH OF PEOPLE.
ELIOT NESS VS. A SERIAL KILLER?
THAT'S A GODDAMN MOVIE.
YOU THINK?
"UNTOUCHABLES" MADE A FORTUNE.
BIG HIT

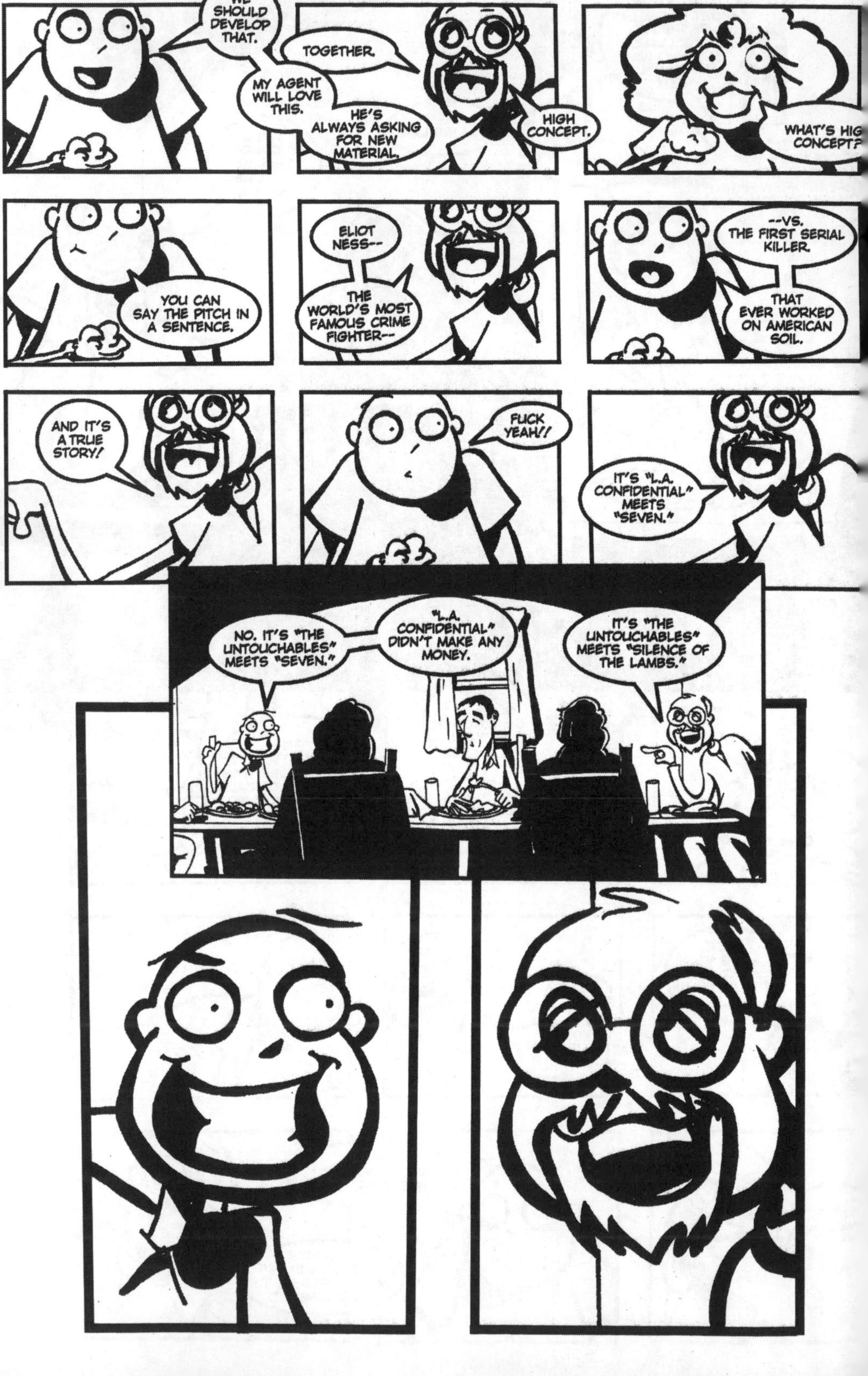
WE SHOULD DEVELOP THAT.
TOGETHER.
MY AGENT WILL LOVE THIS.
HE'S ALWAYS ASKING FOR NEW MATERIAL.
HIGH CONCEPT.
WHAT'S HIG CONCEPT?
YOU CAN SAY THE PITCH IN A SENTENCE.
ELIOT NESS--
THE WORLD'S MOST FAMOUS CRIME FIGHTER--
--VS. THE FIRST SERIAL KILLER.
THAT EVER WORKED ON AMERICAN SOIL.
AND IT'S A TRUE STORY!
FUCK YEAH!!
IT'S "L.A. CONFIDENTIAL" MEETS "SEVEN."
NO. IT'S "THE UNTOUCHABLES" MEETS "SEVEN."
"L.A. CONFIDENTIAL" DIDN'T MAKE ANY MONEY.
IT'S "THE UNTOUCHABLES" MEETS "SILENCE OF THE LAMBS."

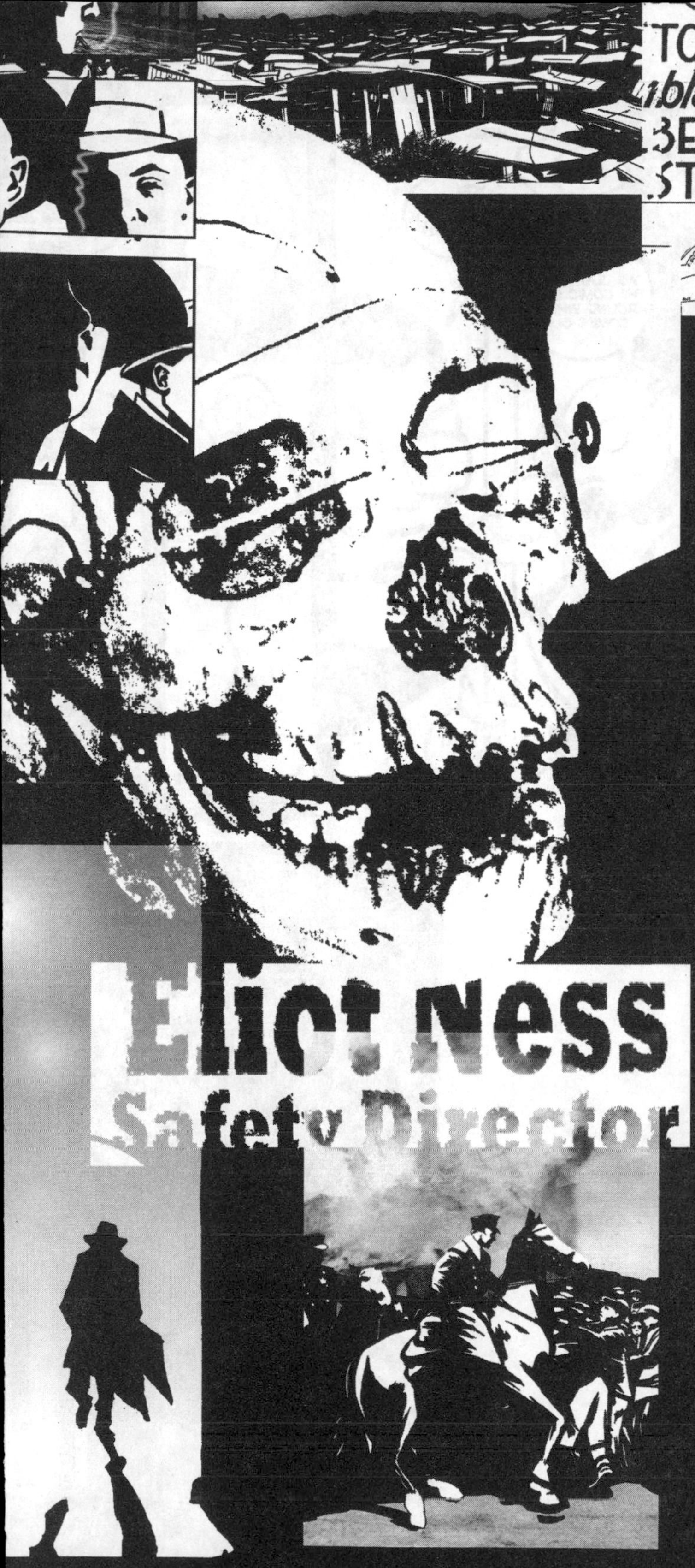
Eliot Ness
Safety Director

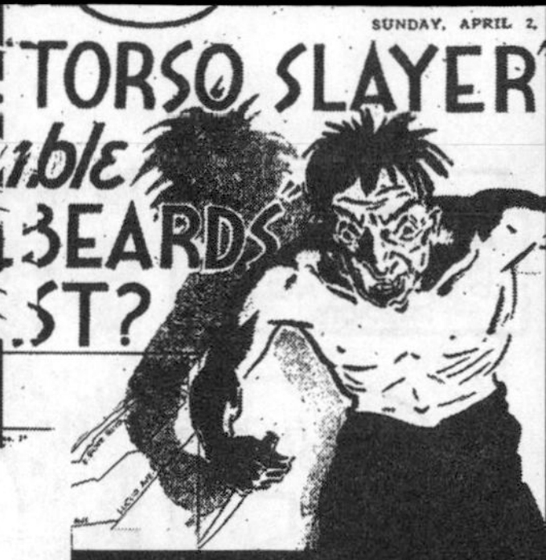
SUNDAY, APRIL 2,
'TORSO SLAYER'

SO WE GOT TO WORK. DID THE RESEARCH.

I WAS WORKING AS AN EDITORIAL CARTOONIST FOR THE CLEVELAND PLAIN DEALER'S SUNDAY MAGAZINE.

MY VERY HIP EDITOR UNEARTHED THE ORIGINAL FILES OF THE CASE FOR ME.

THE STORY WAS WRITING ITSELF.

IT HAD EVERYTHING YOU COULD WANT.

BIG SET PIECES.

COOL CHARACTERS.

COOL CARS
COOL CLOTHES

A KILLER.

A HUNT FOR A KILLER.

AND IT WAS ALL TRUE.

WE TOTALLY FELL IN LOVE WITH THE STORY

THE STORY WAS SO DENSE AND VISUALLY INTERESTING

AND IT WAS FULL OF ALL THESE INTERESTING THINGS I HAD NEVER DRAWN BEFORE.

I THOUGHT IT WOULD BE A DAMN GOOD READ AS WELL AS A DAMN GOOD MOVIE.

I COMMITTED TO DRAWING IT AS A COMIC BOOK SERIES/ GRAPHIC NOVEL FOR US.

A GOOD STORY IS A GOOD STORY.

I WANTED TO SEE THIS STORY. I WANTED TO READ IT.

AND THE IDEA OF CO-WRITING IT WAS INVIGORATING.

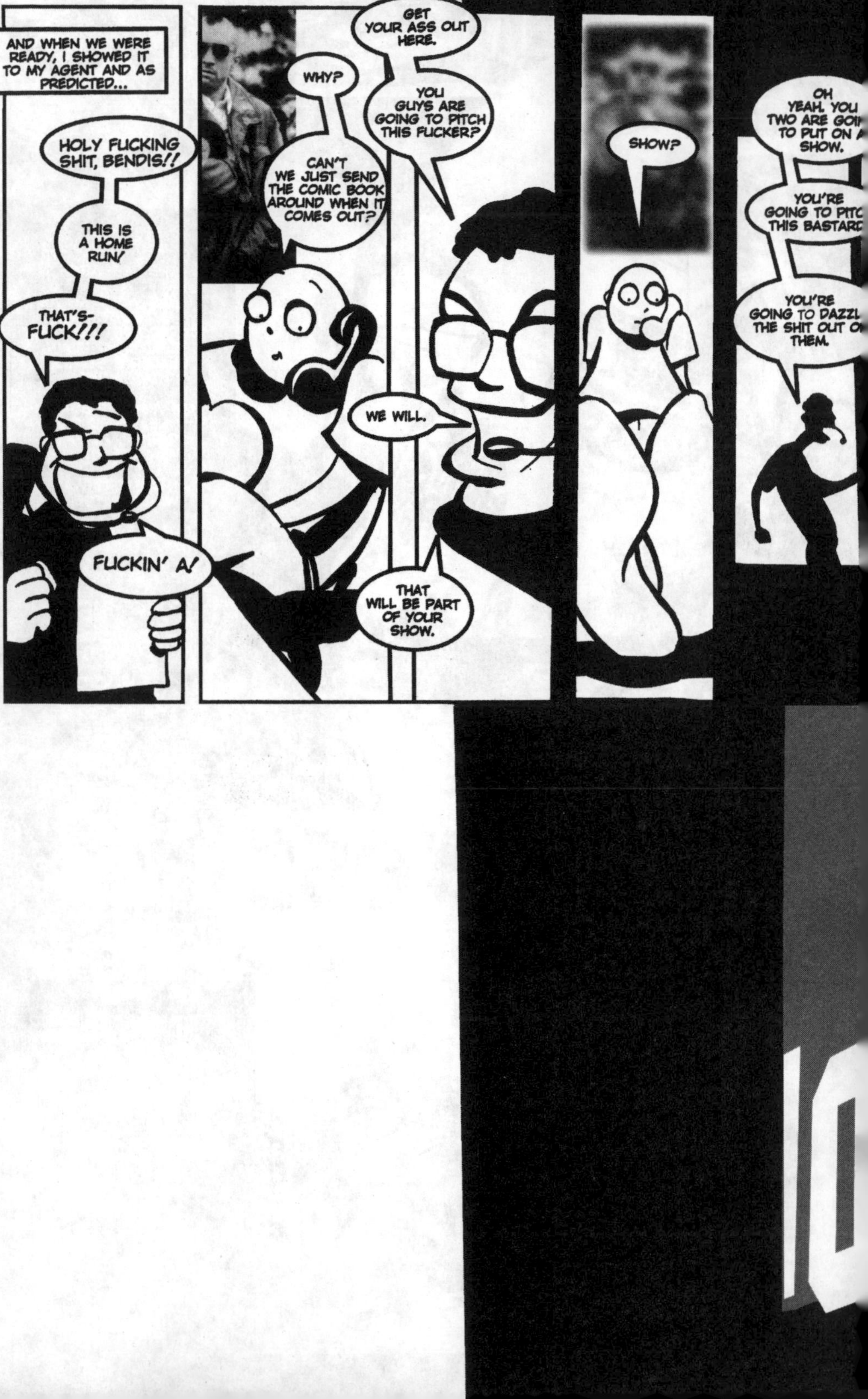
AND WHEN WE WERE READY, I SHOWED IT TO MY AGENT AND AS PREDICTED...
HOLY FUCKING SHIT, BENDIS!!
THIS IS A HOME RUN!
THAT'S- FUCK!!!
FUCKIN' A!
WHY?
CAN'T WE JUST SEND THE COMIC BOOK AROUND WHEN IT COMES OUT?
GET YOUR ASS OUT HERE.
YOU GUYS ARE GOING TO PITCH THIS FUCKER?
WE WILL.
THAT WILL BE PART OF YOUR SHOW.
SHOW?

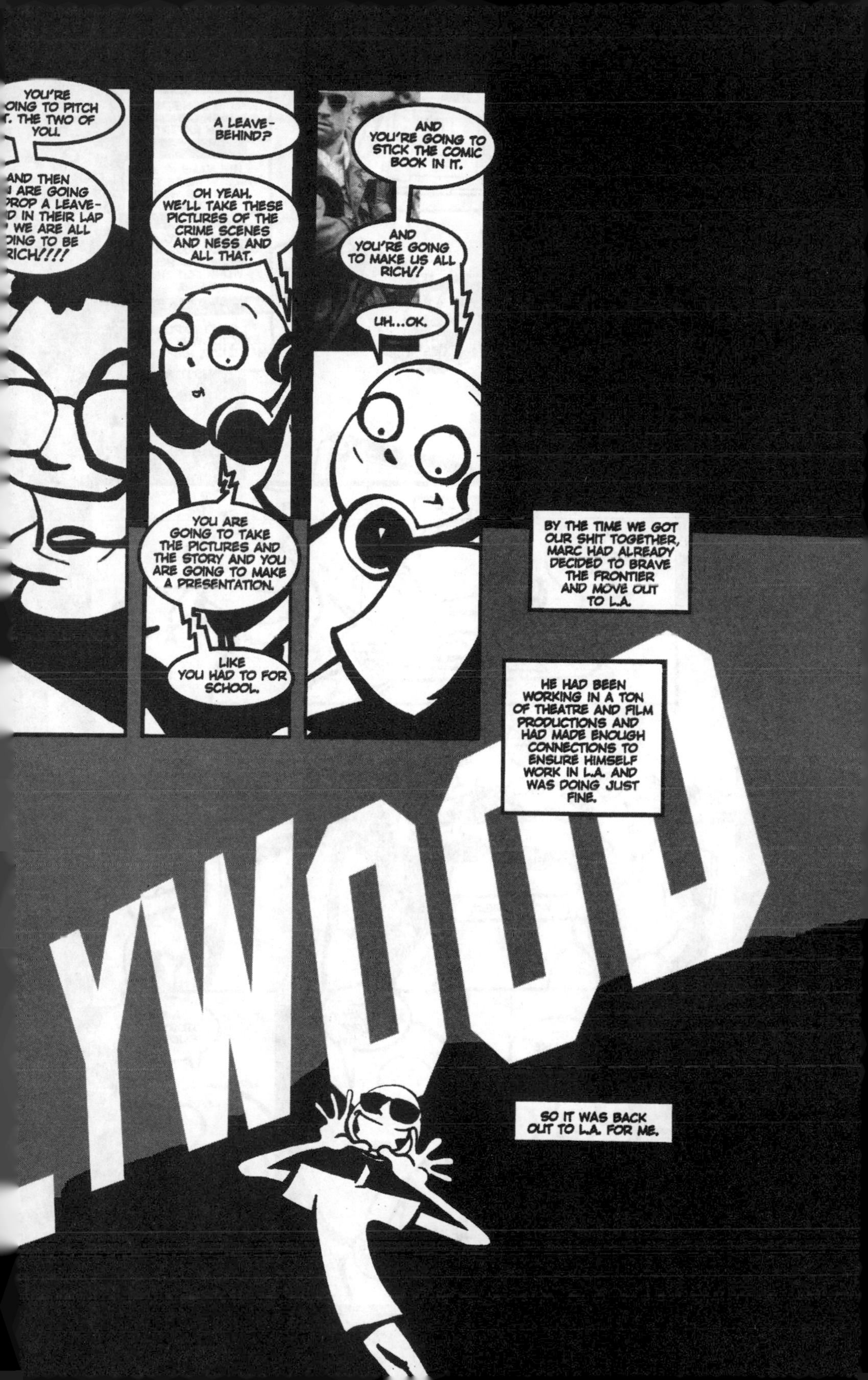
YOU'RE
OING TO PITCH
T. THE TWO OF
YOU.
AND THEN
U ARE GOING
DROP A LEAVE-
D IN THEIR LAP
WE ARE ALL
OING TO BE
RICH!!!!
A LEAVE-
BEHIND?
OH YEAH.
WE'LL TAKE THESE
PICTURES OF THE
CRIME SCENES
AND NESS AND
ALL THAT.
YOU ARE
GOING TO TAKE
THE PICTURES AND
THE STORY AND YOU
ARE GOING TO MAKE
A PRESENTATION.
LIKE
YOU HAD TO FOR
SCHOOL.
AND
YOU'RE GOING TO
STICK THE COMIC
BOOK IN IT.
AND
YOU'RE GOING
TO MAKE US ALL
RICH!!
UH...OK.
BY THE TIME WE GOT OUR SHIT TOGETHER, MARC HAD ALREADY DECIDED TO BRAVE THE FRONTIER AND MOVE OUT TO L.A.
HE HAD BEEN WORKING IN A TON OF THEATRE AND FILM PRODUCTIONS AND HAD MADE ENOUGH CONNECTIONS TO ENSURE HIMSELF WORK IN L.A. AND WAS DOING JUST FINE.
YWOOD
SO IT WAS BACK OUT TO L.A. FOR ME.

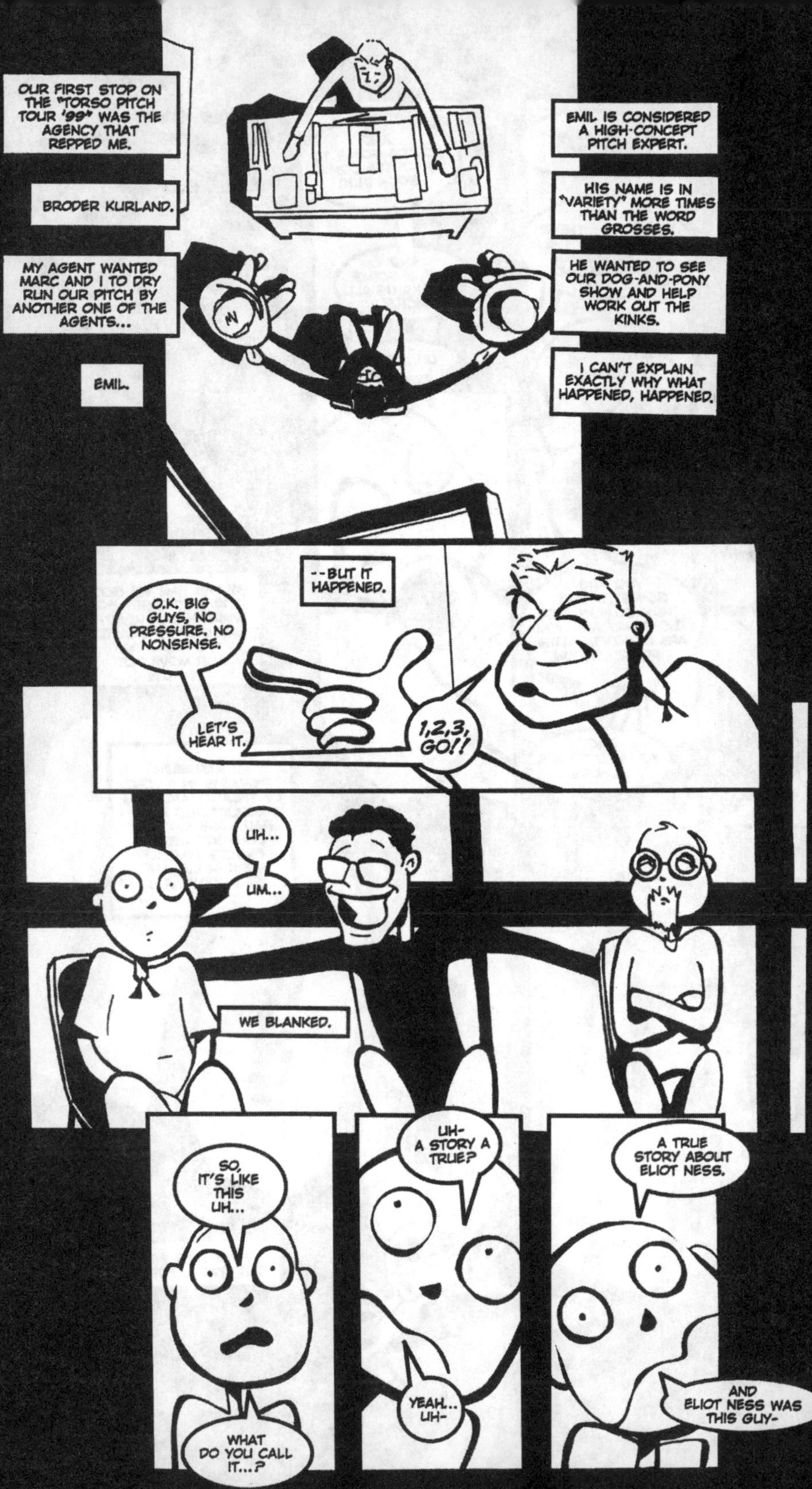
OUR FIRST STOP ON THE "TORSO PITCH TOUR '99" WAS THE AGENCY THAT REPPED ME.
BRODER KURLAND.
MY AGENT WANTED MARC AND I TO DRY RUN OUR PITCH BY ANOTHER ONE OF THE AGENTS...
EMIL.
EMIL IS CONSIDERED A HIGH-CONCEPT PITCH EXPERT.
HIS NAME IS IN "VARIETY" MORE TIMES THAN THE WORD GROSSES.
HE WANTED TO SEE OUR DOG-AND-PONY SHOW AND HELP WORK OUT THE KINKS.
I CAN'T EXPLAIN EXACTLY WHY WHAT HAPPENED, HAPPENED.
--BUT IT HAPPENED.
O.K. BIG GUYS, NO PRESSURE. NO NONSENSE.
LET'S HEAR IT.
1,2,3, GO!!
UH...
UM...
WE BLANKED.
SO, IT'S LIKE THIS UH...
WHAT DO YOU CALL IT...?
UH- A STORY A TRUE?
YEAH... UH-
A TRUE STORY ABOUT ELIOT NESS.
AND ELIOT NESS WAS THIS GUY-

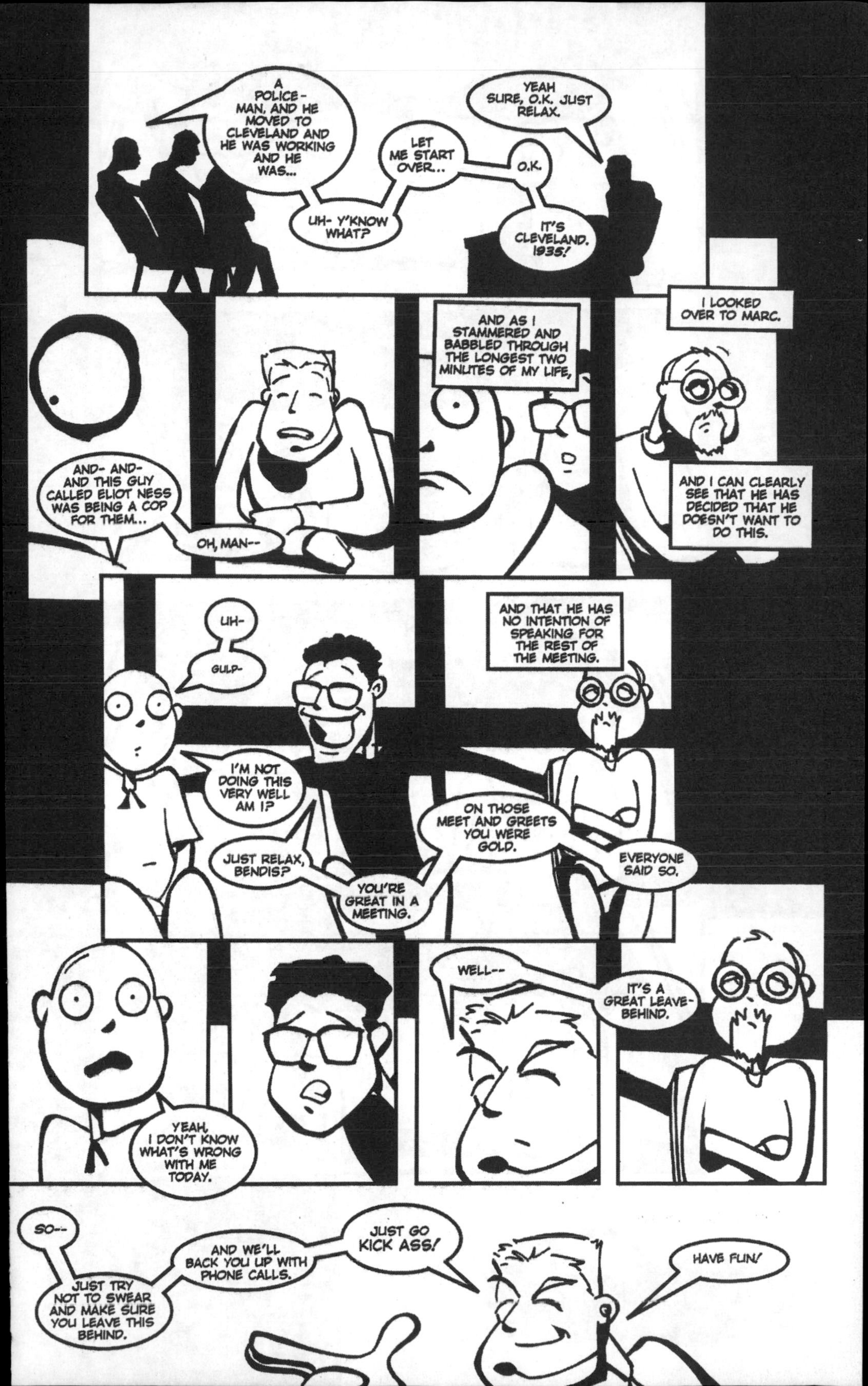
A POLICE-MAN, AND HE MOVED TO CLEVELAND AND HE WAS WORKING AND HE WAS...
UH- Y'KNOW WHAT?
LET ME START OVER...
O.K.
IT'S CLEVELAND. 1935!
YEAH SURE, O.K. JUST RELAX.
AND- AND- AND THIS GUY CALLED ELIOT NESS WAS BEING A COP FOR THEM...
OH, MAN--
AND AS I STAMMERED AND BABBLED THROUGH THE LONGEST TWO MINUTES OF MY LIFE,
I LOOKED OVER TO MARC.
AND I CAN CLEARLY SEE THAT HE HAS DECIDED THAT HE DOESN'T WANT TO DO THIS.
UH-
GULP-
I'M NOT DOING THIS VERY WELL AM I?
AND THAT HE HAS NO INTENTION OF SPEAKING FOR THE REST OF THE MEETING.
JUST RELAX, BENDIS?
YOU'RE GREAT IN A MEETING.
ON THOSE MEET AND GREETS YOU WERE GOLD.
EVERYONE SAID SO.
YEAH, I DON'T KNOW WHAT'S WRONG WITH ME TODAY.
WELL--
IT'S A GREAT LEAVE-BEHIND.
SO--
JUST TRY NOT TO SWEAR AND MAKE SURE YOU LEAVE THIS BEHIND.
AND WE'LL BACK YOU UP WITH PHONE CALLS.
JUST GO KICK ASS!
HAVE FUN!

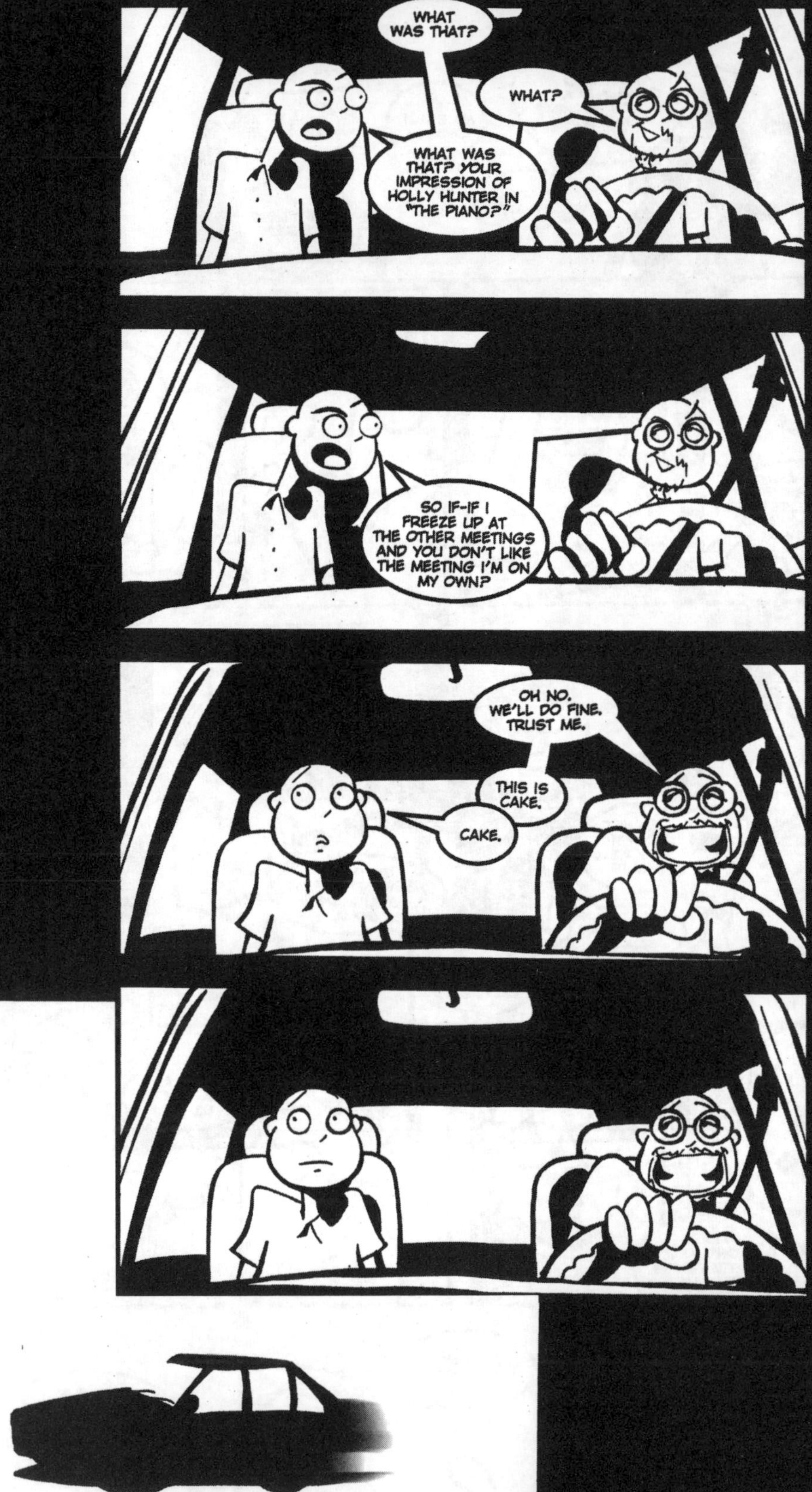
WHAT WAS THAT?
WHAT?
WHAT WAS THAT? YOUR IMPRESSION OF HOLLY HUNTER IN "THE PIANO?"
SO IF-IF I FREEZE UP AT THE OTHER MEETINGS AND YOU DON'T LIKE THE MEETING I'M ON MY OWN?
OH NO. WE'LL DO FINE. TRUST ME.
THIS IS CAKE.
CAKE.

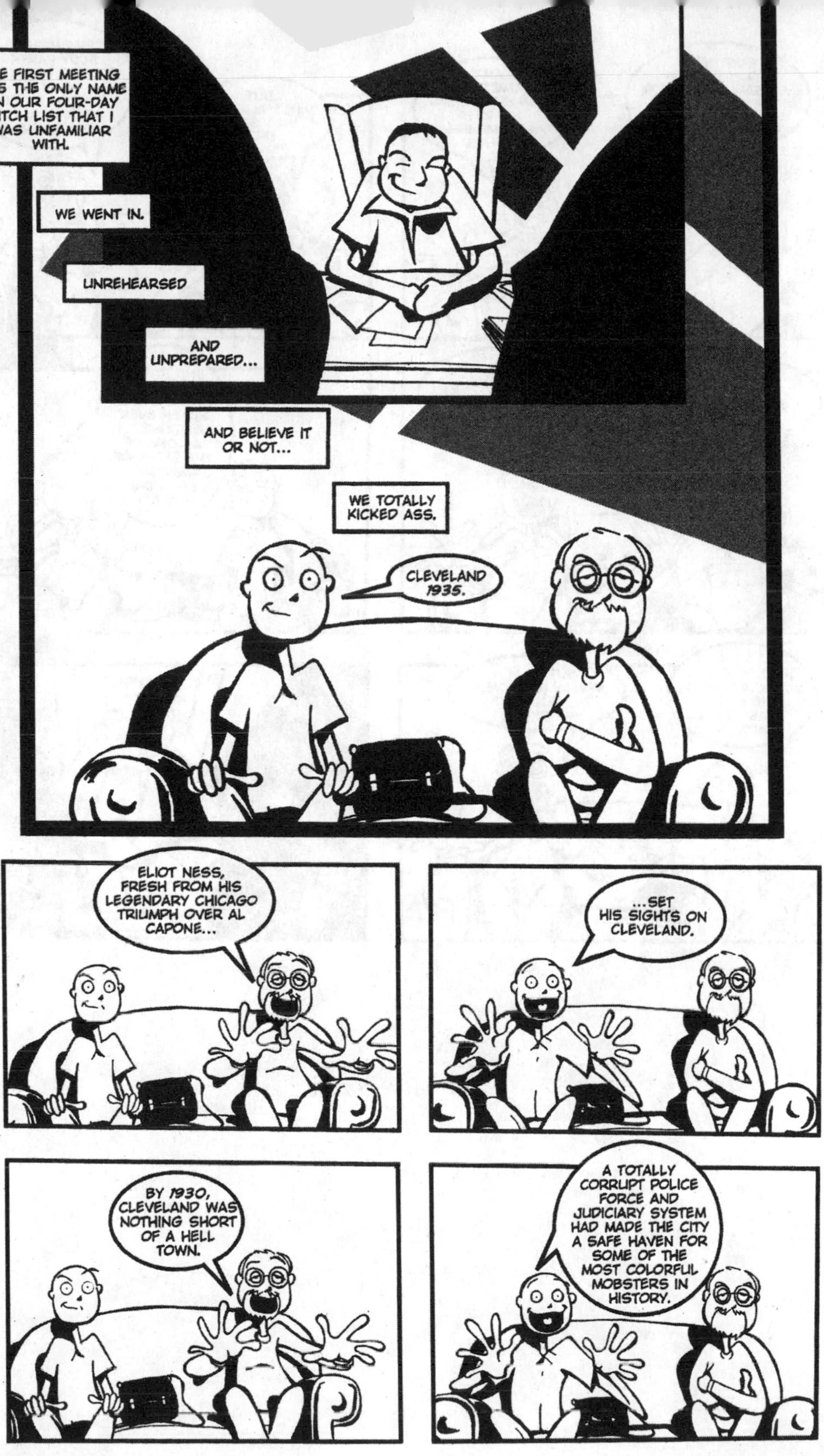
THE FIRST MEETING WAS THE ONLY NAME ON OUR FOUR-DAY PITCH LIST THAT I WAS UNFAMILIAR WITH.
WE WENT IN.
UNREHEARSED
AND UNPREPARED...
AND BELIEVE IT OR NOT...
WE TOTALLY KICKED ASS.
CLEVELAND 1935.
ELIOT NESS, FRESH FROM HIS LEGENDARY CHICAGO TRIUMPH OVER AL CAPONE...
...SET HIS SIGHTS ON CLEVELAND.
BY 1930, CLEVELAND WAS NOTHING SHORT OF A HELL TOWN.
A TOTALLY CORRUPT POLICE FORCE AND JUDICIARY SYSTEM HAD MADE THE CITY A SAFE HAVEN FOR SOME OF THE MOST COLORFUL MOBSTERS IN HISTORY.

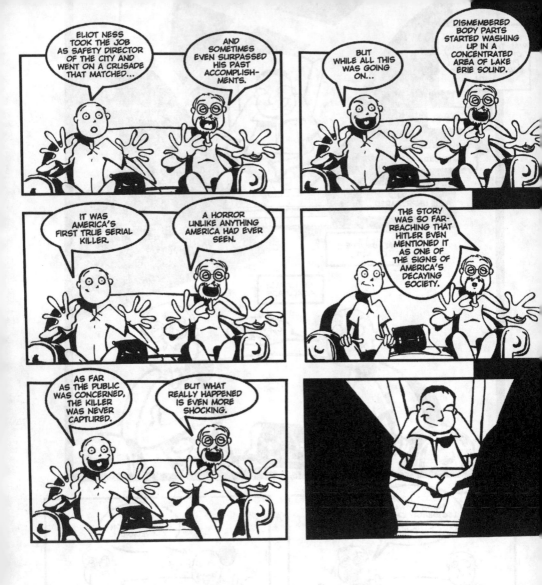

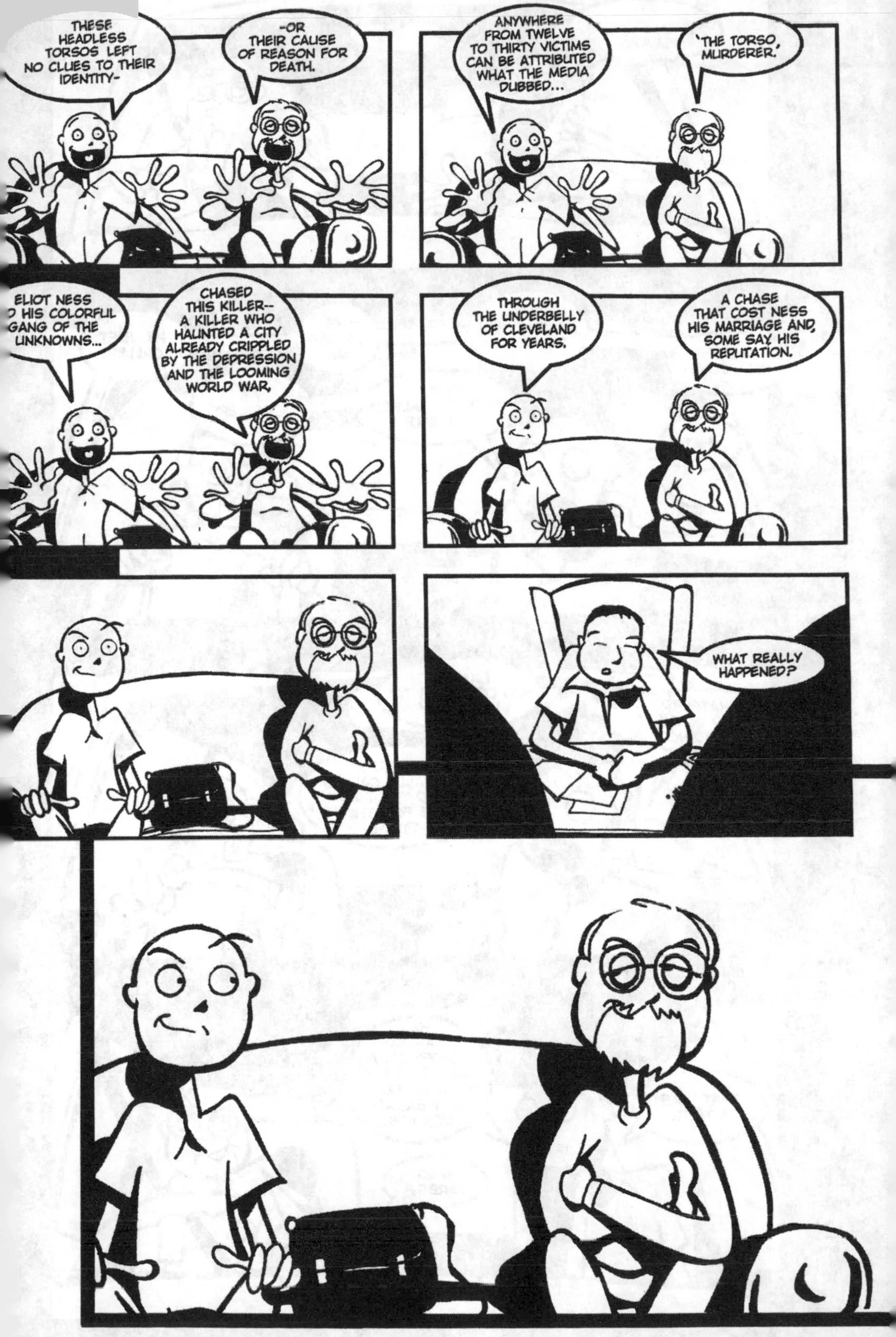
THESE HEADLESS TORSOS LEFT NO CLUES TO THEIR IDENTITY-
-OR THEIR CAUSE OF REASON FOR DEATH.
ANYWHERE FROM TWELVE TO THIRTY VICTIMS CAN BE ATTRIBUTED WHAT THE MEDIA DUBBED...
'THE TORSO MURDERER.'
ELIOT NESS AND HIS COLORFUL GANG OF THE UNKNOWNS...
CHASED THIS KILLER-- A KILLER WHO HAUNTED A CITY ALREADY CRIPPLED BY THE DEPRESSION AND THE LOOMING WORLD WAR,
THROUGH THE UNDERBELLY OF CLEVELAND FOR YEARS.
A CHASE THAT COST NESS HIS MARRIAGE AND, SOME SAY, HIS REPUTATION.
WHAT REALLY HAPPENED?

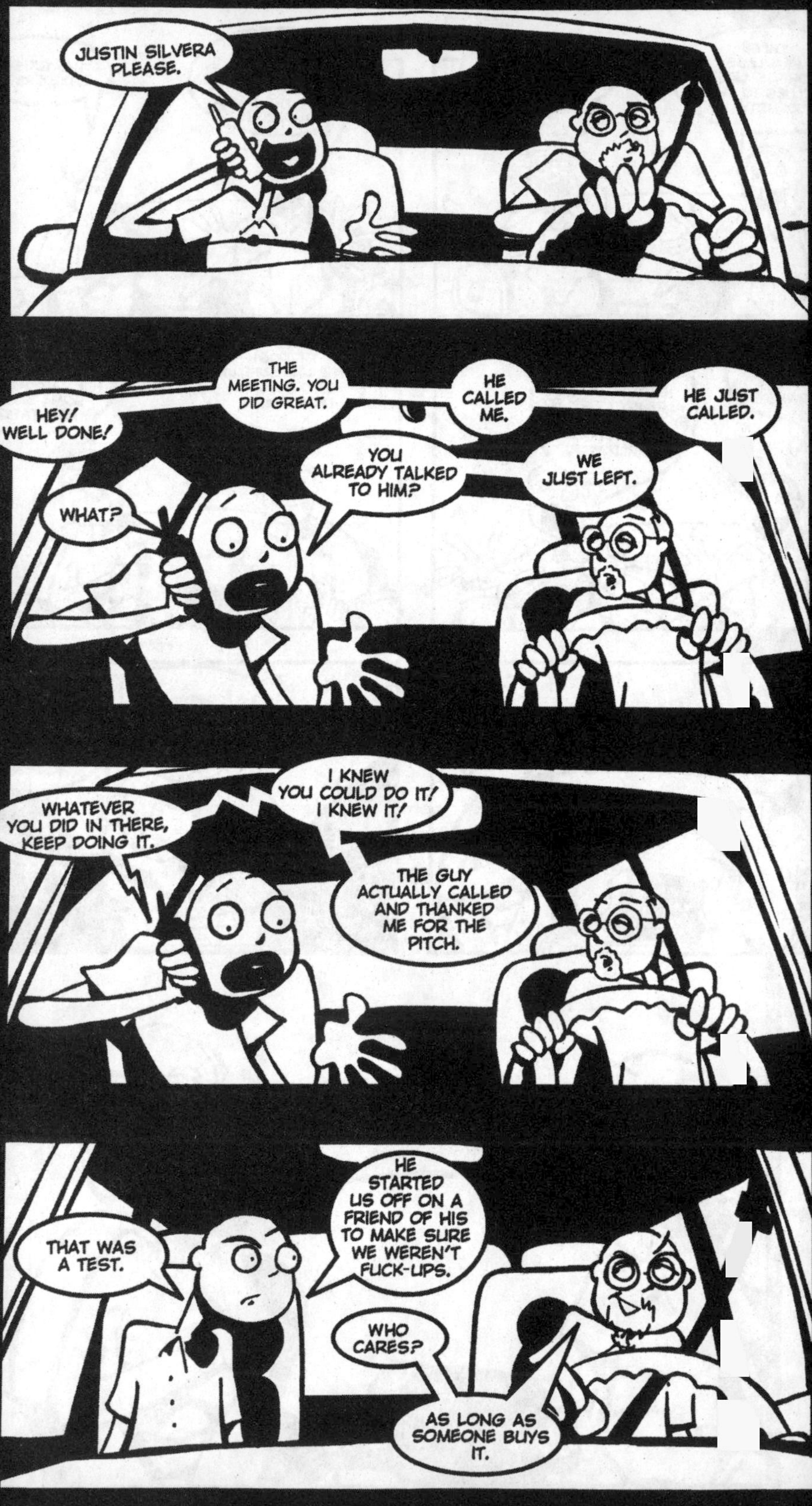

JUSTIN SILVERA PLEASE.
HEY! WELL DONE!
THE MEETING. YOU DID GREAT.
HE CALLED ME.
HE JUST CALLED.
WHAT?
YOU ALREADY TALKED TO HIM?
WE JUST LEFT.
WHATEVER YOU DID IN THERE, KEEP DOING IT.
I KNEW YOU COULD DO IT! I KNEW IT!
THE GUY ACTUALLY CALLED AND THANKED ME FOR THE PITCH.
THAT WAS A TEST.
HE STARTED US OFF ON A FRIEND OF HIS TO MAKE SURE WE WEREN'T FUCK-UPS.
WHO CARES?
AS LONG AS SOMEONE BUYS IT.

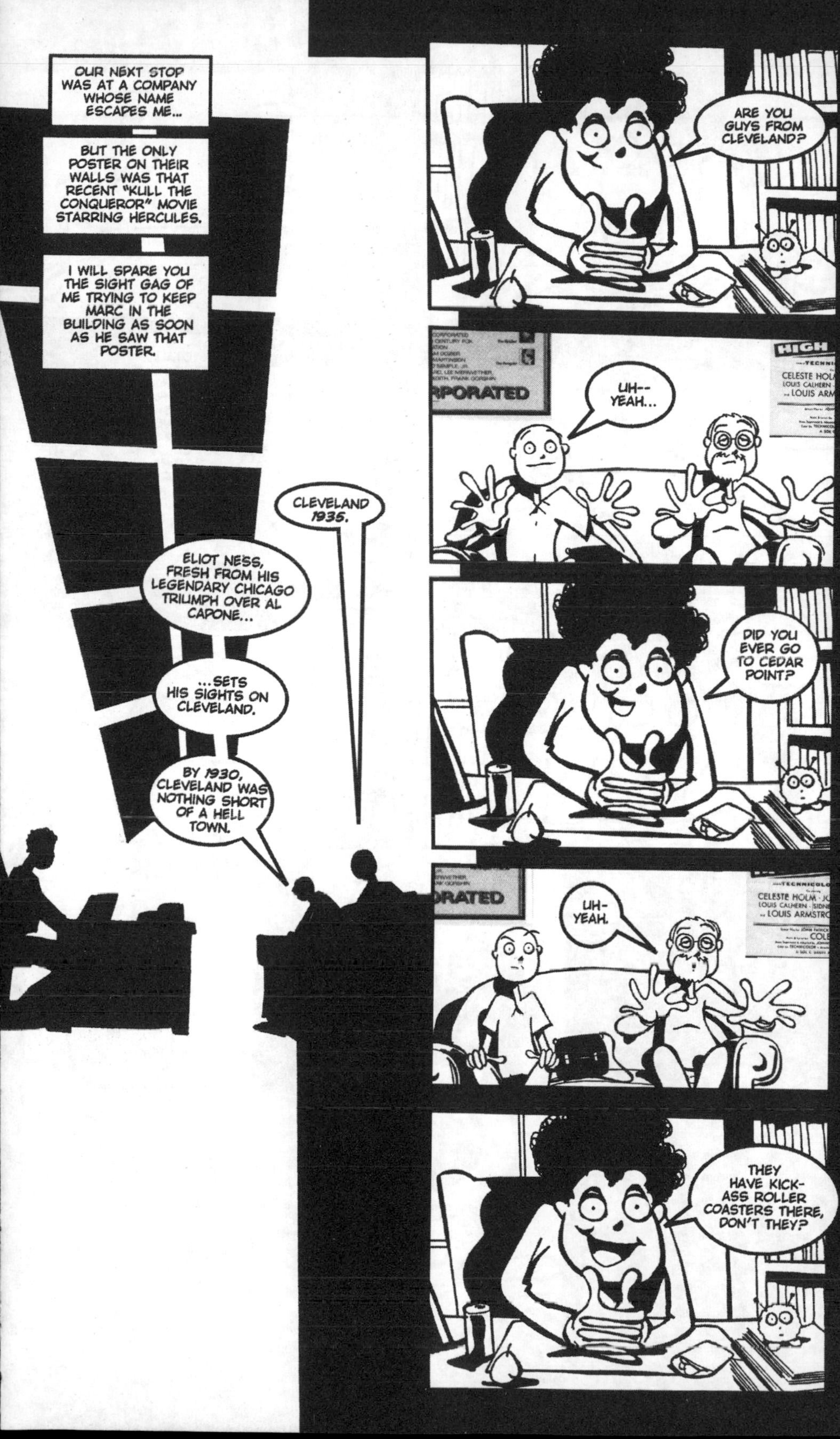
OUR NEXT STOP WAS AT A COMPANY WHOSE NAME ESCAPES ME...
BUT THE ONLY POSTER ON THEIR WALLS WAS THAT RECENT "KULL THE CONQUEROR" MOVIE STARRING HERCULES.
I WILL SPARE YOU THE SIGHT GAG OF ME TRYING TO KEEP MARC IN THE BUILDING AS SOON AS HE SAW THAT POSTER.
CLEVELAND 1935.
ELIOT NESS, FRESH FROM HIS LEGENDARY CHICAGO TRIUMPH OVER AL CAPONE...
...SETS HIS SIGHTS ON CLEVELAND.
BY 1930, CLEVELAND WAS NOTHING SHORT OF A HELL TOWN.
ARE YOU GUYS FROM CLEVELAND?
UH-- YEAH...
DID YOU EVER GO TO CEDAR POINT?
UH- YEAH.
THEY HAVE KICK-ASS ROLLER COASTERS THERE, DON'T THEY?

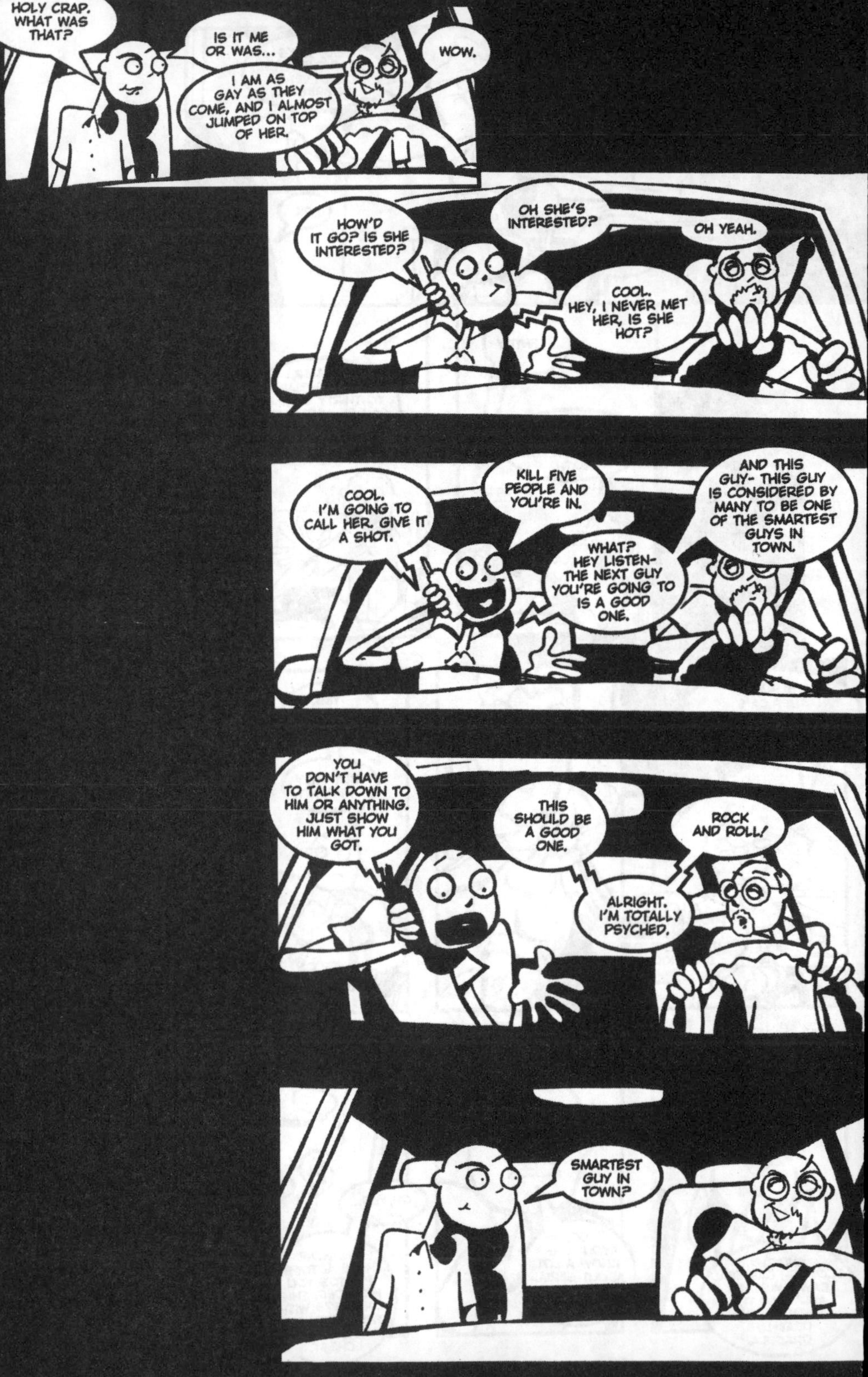
HOLY CRAP. WHAT WAS THAT?
IS IT ME OR WAS...
I AM AS GAY AS THEY COME, AND I ALMOST JUMPED ON TOP OF HER.
WOW.
HOW'D IT GO? IS SHE INTERESTED?
OH SHE'S INTERESTED?
OH YEAH.
COOL. HEY, I NEVER MET HER, IS SHE HOT?
COOL. I'M GOING TO CALL HER. GIVE IT A SHOT.
KILL FIVE PEOPLE AND YOU'RE IN.
AND THIS GUY- THIS GUY IS CONSIDERED BY MANY TO BE ONE OF THE SMARTEST GUYS IN TOWN.
WHAT? HEY LISTEN- THE NEXT GUY YOU'RE GOING TO IS A GOOD ONE.
YOU DON'T HAVE TO TALK DOWN TO HIM OR ANYTHING. JUST SHOW HIM WHAT YOU GOT.
THIS SHOULD BE A GOOD ONE.
ROCK AND ROLL!
ALRIGHT. I'M TOTALLY PSYCHED.
SMARTEST GUY IN TOWN?

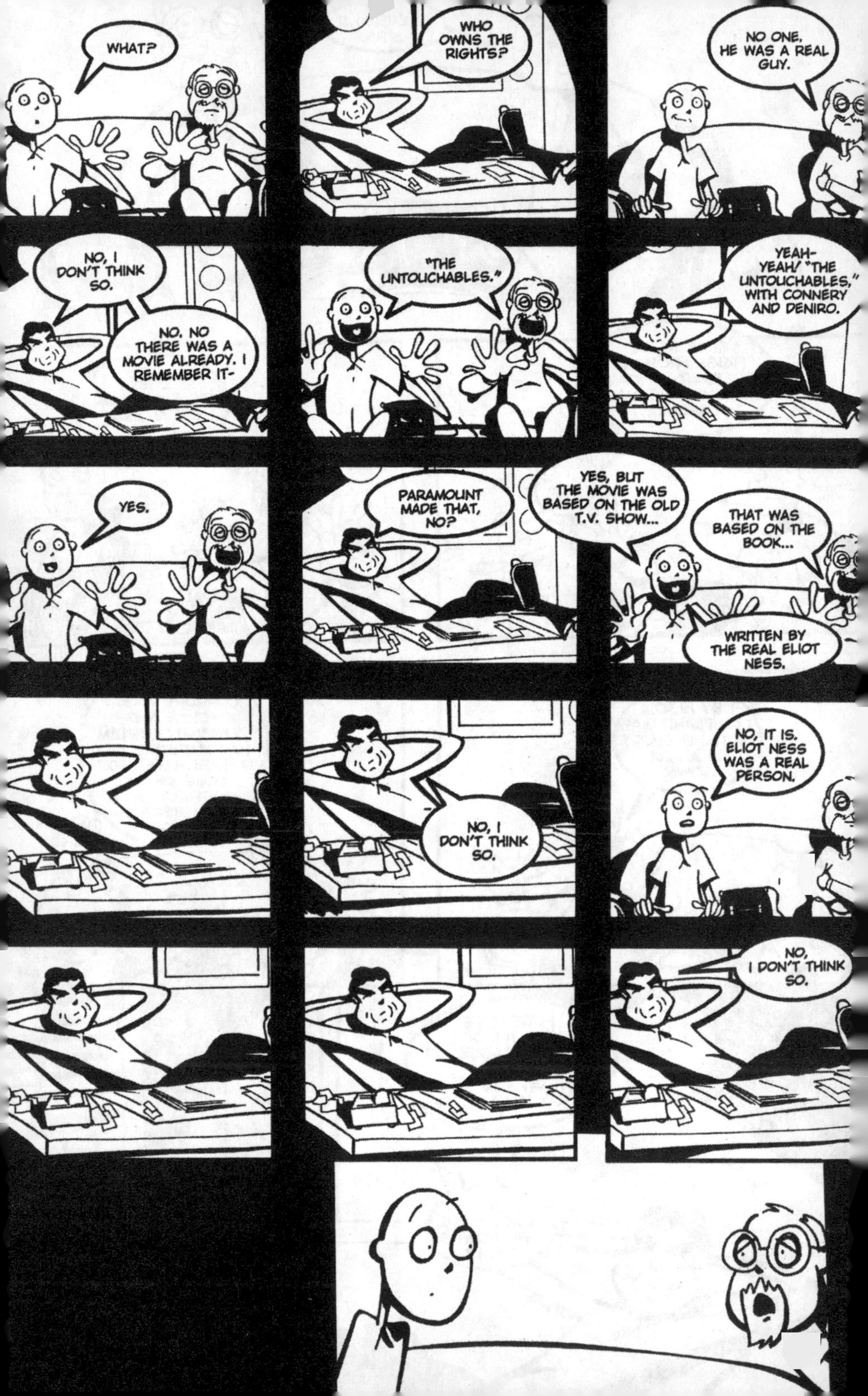
WHAT?
WHO OWNS THE RIGHTS?
NO ONE. HE WAS A REAL GUY.
NO, I DON'T THINK SO.
NO. NO THERE WAS A MOVIE ALREADY. I REMEMBER IT-
"THE UNTOUCHABLES."
YEAH-YEAH! "THE UNTOUCHABLES," WITH CONNERY AND DENIRO.
YES.
PARAMOUNT MADE THAT, NO?
YES, BUT THE MOVIE WAS BASED ON THE OLD T.V. SHOW...
THAT WAS BASED ON THE BOOK...
WRITTEN BY THE REAL ELIOT NESS.
NO, I DON'T THINK SO.
NO, IT IS. ELIOT NESS WAS A REAL PERSON.
NO, I DON'T THINK SO.

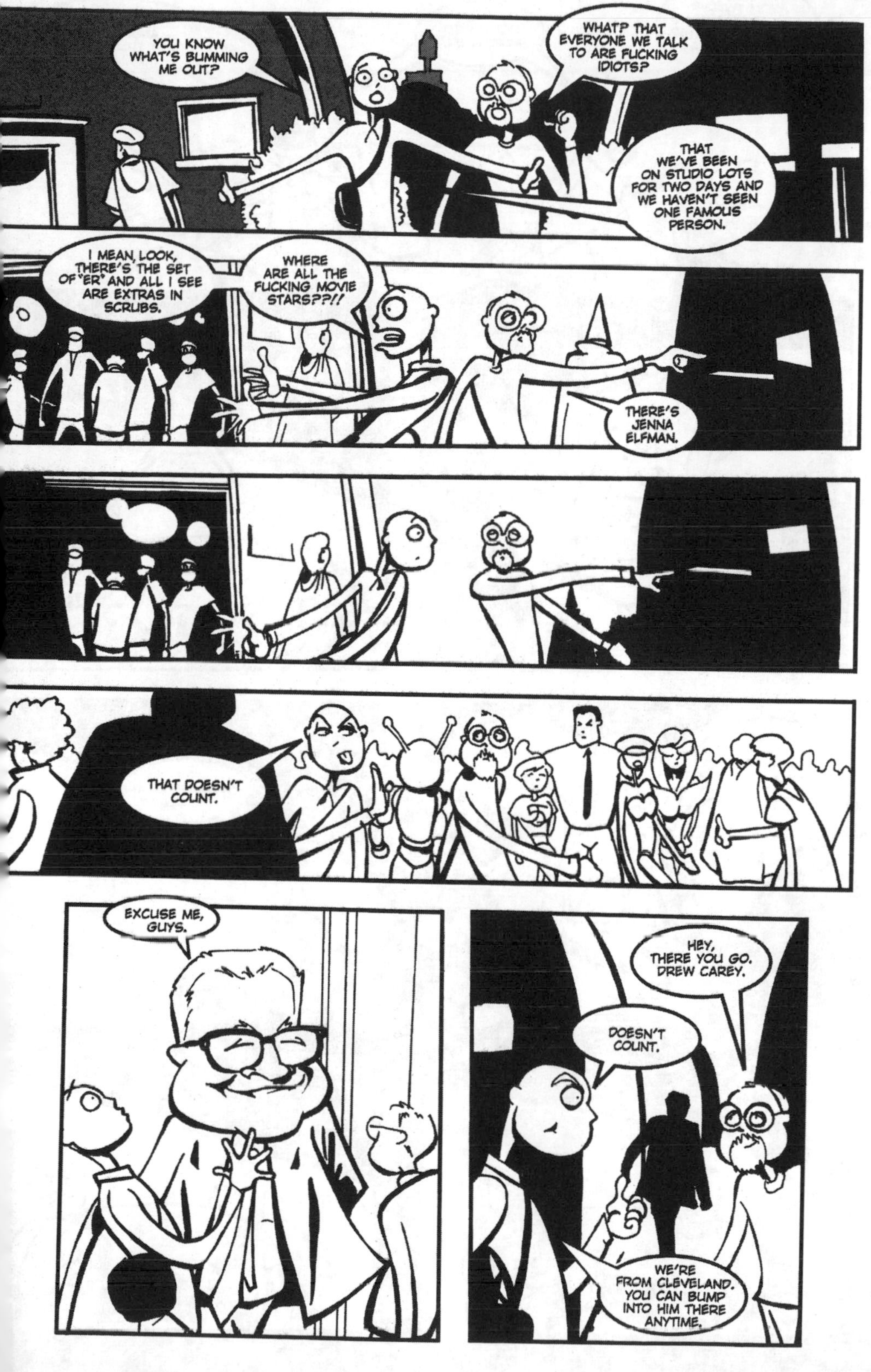
YOU KNOW WHAT'S BUMMING ME OUT?
WHAT? THAT EVERYONE WE TALK TO ARE FUCKING IDIOTS?
THAT WE'VE BEEN ON STUDIO LOTS FOR TWO DAYS AND WE HAVEN'T SEEN ONE FAMOUS PERSON.
I MEAN, LOOK, THERE'S THE SET OF "ER" AND ALL I SEE ARE EXTRAS IN SCRUBS.
WHERE ARE ALL THE FUCKING MOVIE STARS??!!
THERE'S JENNA ELFMAN.
THAT DOESN'T COUNT.
EXCUSE ME, GUYS.
HEY, THERE YOU GO. DREW CAREY.
DOESN'T COUNT.
WE'RE FROM CLEVELAND. YOU CAN BUMP INTO HIM THERE ANYTIME.

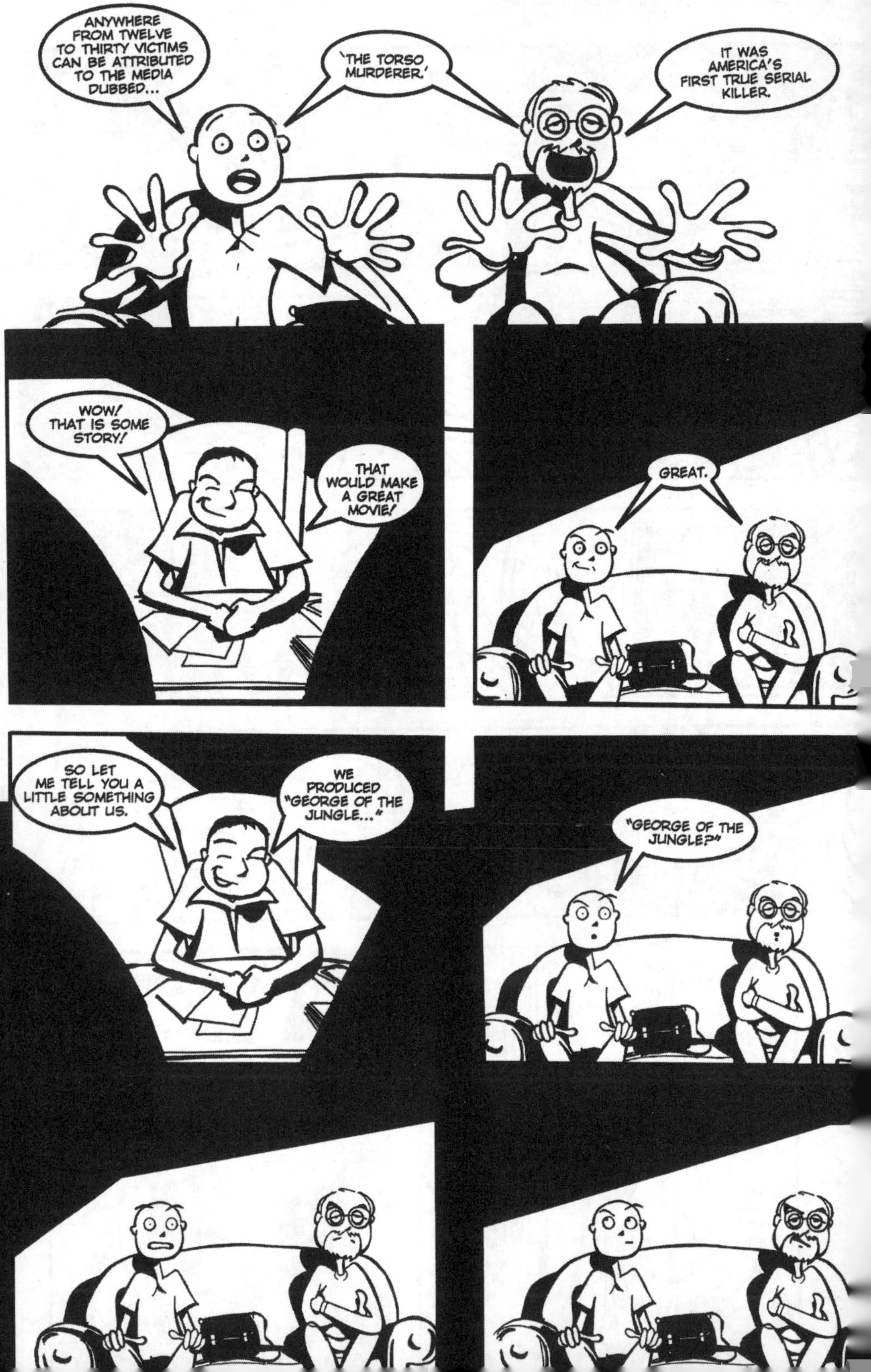
ANYWHERE FROM TWELVE TO THIRTY VICTIMS CAN BE ATTRIBUTED TO THE MEDIA DUBBED...
`THE TORSO MURDERER.'
IT WAS AMERICA'S FIRST TRUE SERIAL KILLER.
WOW! THAT IS SOME STORY!
THAT WOULD MAKE A GREAT MOVIE!
GREAT.
SO LET ME TELL YOU A LITTLE SOMETHING ABOUT US.
WE PRODUCED "GEORGE OF THE JUNGLE..."
"GEORGE OF THE JUNGLE?"

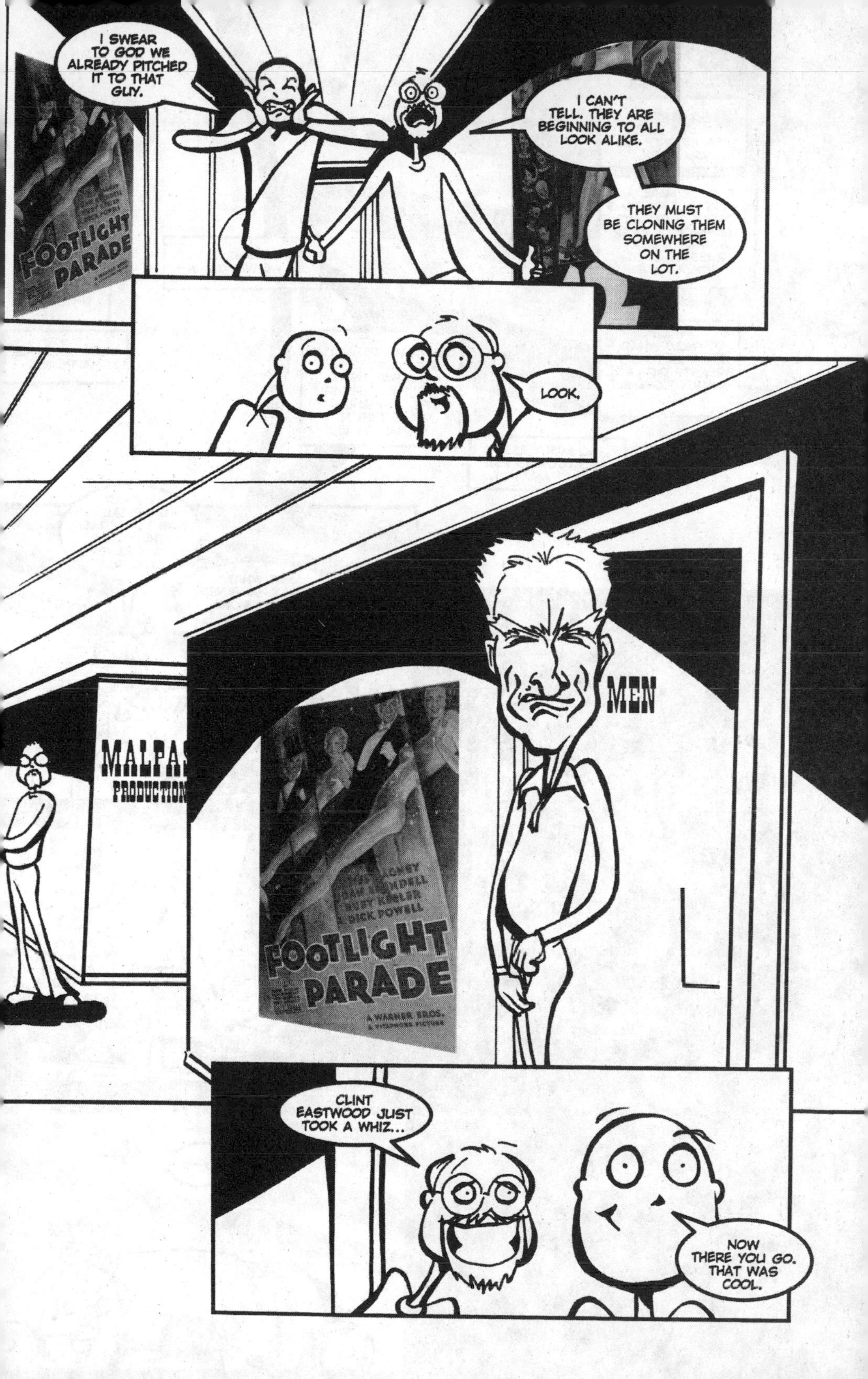
I SWEAR TO GOD WE ALREADY PITCHED IT TO THAT GUY.
I CAN'T TELL. THEY ARE BEGINNING TO ALL LOOK ALIKE.
THEY MUST BE CLONING THEM SOMEWHERE ON THE LOT.
FOOTLIGHT PARADE
LOOK.
MALPAS
PRODUCTION
MEN
FOOTLIGHT PARADE
A WARNER BROS.
CLINT EASTWOOD JUST TOOK A WHIZ...
NOW THERE YOU GO. THAT WAS COOL.

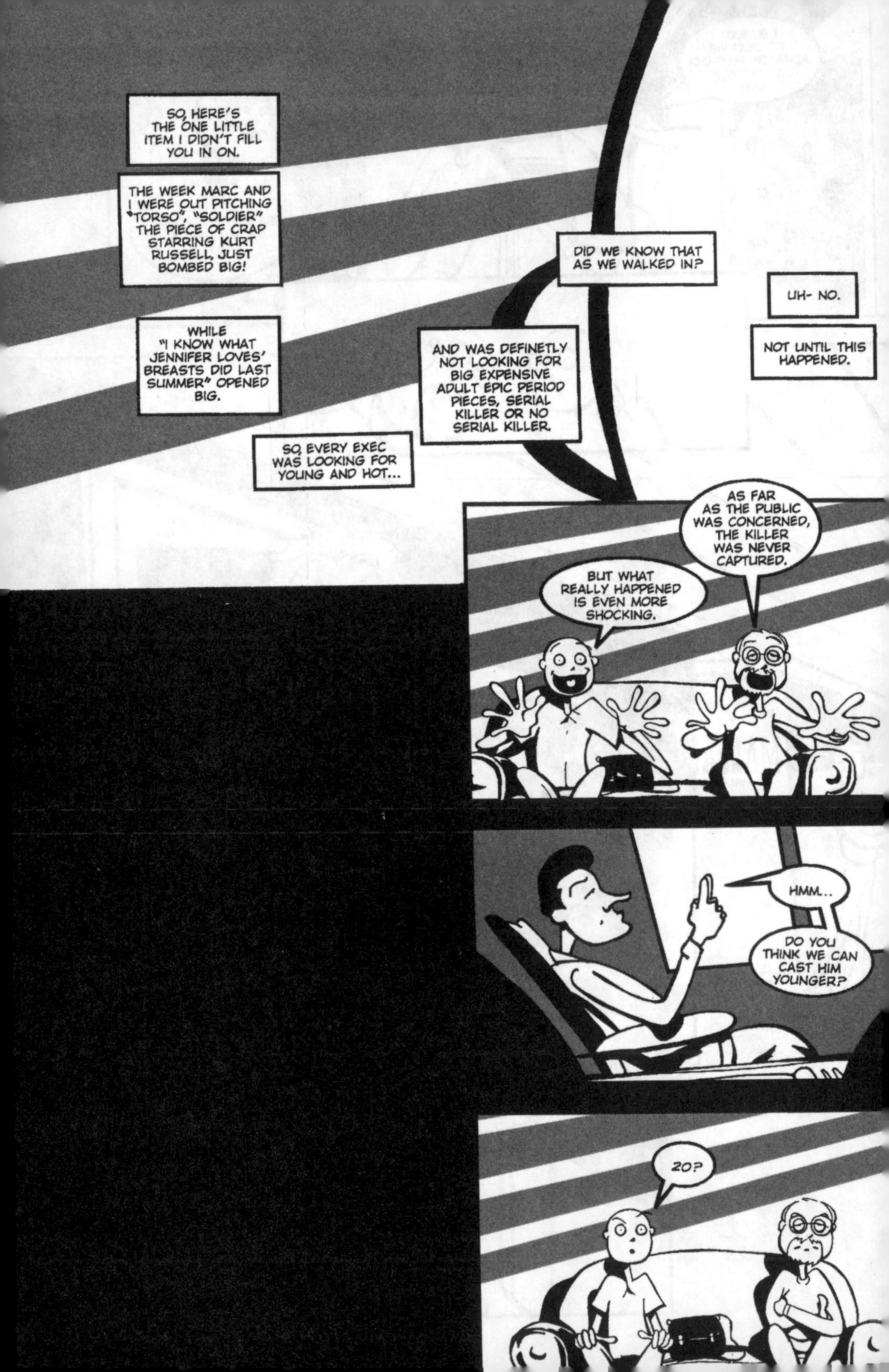
SO, HERE'S THE ONE LITTLE ITEM I DIDN'T FILL YOU IN ON.
THE WEEK MARC AND I WERE OUT PITCHING "TORSO", "SOLDIER" THE PIECE OF CRAP STARRING KURT RUSSELL, JUST BOMBED BIG!
WHILE "I KNOW WHAT JENNIFER LOVES' BREASTS DID LAST SUMMER" OPENED BIG.
SO, EVERY EXEC WAS LOOKING FOR YOUNG AND HOT...
AND WAS DEFINETLY NOT LOOKING FOR BIG EXPENSIVE ADULT EPIC PERIOD PIECES, SERIAL KILLER OR NO SERIAL KILLER.
DID WE KNOW THAT AS WE WALKED IN?
UH- NO.
NOT UNTIL THIS HAPPENED.
AS FAR AS THE PUBLIC WAS CONCERNED, THE KILLER WAS NEVER CAPTURED.
BUT WHAT REALLY HAPPENED IS EVEN MORE SHOCKING.
HMM...
DO YOU THINK WE CAN CAST HIM YOUNGER?
20?

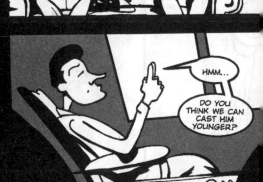

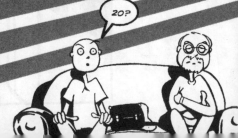

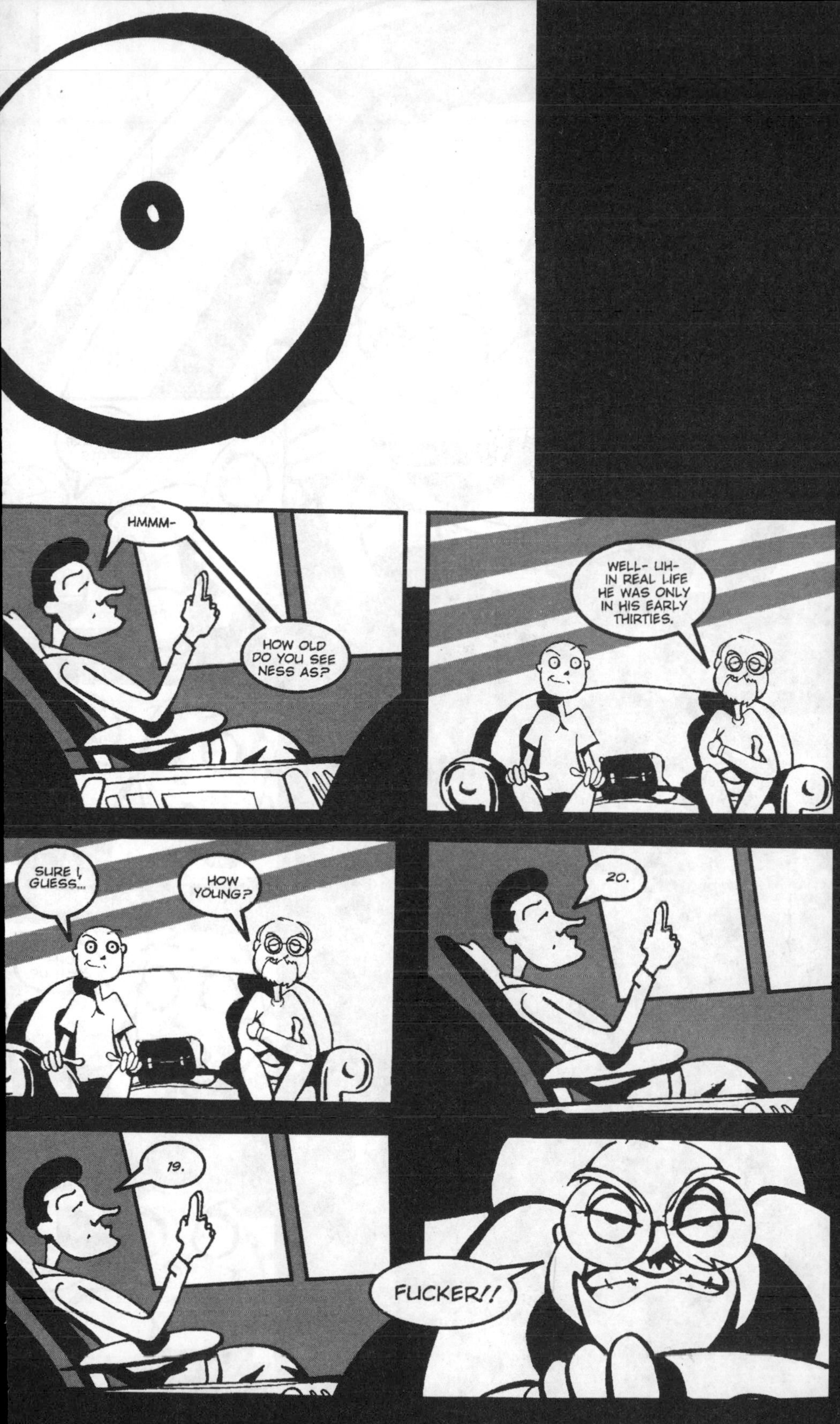
HMMM-
HOW OLD DO YOU SEE NESS AS?
WELL- UH- IN REAL LIFE HE WAS ONLY IN HIS EARLY THIRTIES.
SURE I, GUESS...
HOW YOUNG?
20.
19.
FUCKER!!

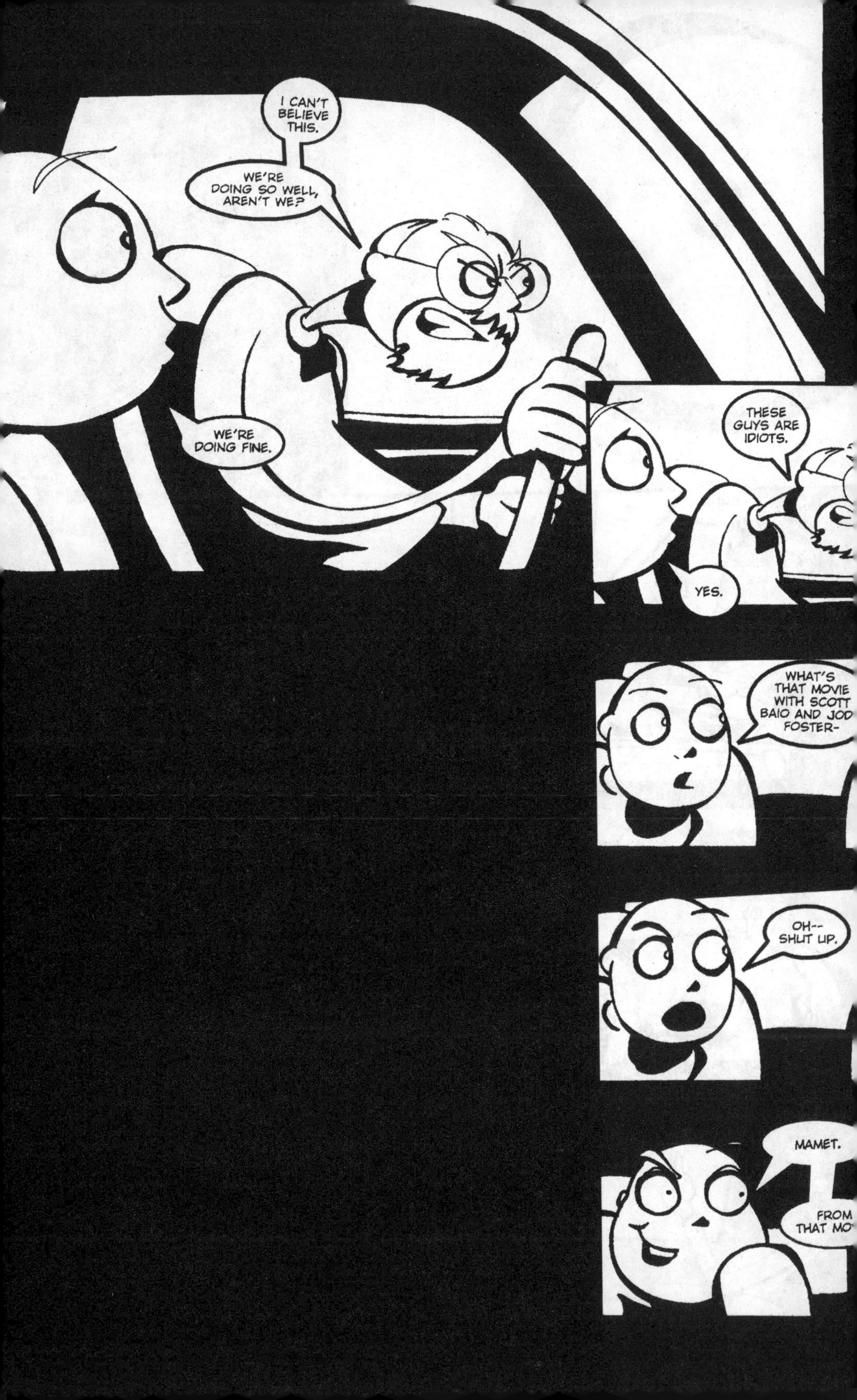
I CAN'T BELIEVE THIS.
WE'RE DOING SO WELL, AREN'T WE?
WE'RE DOING FINE.
THESE GUYS ARE IDIOTS.
YES.
WHAT'S THAT MOVIE WITH SCOTT BAIO AND JOD
FOSTER-
OH-- SHUT UP.
MAMET.
FROM THAT MO

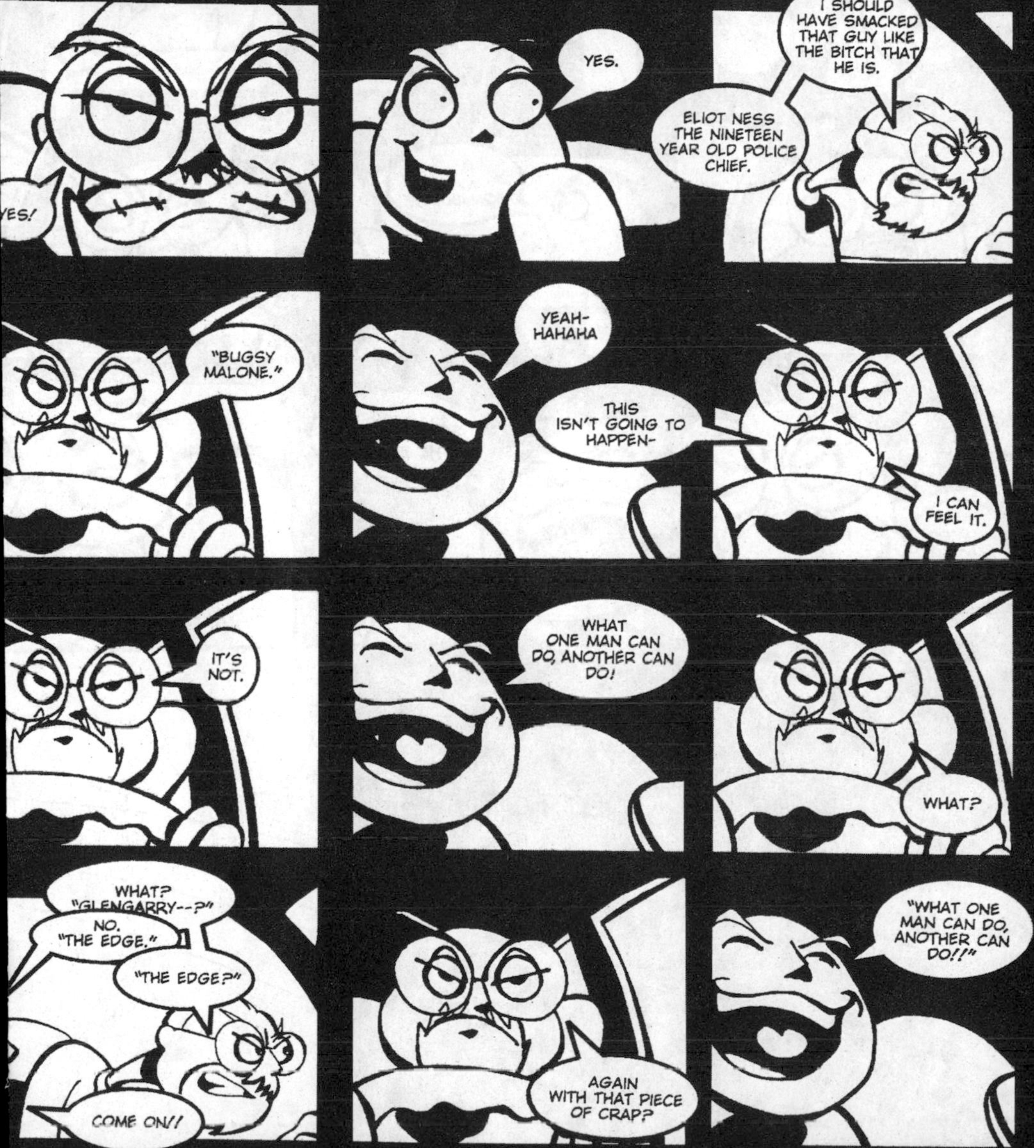
YES!
YES.
I SHOULD HAVE SMACKED THAT GUY LIKE THE BITCH THAT HE IS.
ELIOT NESS THE NINETEEN YEAR OLD POLICE CHIEF.
"BUGSY MALONE."
YEAH-HAHAHA
THIS ISN'T GOING TO HAPPEN-
I CAN FEEL IT.
IT'S NOT.
WHAT ONE MAN CAN DO, ANOTHER CAN DO!
WHAT?
WHAT? "GLENGARRY--?"
NO. "THE EDGE."
"THE EDGE?"
COME ON!!
AGAIN WITH THAT PIECE OF CRAP?
"WHAT ONE MAN CAN DO, ANOTHER CAN DO!!"

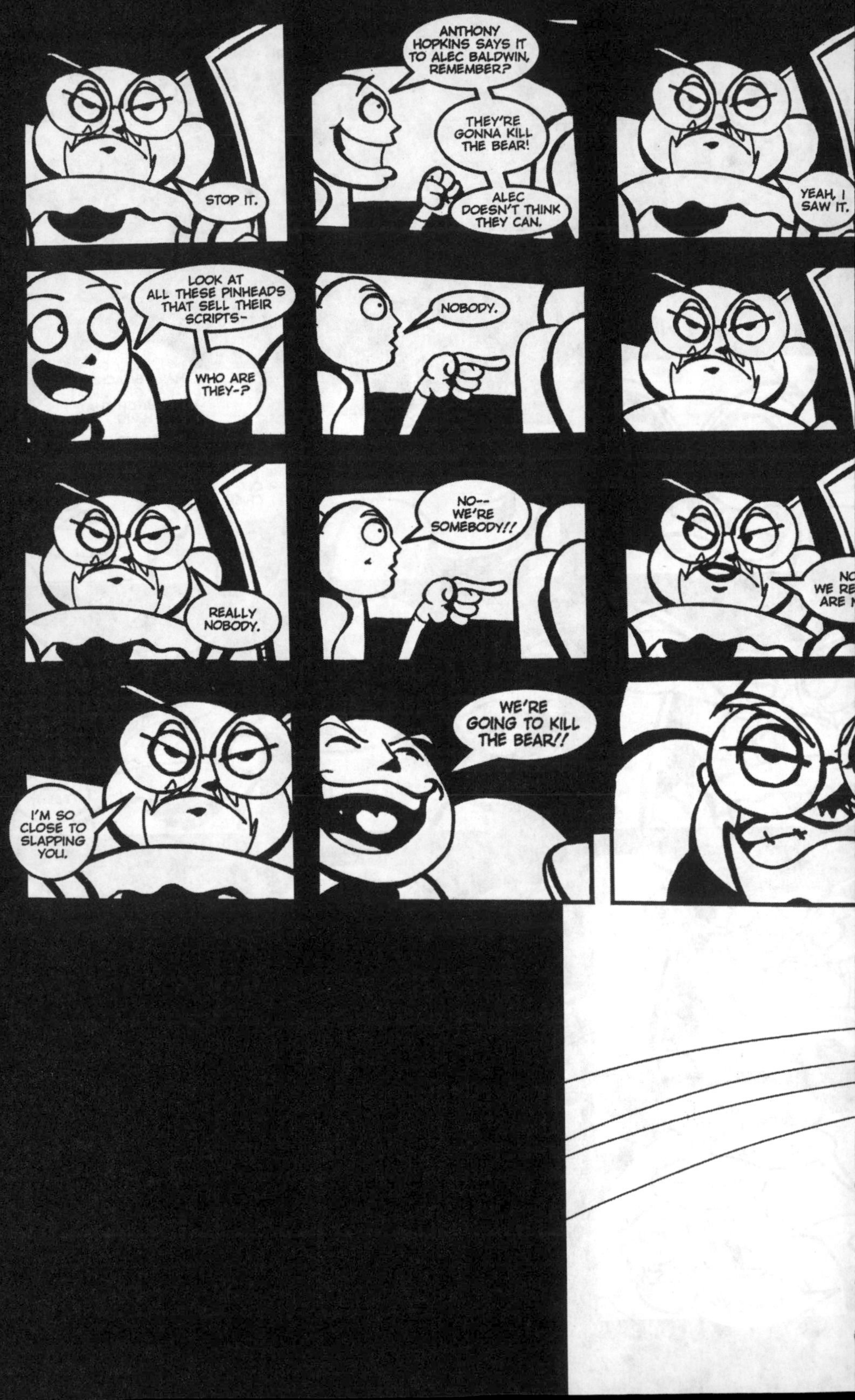
STOP IT.
ANTHONY HOPKINS SAYS IT TO ALEC BALDWIN, REMEMBER?
THEY'RE GONNA KILL THE BEAR!
ALEC DOESN'T THINK THEY CAN.
YEAH, I SAW IT.
LOOK AT ALL THESE PINHEADS THAT SELL THEIR SCRIPTS-
WHO ARE THEY-?
NOBODY.
REALLY NOBODY.
NO-- WE'RE SOMEBODY!!
I'M SO CLOSE TO SLAPPING YOU.
WE'RE GOING TO KILL THE BEAR!!

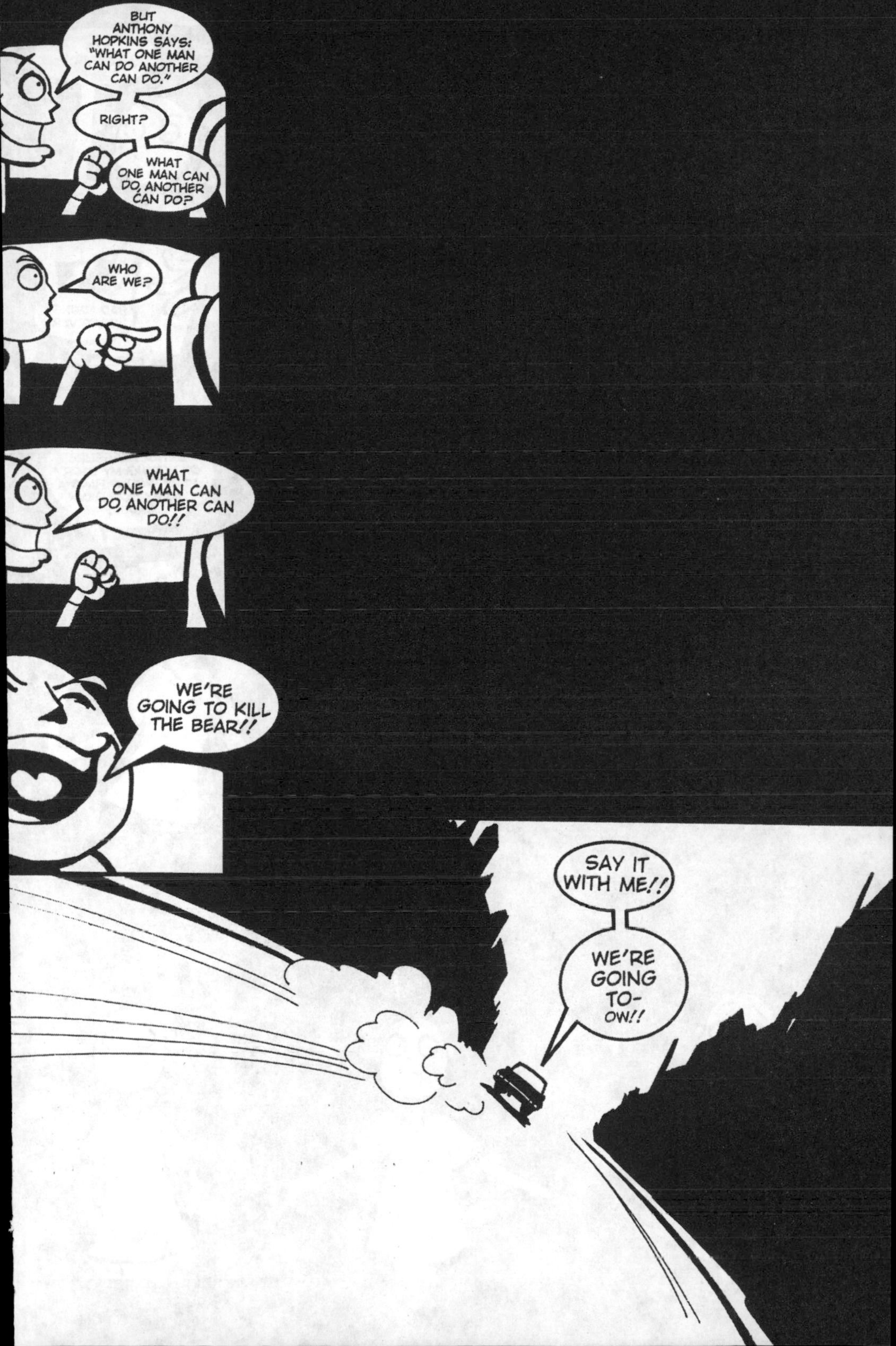
BUT ANTHONY HOPKINS SAYS: "WHAT ONE MAN CAN DO ANOTHER CAN DO."
RIGHT?
WHAT ONE MAN CAN DO, ANOTHER CAN DO?
WHO ARE WE?
WHAT ONE MAN CAN DO, ANOTHER CAN DO!!
WE'RE GOING TO KILL THE BEAR!!
SAY IT WITH ME!!
WE'RE GOING TO-
OW!!

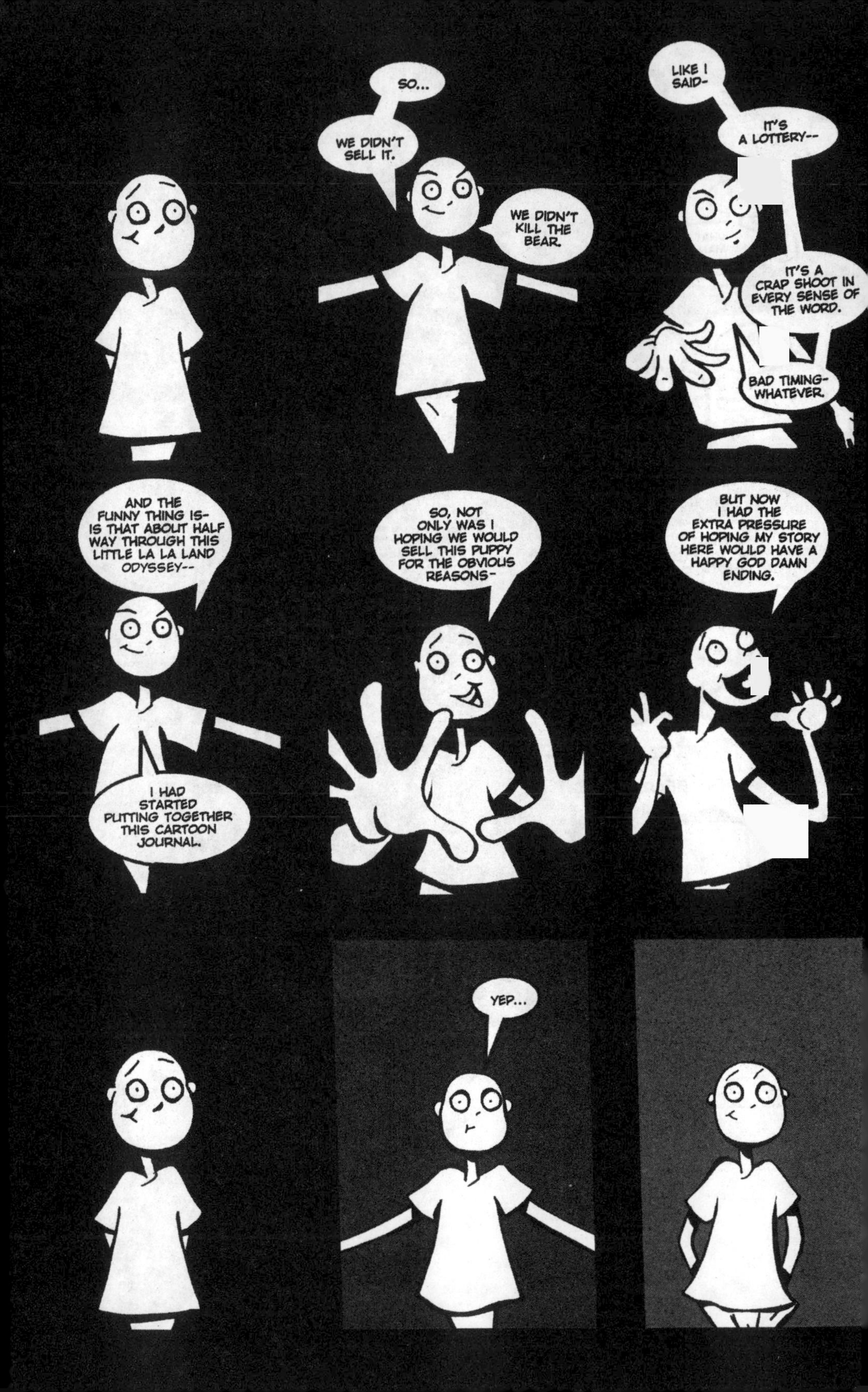
SO...
WE DIDN'T SELL IT.
WE DIDN'T KILL THE BEAR.
LIKE I SAID-
IT'S A LOTTERY--
IT'S A CRAP SHOOT IN EVERY SENSE OF THE WORD.
BAD TIMING- WHATEVER.
AND THE FUNNY THING IS- IS THAT ABOUT HALF WAY THROUGH THIS LITTLE LA LA LAND ODYSSEY--
I HAD STARTED PUTTING TOGETHER THIS CARTOON JOURNAL.
SO, NOT ONLY WAS I HOPING WE WOULD SELL THIS PUPPY FOR THE OBVIOUS REASONS-
BUT NOW I HAD THE EXTRA PRESSURE OF HOPING MY STORY HERE WOULD HAVE A HAPPY GOD DAMN ENDING.
YEP...

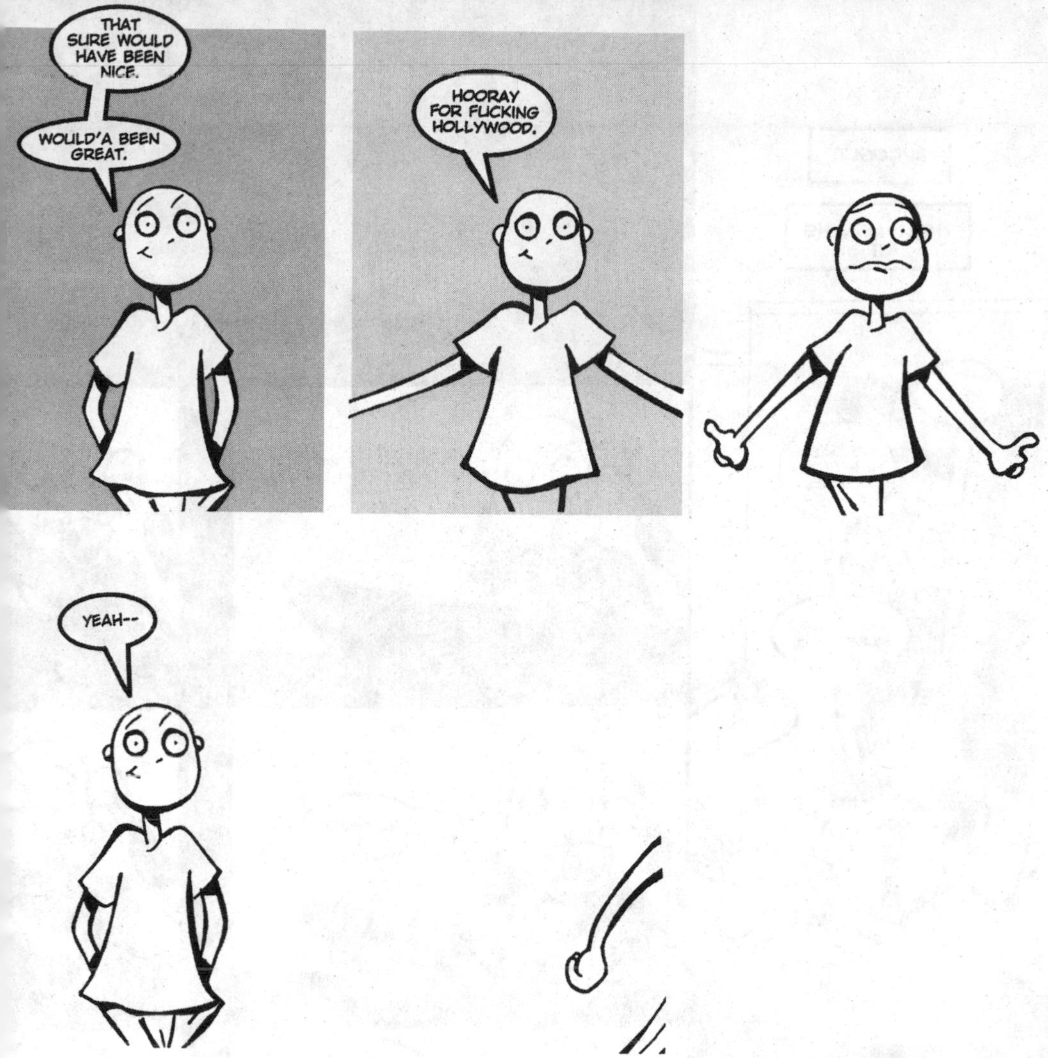
THAT SURE WOULD HAVE BEEN NICE.
WOULD'A BEEN GREAT.
HOORAY FOR FUCKING HOLLYWOOD.
YEAH--

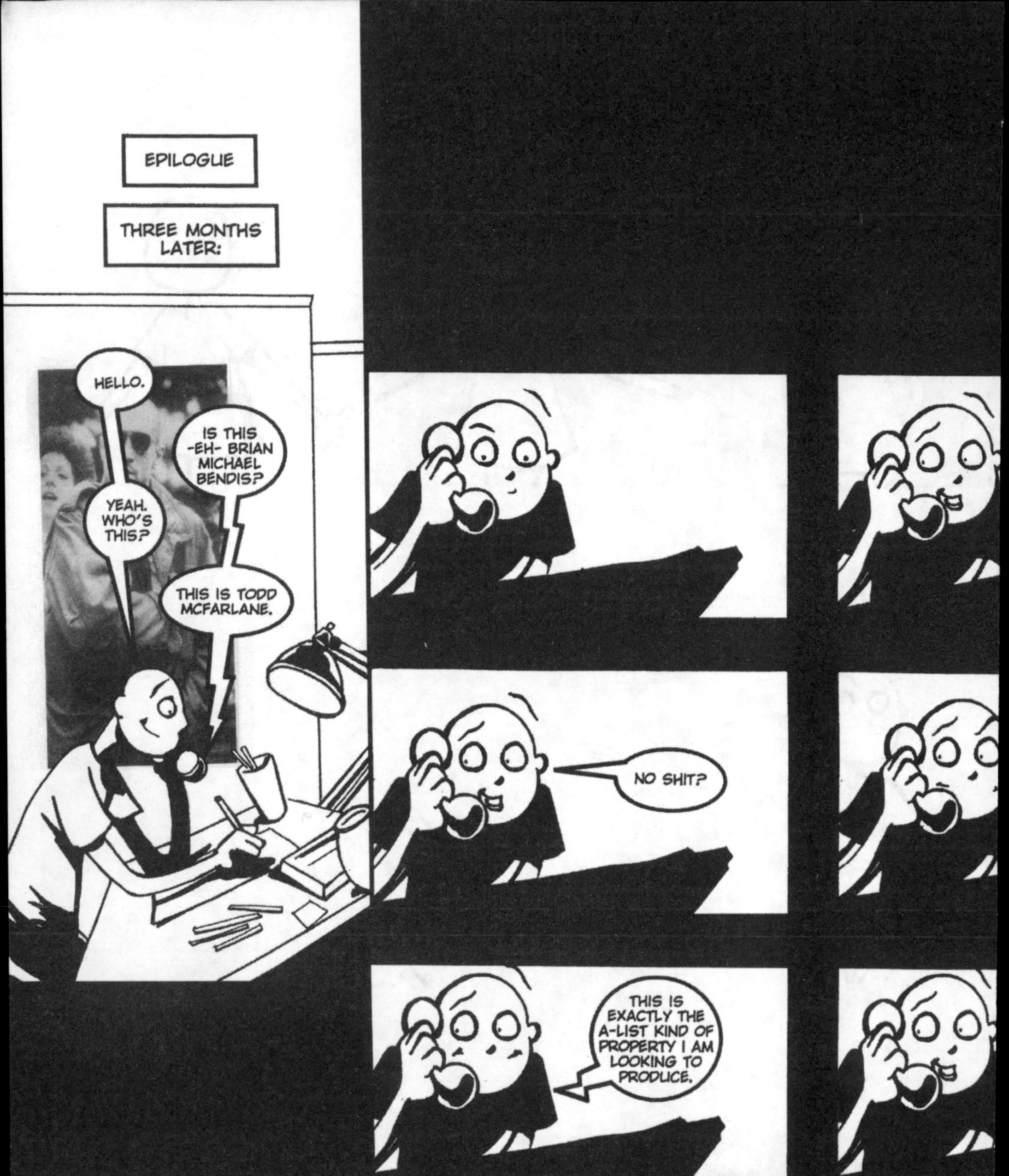
EPILOGUE
THREE MONTHS LATER:
HELLO.
IS THIS -EH- BRIAN MICHAEL BENDIS?
YEAH. WHO'S THIS?
THIS IS TODD MCFARLANE.
NO SHIT?
THIS IS EXACTLY THE A-LIST KIND OF PROPERTY I AM LOOKING TO PRODUCE.

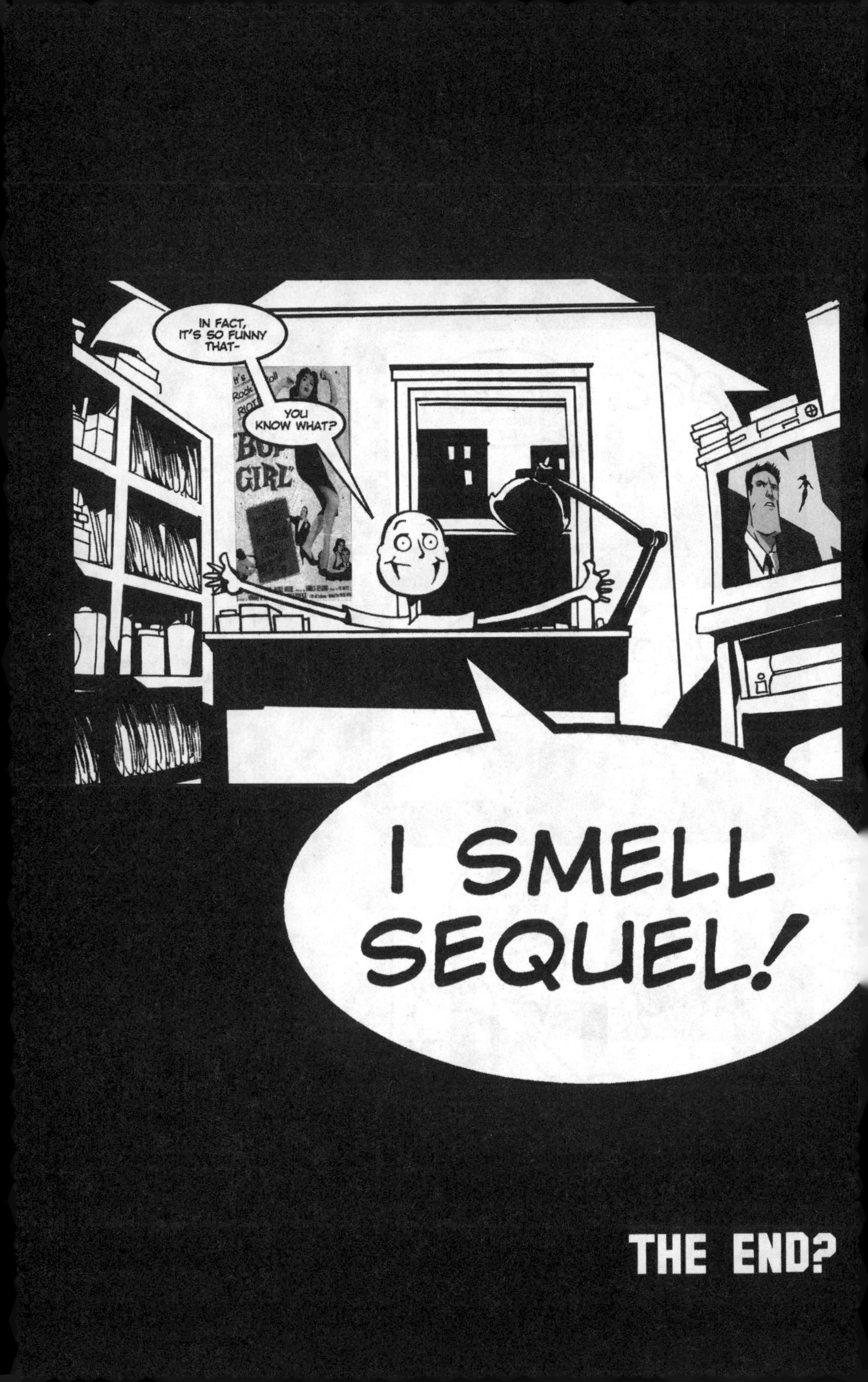
IN FACT, IT'S SO FUNNY THAT-
YOU KNOW WHAT?
I SMELL SEQUEL!
THE END?

EPILOGUE

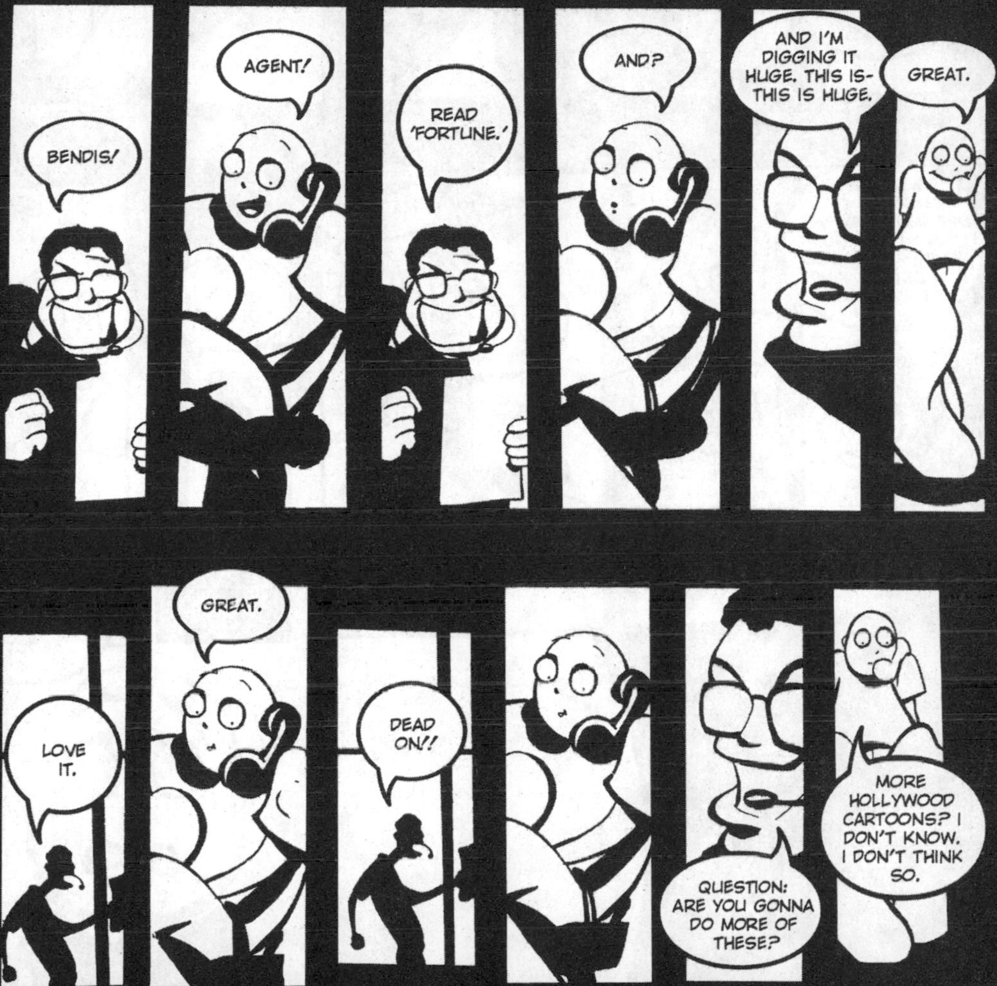
BENDIS!
AGENT!
READ 'FORTUNE.'
AND?
AND I'M DIGGING IT HUGE. THIS IS- THIS IS HUGE.
GREAT.
LOVE IT.
GREAT.
DEAD ON!!
QUESTION: ARE YOU GONNA DO MORE OF THESE?
MORE HOLLYWOOD CARTOONS? I DON'T KNOW. I DON'T THINK SO.

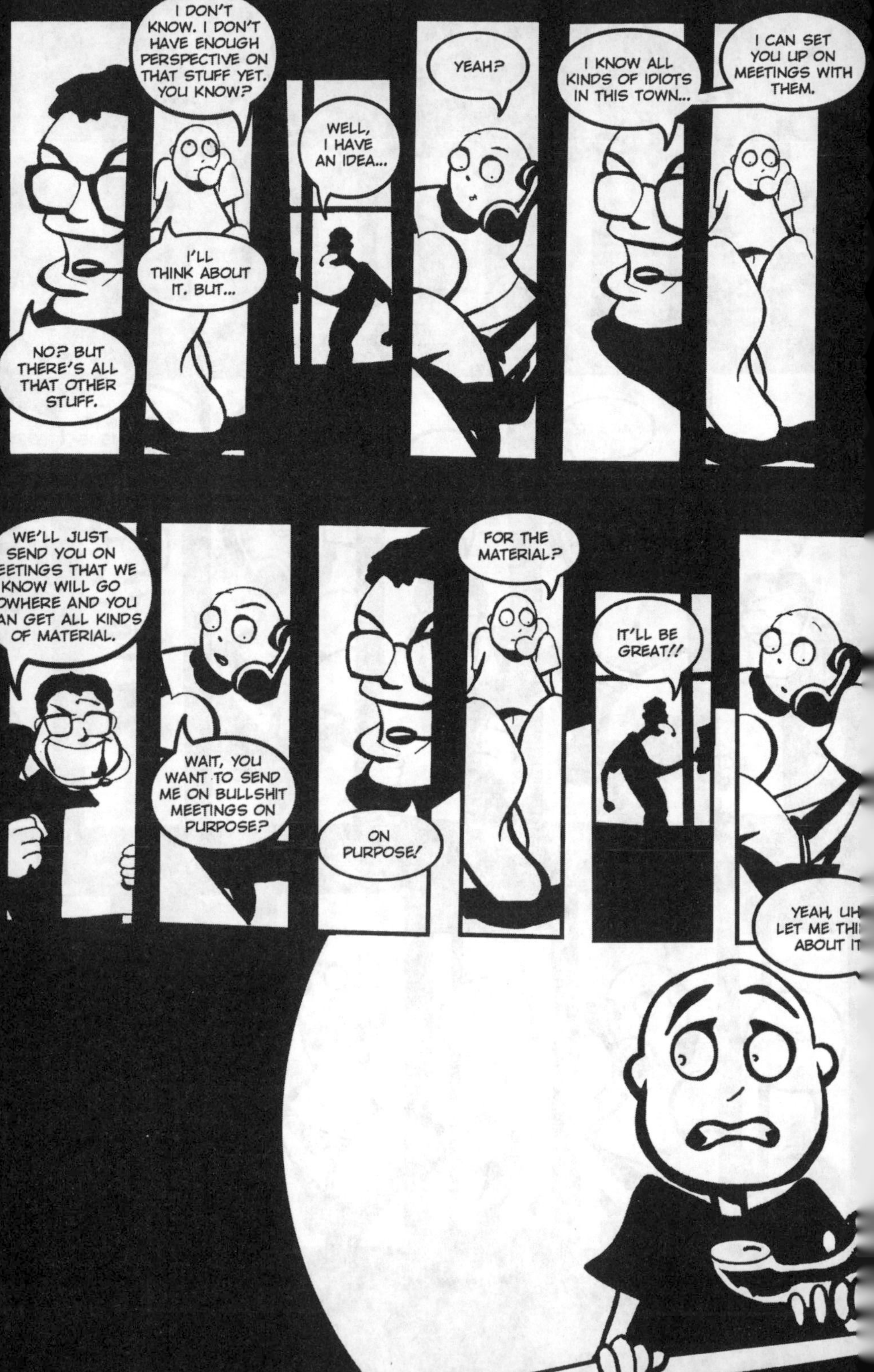
I DON'T KNOW. I DON'T HAVE ENOUGH PERSPECTIVE ON THAT STUFF YET. YOU KNOW?
NO? BUT THERE'S ALL THAT OTHER STUFF.
I'LL THINK ABOUT IT. BUT...
WELL, I HAVE AN IDEA...
YEAH?
I KNOW ALL KINDS OF IDIOTS IN THIS TOWN...
I CAN SET YOU UP ON MEETINGS WITH THEM.
WE'LL JUST SEND YOU ON MEETINGS THAT WE KNOW WILL GO NOWHERE AND YOU CAN GET ALL KINDS OF MATERIAL.
WAIT, YOU WANT TO SEND ME ON BULLSHIT MEETINGS ON PURPOSE?
ON PURPOSE!
FOR THE MATERIAL?
IT'LL BE GREAT!!

Thank you

First, a huge salute to the very brave, very generous, and very very multi-talented Mr. Marc Andreyko. Part of this is his story as well and I thank him for his good humor in my portrayal of him.

The same goes ten-fold for my smart and beautiful wife Alisa, whose love, support and belief in me never fails. It takes a special kind of cool chick to be open to a little comic- book ribbing. Man, did I marry well.

Also, thanks to my super-agents Justin and Chris. They were the biggest fans of this book, and I thank them for their good humor and support. Now go book me some meetings and sell, sell, sell!!! I need some extra material for the collected edition.

David Spree has seen his career skyrocket in Hollywood since our meager beginnings, and no one deserves it more than he. He is a good friend and deserves all of his career success. But for the record, he was the only douchebag, yellow-bellied scaredy cat who wouldn't let me use his real name. CHICKEN!!

A big thank-you to my new step-family at Oni. I was a huge fan of the company before I published a book with them. And one of the best parts of doing this comic was finding out what excellent guys Joe and Jamie really are. I plan to return to Oni sometime in the not-so-distant future with a brand-new project.

Not to mention my other wife: the lovely and talented K.C. McCrory who, you will notice, has come aboard this year as the much, much, much, needed copy editor. You are a wonderful friend and excellent masseuse for whose contributions all my fans thank you for.

I also would like to thank Todd Mcfarlane, Terry Fitzgerald, Larry Marder, David Mack, Joe Quesada, James Hudnall, Greg Horn, Jared Bendis, Randy Lander, Marc Ricketts, Scott Morse, Michael Hahn, James Valentino, Anthony Bozzi, Judd Winick, Ashley Wood, Michael Avon Oeming, Pat Garahy, Jeff Jensen, and my mom. To be honest, most of these people really didn't do anything worth mentioning , but they'll give me shit if they don't see their names in the book.

If I forgot to thank you and you think you deserve it, it's just that I feel our relationship is so special that I didn't want to cheapen it by publically acknowledging it.

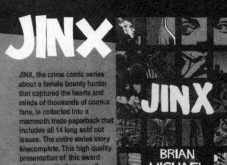

JINX STORE

SEND ALL CHECKS OR MONEY ORDERS TO

BRIAN BENDIS
P.O. BOX 14736
CLEVELAND, OHIO
44114

SHIPPING-.95 PER ISSUE. 3.00 PER TRADE.
2-3 WEEKS FOR DELIVERY
BOOKS SIGNED UPON REQUEST

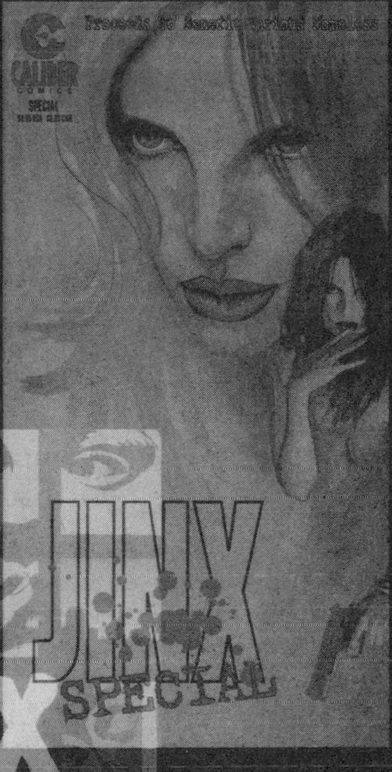

CALIBER COMICS
SPECIAL
JINX
SPECIAL

ORIGINAL GRAPHIC NOVELS

ESSENTIAL JINX
A GIRL, TWO GUYS, AND A TREASURE HUNT. EVERY SINGLE PAGE OF THE JINX STORY LINE IN ONE HUGE, INEXPENSIVE VOLUME.
INCLUDES JINX 1-7 IMAGE, JINX 1-5, AND THE JINX CHARITY SPECIAL.
17.95 440 PGS.

GOLDFISH
THE SAVVY GRIFTER RETURNS HOME. THE ENTIRE GOLDFISH GRAPHIC NOVEL PLUS A NEW PROSE STORY.
16.95 272 PGS

FIRE
THE REALITY BASED SPY THRILLER.
REMASTERED, RELETTERED, ON HIGH GRADE PAPER.
9.95 112 PGS.

JINX

BRIAN
MICHAEL
BENDIS

SINGLE ISSUES
IF IT NOT LISTED, IT IS SOLD OUT. PRICE PER BOOK.

CALIBER JINX
ISSUE 2-4- 2.95
ISSUE 6-7- 2.95

IMAGE JINX
ISSUE 1-2- 2.95
ISSUE 3- 3.95
ISSUE 4- 2.95
ISSUE 5- 3.95

JINX: TORSO
ISSUE 1-3 3.95
ISSUE 4-6- 4.95

JINX SPECIAL ISSUES

CHARITY SPECIAL 4.95
DAVID MACK COVER- HOMELESS
KEN MEYER JR COVER- ENVIRONMENT

BURIED TREASURE SPECIAL- 3.95
W/ WARREN ELLIS, JAMES HUDNALL, MARK RICKETTS

TRUE CRIME CONFESSION- 3.95

POP CULTURE HOO HAH- 3.95

ORIGINAL ART PAGES
LIST ALTERNATIVES

$80 PER PAGE
$150 PER PAGE

FOR AN ILLUSTRATED VERSION OF THE JINX STORE VISIT THE OFFICIAL JINX SITE.

WWW.JINXWORLD.COM